Jazz Internationalism

THE NEW BLACK STUDIES SERIES

Edited by Darlene Clark Hine and Dwight A. McBride

A list of books in the series appears at the end of this book.

Jazz Internationalism

*Literary Afro-Modernism and the
Cultural Politics of Black Music*

JOHN LOWNEY

UNIVERSITY OF
ILLINOIS PRESS
Urbana, Chicago, and Springfield

Library of Congress Cataloging-in-Publication Data
Names: Lowney, John, 1957– author.
Title: Jazz internationalism : literary Afro-modernism
    and the cultural politics of black music / John
    Lowney.
Description: Urbana : University of Illinois Press,
    2017. | Series: New black studies series | Includes
    bibliographical references and index. | Identifiers:
    LCCN 2017017753 (print) | LCCN 2017033267 (ebook)
    | ISBN 9780252099939 (e-book) | ISBN 9780252041334
    (hardback) | ISBN 9780252082863 (paperback)
Subjects: LCSH: American literature—African American
    authors—History and criticism. | Jazz in literature.
    | Modernism (Literature)—United States. | African
    Americans—Music—History and criticism. | Black
    nationalism—United States—History—20th century.
    | African Americans—Social life and customs—20th
    century. | BISAC: LITERARY CRITICISM / American
    / African American. | MUSIC / Genres & Styles /
    Jazz. | LITERARY CRITICISM / Poetry.
Classification: LCC PS153.N5 (ebook) | LCC PS153.N5 L73
    2017 (print) | DDC 810.9/896073—dc23
LC record available at https://lccn.loc.gov/2017017753

for Jasmine

Contents

Acknowledgments   ix

Introduction   1

1   "Harlem Jazzing": Claude McKay, *Home to Harlem*,
    and Jazz Internationalism   27

2   "Black Man's Verse": The Black Chicago Renaissance
    and the Popular Front Jazz Poetics of Frank Marshall Davis   59

3   "Do You Sing for a Living?": Ann Petry, *The Street*,
    and the Gender Politics of World War II Jazz   89

4   "Cultural Exchange": Cold War Jazz and the
    Political Aesthetics of Langston Hughes's Long Poems   111

5   "A Silent Beat in Between the Drums": Bebop, Post-Bop,
    and the Black Beat Poetics of Bob Kaufman   131

    Conclusion   "A New Kind of Music": Paule Marshall,
    The Fisher King, and the Dissonance of Diaspora   159

Notes   181

Works Cited   205

Index   221

Acknowledgments

The writers and musicians I discuss in this book all experienced significant struggle as well as success in their lives, and I want to begin by acknowledging their inspirational art and activism. I hope that this book succeeds not only in furthering recognition of underappreciated jazz writers and texts but also in celebrating the vitally collaborative dynamic of jazz practice. Researching and writing this book has reminded me how scholarship is by definition collaborative, and I appreciate the opportunity I have had to interact with scholars and artists whose exemplary work and sage advice have likewise been inspirational.

Jazz Internationalism began with research on Langston Hughes, and I thank Mark Sanders and Joseph Skerrett for their early support of this project. This book is indebted to numerous individuals and scholarly communities, within African American studies, African diaspora studies, American studies, and modernist studies. I want to thank specifically those who have shared their research, responded to my research, and encouraged me as I was working on this book: Houston Baker Jr., Martha Cutter, Joseph Entin, Gregory Fraser, Cheryl Higashida, Matt Hofer, Gary Holcomb, Tsitsi Jaji, Gillian Johns, Jean-Phillippe Marcoux, Jane Marcus, Dellita Martin-Ogunsola, William Maxwell, Ron Miller, Nathaniel Mills, Daniel Morris, Aldon Nielsen, Richard Purcell, Arnold Rampersad, Rachel Rubin, James Smethurst, Edgar Tidwell, Henry Veggian, Priscilla Wald, and Tyrone Williams. I also want to thank the two readers for the University of Illinois Press, whose careful reading and specific advice have made this a stronger book.

This book would not exist without the wisdom and camaraderie of my colleagues at St. John's University. I extend my gratitude especially to Stephen Sicari, the chair of the university's English department, whose leadership and judgment have been so important to the development of our department and whose thoughtfulness as a friend means so much to me. I also want to thank Dean Jeffrey Fagen of St. John's College of Liberal Arts and Sciences for his generous support of my work and of the English department. I am fortunate to have colleagues at St. John's who are as congenial as they are accomplished in their research areas. I thank especially those whose specific knowledge and advice have enhanced the development of this book: Dohra Ahmad, Lee Ann Brown, Rod Bush, Scott Combs, Josh Gosciak, Lawrence Joseph, Amy King, Sharon Marshall, and Elda Tsou. I also appreciate the expertise and energy of my most recent colleagues in English and Africana studies, Raj Chetty and Shante Paradigm Smalls. Finally, my undergraduate and graduate students in the African American studies courses I have taught at St. John's have been so important for my conceptualization of this book.

I would like to acknowledge the support I received as a Donald C. Gallop Fellow in American Literature at the Beinecke Rare Book and Manuscript Library, Yale University. I thank especially Patricia Willis and Nancy Kuhl. I have also received expert assistance from staff members of the St. John's University Library; the Howard Gotlieb Archival Research Center, Boston University; and the following research collections of the New York Public Library: the General Research Division, the Library for the Performing Arts, and the Schomburg Center for Research in Black Culture.

It has been a pleasure to work with such a dedicated staff at the University of Illinois Press. I want to begin by thanking Darlene Clark Hine and Dwight A. McBride for their outstanding work in editing the New Black Studies Series. It is an honor for this book to be included in this series. I am extraordinarily grateful for the patient guidance and astute judgment of Dawn Durante, whose exemplary editorial work has been so beneficial for this book. I also want to thank Brigette Brown and Tad Ringo for their editorial expertise. Jill R. Hughes has been an exceptionally thorough and thoughtful copyeditor. Finally, I want to thank the two anonymous readers of this manuscript, as their insightful questions and suggestions have improved this book.

I especially want to express my gratitude to my extended family for their support as I was working on this book. Thanks especially to Susan Cain and Vaughn Neville, Mark and Cheryl Lowney, Debbie and Mitch Suzan, and the late Kay Lowney. Your love—and your love of jazz—has made this project especially meaningful. I also want to thank Ashley Cross, whose exemplary intellectual judgment and feminist social consciousness have greatly influenced my work as a scholar and teacher. Finally, I want to thank my favorite acrobat, artist, and musician, our daughter, Jasmine Cross Lowney, to whom this book is dedicated. Her lifetime has coincided with the development of this book, and her presence has brought new meaning to my scholarship as well as my life more generally.

Parts of several chapters in *Jazz Internationalism* were previously published as articles. They have since been substantially revised for this book. Part of chapter 1 was first published as "Haiti and Black Transnationalism: Remapping the Migrant Geography of *Home to Harlem*," *African American Review* 34.3 (2000): 413–29. Part of chapter 4 was originally published as "Jazz, Black Transnationalism, and the Political Aesthetics of Langston Hughes's *Ask Your Mama*," in *American Literature* 84:3 (2012): 563–87, copyright © 2012, Duke University Press; republished by permission of the copyright holder. Part of chapter 6 was originally published as "'A New Kind of Music': Jazz Improvisation and the Diasporic Dissonance of Paule Marshall's *The Fisher King*," in *MELUS* (*Multi-Ethnic Literature of the United States*) 40.1 (2015): 99–123, copyright © 2015, Oxford University Press; reprinted by permission of the copyright holder. I am grateful to the editors of these journals for their permission to reprint these materials.

I thankfully acknowledge the following for permission to quote from copyrighted works:

Excerpts from the following poems in *Black Moods: Collected Poems by Frank Marshall Davis*, edited by John Edgar Tidwell, Copyright © 2002 by the Board of Trustees of the University of Illinois: "Chicago's Congo"; "Gary, Indiana"; "Jazz Band"; "Cabaret"; "Creation"; "Dancing Gal"; "Louis Armstrong"; and "Billie Holiday"; used with permission of the University of Illinois Press.

Excerpts from "Cultural Exchange," "Shades of Pigmeat," "Ride, Red, Ride," "Horn of Plenty," and "Bird in Orbit," in *The Collected Poems of Langston Hughes*, edited by Arnold Rampersad with David Roessel, associate editor, copyright © 1994 by the Estate of Langston Hughes; used by permission of Alfred A. Knopf, an imprint of the Knopf Doubleday Publishing Group, a division of Penguin Random House LLC; all rights reserved; additional rights and territories by permission of Harold Ober Associates Incorporated.

Excerpts from "Oct. 5th, 1963," "O-Jazz-O," and "O-Jazz-O War Memoir" are reprinted by permission from *Cranial Guitar* (Coffee House Press, 1996), copyright © 1996 by Bob Kaufman.

Excerpts from "A Remembered Beat," "African Dream," "Bagel Shop Jazz," "Walking Parker Home," and "War Memoir," by Robert Kaufman, from *Solitudes Crowded with Loneliness*, copyright © 1965 by Bob Kaufman; reprinted by permission of New Directions Publishing Corp.

Excerpt from *Mexico City Blues*, by Jack Kerouac, copyright © 1959 by Jack Kerouac; used by permission of Grove/Atlantic, Inc. Any third-party use of this material, outside of this publication, is prohibited.

Jazz Internationalism

Introduction

I have come back from France more firmly convinced than ever
that negroes should write negro music. We have our own racial
feeling and if we try to copy whites we will make bad copies. I
noticed that the Morocco negro bands played music which had
an affinity to ours. One piece, "In Zanzibar," I took for my band,
and though white audiences found it discordant, I found it most
sympathetic. We won France by playing music which was ours and
not a pale imitation of others, and if we are to develop in America
we must develop along our own lines. . . . The music of our race
springs from the soil, and this is true today of no other race, except
possibly the Russians, and it is because of this that I and all my
musicians have come to love Russian music.

—James Reese Europe, quoted in Grenville Vernon, "A Negro
    Explains 'Jazz'"

Overwhelmed at first by the mere volume of barbaric sound she
found herself after a time trying to analyze jazz. It seemed to her to
be musical Bolshevism—a revolt against law and order in music.
Apparently, too, the jazz Bolsheviks were looters, pillaging the
treasure houses of music's aristocracy. One piece was based upon
a Chopin waltz, another was a distortion of an aria from "Tosca,"
another had been filched from Strauss's "Rosenkavalier." Had
something gone wrong with the mind of the world? Was there a
connection between the various disturbing elements—free verse,
futuristic painting, radicalism, crime waves, obstreperous youth,
jazz music, jazz dancing, jazz thinking?

—Julian Street, "The Jazz Baby"

In one of the earliest public statements about jazz by an African American
musician, renowned band leader James Reese Europe explains the African
American sources of jazz and its growing international prominence during World War I. Europe speaks in the wake of the historic contribution
of the 369th Infantry Jazz Band, also known as the "Hellfighters Band," to
the U.S. war effort in France. Europe's 1919 account of jazz, especially in
his concluding statement about "negro music," suggests how complicated

it was to conceptualize the cultural geography of early jazz. The fact that Europe became the most celebrated jazz bandleader in the world because of his reception in France is one point of departure for considering the internationalism of jazz. The value of jazz is confirmed by the enthusiastic response of European audiences, a pattern that would be reiterated in subsequent jazz autobiographies, beginning with Louis Armstrong's *Swing That Music* (1936). Europe insists on the emergence of jazz from "the soil," however—presumably the African American soil where ragtime and jazz emerged—yet he also suggests that "negro music" is as much African music as American music. The "racial feeling" he attributes to jazz is comparable to that of the "black Morocco bands," and he makes a clear distinction between the adaptation of Moroccan music from the imitation of "white music." Indeed, the sound of "In Zanzibar," "sympathetic" to Europe but "discordant" to white audiences, underscores the racial divide between black and white jazz listeners. To further complicate this black internationalist understanding of jazz, Europe concludes by comparing "the soil" of "negro music" to that of Russian music, suggesting that music that sustains its folk roots is, paradoxically, most likely to travel across cultures. To compare African American music with Russian music in 1919 inevitably invokes dual conceptualizations of internationalism, black and red, and although Europe's argument is not overtly political, he suggests that music is a mode of both national self-determination and internationalism.[1]

Europe can be considered one of the first critics and historians of jazz as it was evolving from ragtime, and his assertions about the distinctiveness of black music are based on his musicological knowledge and his comparative perspective as an international traveler.[2] In "A Negro Explains Jazz," he discusses the importance of collective improvisation in jazz, beginning in New Orleans, and he explains the distinctive instrumentation in jazz orchestras like his as well as the rhythmic role of syncopation. His cultural commentary on jazz, then, is quite different from the response to jazz in popular journalism and fiction of the early 1920s, in which jazz is more likely to be considered foreign or alien rather than a product of "the soil" of America. A good example of this is one of the earliest stories about jazz, Julian Street's "The Jazz Baby." Published in the July 15, 1922, *Saturday Evening Post*, the story represents anxiety and skepticism about jazz from a Eurocentric musical perspective. What is remarkable about this story, though, is the political resonance it attributes to jazz. "The Jazz Baby" features an upper-class Manhattan mother, a classical pianist, who initially anticipates her son's return home from college for the Easter holiday. She is especially excited about the prospect of performing Grieg and Beethoven with her son, who is an accomplished cello player. To her horror, he returns home without his cello and instead produces a "shining, tubular, twisted, bell-mouthed something scaffolded with metal bars and disks" (422). When the befuddled mother asks, "Is it a fire extinguisher or a home-brew outfit?" he answers, "No—home blew," and begins "undulating his body in a negroid manner" and sings a song about the "home-brew blues" (422). He follows this initial performance with a more extensive rendition of a song called "You Gorilla-Man," this time in a combo with several friends. It is the lyrics as much as the music that provoke the mother's reflection on the politics of jazz, which conclude with the appeal of the female singer to her "Gorilla-Man": "Oh, swing me through the trees, beneath the moon serene; / You're my Gorilla-Man and I'm your Jungle Queen" (436). "Jazz Baby" is absurdly primitivist, and it is absurdly dismissive of jazz, as it ultimately identifies this "jungle" music as nonsense, as evidence of the musical inferiority and moral depravity of music derived from African modes of expression. As such, it resembles even as it mocks the often hysterical response to jazz in popular print media of the early 1920s.[3]

As much as "The Jazz Baby" suggests that jazz is at best frivolous, the mother's rendering of its threat to tradition is not limited to its impact on music. Jazz seems "barbaric" because it is loud and discordant, but when she reflects on the meaning of this barbarism, jazz becomes "musical Bolshevism—a revolt against law and order in music." "Bolshevism" here implies disrespect for class hierarchy, evident in "pillaging the treasure houses of music's aristocracy." This "musical Bolshevism" is exemplified by the pastiche of European musical genres that are adapted and thus "distorted" by jazz. "Bolshevism" is at once an aggressive act of thievery and an attitude toward the rule of property. As overtly ludicrous as it is to characterize the act of appropriating conventions of classical music with a revolutionary social movement, the term "Bolshevism" suggests both a cultural politics and an anxiety about modernism and modernity. Aligning jazz with "free verse" and "futuristic painting" implies that jazz corresponds with movements in the arts that are likewise assaults on traditional rules. But the underlying fear that jazz is a mode of "radicalism" that undermines European conventions, that it is identified with crime as well as youth, suggests the social as well as cultural threat that music derived from Africa poses. Jazz is variously identified with the working class, with black culture, with bohemia, and with modernity more generally. If its sources are obscure to a Eurocentric understanding of music, its "Bolshevist" impact is more threatening, because it is aligned more broadly with presumably revolutionary social and cultural movements.

"A Negro Explains Jazz" and "The Jazz Baby" exemplify the internationalism of early jazz discourse, even though they represent two divergent but representative approaches to jazz: a serious inquiry into the music's history and its social and artistic significance on the one hand, and a satiric portrayal of the music's popularity and its social and artistic triviality on the other. However, both Europe and Street accentuate how jazz is associated with modes of internationalism that were integral to modernity and modernism, especially in the immediate post–World War I years: black internationalism and socialist internationalism. The rhetorical conflation of these modes of internationalism, "black" and "red," "African" and "Bolshevik," is especially prevalent in skeptical or naive responses to early jazz, when its newness was identified with revolutionary change of various kinds.[4] This correspondence of "black" and "red" also suggests anxiety about the African American Great Migration as well as immigration from Eastern Europe that transformed U.S. cities and the cultural geography of the nation during the 1910s and 1920s. If jazz evoked the Southern "soil" of African American culture, it also represented the urban sites in which it developed, from New Orleans to Chicago and New York and elsewhere. The correlation of jazz with modes of internationalism also suggests an increasingly global awareness that was amplified by the emerging mass media of the 1920s. The response to early jazz, then, by its proponents and practitioners as well as its detractors, demonstrates how jazz was understood politically in ways that were often contradictory but were also responsive to the contradictions of national and international social change.

Because jazz emerged as a mass cultural phenomenon during the period of social and political upheaval associated with World War I and the Bolshevik Revolution, it is not surprising that early commentators disagreed about its origins and popularity. The questions raised about the cultural significance of jazz concerned both its African American roots and its international appeal, and while early responses to jazz were sometimes wildly speculative about what was new or even radical about the music, these initial questions prompted debates about jazz that would recur in subsequent generations. Early jazz commentary is especially concerned with the cultural geography of jazz, as a mode of African American cultural expression that is also modern and international, as Afro-modern music. Beginning with the earliest formulations of "jazz internationalism," this book reconsiders the significance of jazz for Afro-modernist literature from the New Negro Renaissance through the radical social movements of the 1960s.[5] In proposing a black internationalist history of Afro-modernist jazz writing, *Jazz Internationalism* draws from scholarship on black radicalism in African American literary and cultural studies, black transnationalist studies, and recent jazz studies (especially scholarship on jazz and anticolonialism). Through the examination of writing that features jazz as a critical social discourse as well as a mode of artistic expression, I explore how jazz functions as a discourse of radical internationalism and black modernism in leftist African American literature. This book redefines the importance of jazz for African American literary modernism, as it relates recent jazz historiography to current theoretical articulations of black internationalism, including articulations of black Atlantic, socialist, and diasporic models of internationalism. In discussing how jazz is invoked as a mode of utopian thought as well as social and political criticism in radical African American writing, I consider how writers such as Claude McKay, Frank Marshall Davis, Ann Petry, Langston Hughes, Bob Kaufman, and Paule Marshall explore the possibilities and challenges of black internationalism through their innovative adaptations of black music.

There have been a number of outstanding studies that articulate the importance of black music for Afro-modernist literary production since Paul Gilroy's widely influential *The Black Atlantic: Modernity and Double Consciousness* (1993), most of which concentrate on a specific historical period.[6] What differentiates *Jazz Internationalism* from previous literary and cultural studies of jazz writing is its historical scope, which begins with the New Negro Renaissance but concentrates most intensively on the historical period from the 1930s through the early 1960s, the period that literary historian Lawrence P. Jackson has identified with "the indignant generation" of African American writing.[7] These decades feature the development and impact, nationally and internationally, of the modern African American civil rights movement. What has become increasingly recognized as the "long civil rights movement" coincides with the period in which jazz achieved its greatest popularity and respect as an African American mode of cultural and artistic expression. As Nikhil Pak Singh, Jacquelyn Dowd Hall, Glenda Elizabeth Gilmore, and other long civil rights historians have argued, extending the civil rights movement historically, to include 1930s activism, and geographically, to encompass urban sites in the North, restores the impact of radical movements on the civil rights struggle. It also deflates the myth that the South was exceptional in its racist practices. This historical framework has informed African American cultural studies, especially studies of African American radicalism and black transnationalism.[8] It also informs the new jazz studies, particularly in scholarship that addresses the social and political implications of jazz and its reception, from the popularity of early jazz and swing, through the innovations of bebop and hard bop, to the avant-garde emergence of free jazz.[9] It is interesting, then, that the correspondence of the African American civil rights movement with the popularity of jazz has not received more attention in African American literary studies, beyond studies of individual canonical writers such as Ralph Ellison or James Baldwin. The broader impact of jazz on African American literature has been identified primarily with the

Harlem Renaissance of the 1920s and the Black Arts movement of the later 1960s and '70s rather than with the intervening period when jazz reached its largest audience, in the United States and worldwide, and generated the most intensive discussions of its social significance.

This book suggests not only a history of Afro-modernist jazz literature that coincides with the long civil rights movement; it also accentuates the intertextuality of jazz literature, evolving through several generations of black music and writing.[10] The writers whom I situate in dialogue with each other include canonical Afro-modernist figures such as McKay and Hughes, who are most often identified with the Harlem Renaissance but whose international impact extends historically as well as geographically beyond 1920s Harlem. In making the case for Petry and Marshall as left feminist jazz novelists, *Jazz Internationalism* underscores the significance of African American women writers whose contribution to jazz writing has not been sufficiently recognized. Finally, the chapters on Davis and Kaufman suggest how these influential but understudied writers take on new prominence with attention to their deployment of jazz as a mode of radical social criticism. While the primary purpose of *Jazz Internationalism* is not one of recovering overlooked writers or texts, it does make a case for a more expansive understanding of jazz writing for both African American literary history and African diasporic studies more generally.

Jazz Internationalism begins with the underlying premise of political theorist Michael Hanchard's important essay "Afro-Modernity: Temporality, Politics, and the African Diaspora":

> At its broadest parameters, [Afro-modernity] consists of the selective incorporation of technologies, discourses, and institutions of the modern West within the cultural and political practices of African-derived peoples to create a form of relatively autonomous modernity distinct from its counterparts of Western Europe and North America. It is no mere mimicry of Western modernity but an innovation upon its precepts, forces, and features. (247)

Afro-modernity, Hanchard asserts, "can be seen as the negation of the idea of African and African-derived peoples as the antithesis of modernity" (247). This conceptualization of Afro-modernity is based on political and cultural affiliations that transcend the nation-state, that counter the shared African diasporic experience of racial oppression with alternative networks of resistance across national boundaries and, in doing so, underscore the contradictions of Western discourses and practices of modernization. Hanchard critiques as he extends what he identifies as the two primary approaches to African diaspora studies: "the Herskovitzean model, which focuses on African residuals in culture and language, bodily and figurative arts," and "the mobilizational model—studies that have focused on resistance, overt as well as veiled (song, dance, slave revolts, post-emancipation rebellions, or civil rights movements)" (246). Specifically, Hanchard emphasizes three aspects of temporality that have distinguished the transnational Afro-modern response to white supremacy: "first, the distinctive role of history in Afro-Modernity; second, that inequalities visited on African and African-descended populations have often been understood temporally, as impositions on human time; and third, that this temporal understanding . . . affected ideas about freedom, progress, and racial solidarity" (249).

Hanchard's formulation of Afro-modernity concentrates primarily on politics, on modernity rather than modernism, but his emphasis on the importance of temporality has implications for cultural practices such as literature and music as well. Certainly African American literature manifests the importance of history, through inventive practices of recovery and revision, and the politics of temporality are enacted in black music, most notably jazz.[11] However, the correlation of Afro-modernism with Afro-modernity is worth exploring more specifically, especially since African diasporic cultural production has more often than not been figured as an alternative to modernism, whether in the United States or Europe. Until recent decades the term "Afro-modernism" would have been perceived as a contradiction in modernist studies if not African American studies, despite the evident impact of African diasporic cultures on American and European modernisms.

"Afro-modernism" has signified quite different historical parameters as well as aesthetic tendencies in African American studies. Most broadly, it encompasses the artistic response to modernity, to the social, cultural, and political changes that have motivated modernism, especially in the first half of the twentieth century. This would include the disintegration of European empires and the creation of new nation-states in what were European colonies, World War I and its aftermath, the Bolshevik Revolution and the formation of the Soviet Union, massive shifts of population from rural areas to urban centers (including immigration and migration), and the struggle for equal rights for women and racial and ethnic minorities. The impact of new technologies, including technologies of warfare, transportation, and—most importantly for the arts—communication, also have intensified the experience of change and the perception of irrationality, chance, and unpredictability so often associated with modernism. As definitions of "international modernism" have variously posited, this experience of change has motivated the artist's quest for new forms, new styles, and new languages to come to terms with modernity. In responding to this perception of change, art becomes an especially powerful means for ordering what seems like a chaotic world.

Because modernism, especially the New Critical version of modernism that was canonized in academia, has tended to be associated with a sense of cultural crisis, with the collapse of traditional myths and social structures, and with a sense of anxiety about this collapse, it has not adequately accounted for those whose experience of dramatic change is not necessarily alienating. The collapse of traditional myths and social structures was, of course, potentially liberating for women, who were gaining greater access to the public sphere. It was also potentially liberating for the working class, whether or not they saw the Soviet Union as an exemplary communist state. And it was potentially liberating for people of color, whose demands for equality and justice were increasingly organized internationally as well as nationally in countries such as the United States. This inherent tension within modernist studies, then, has informed articulations of literary Afro-modernism and its relation to international modernism.[12] Afro-modernity, after all, is as likely to be identified with hope as with the despair of the World War I years. While the first two decades of the twentieth century represented the nadir of African American life in the South, with intensified racial violence as well as stifling practices of discrimination, segregation, and injustice, the Great Migration offered the hope for a better life in the North or West. As importantly, the New Negro movement asserted a sense of resolve that was based on growing pride in African heritage and an increasingly internationalized resistance to systematic racial oppression. As destructive and disillusioning as the experience of World War I was for African American soldiers, and as deadly as mob violence against African American migrants and returning soldiers throughout the United States was by 1919, the war years were enormously important for developing an international consciousness of racial pride and resistance. The 1919 Pan-African Conference in Paris, the protest of President Woodrow Wilson's hypocritical claims for self-determination while the United States was occupying Haiti, the radical response to the racial assumptions of the League of Nations, and the symbolic success of James Reese Europe's jazz tour of France all increased awareness of the international dimensions of the New Negro movement.[13] As for the modernity and modernism of the New Negro, what was "new" about the New Negro predated Alain Locke's anthology by about thirty years. The New Negro was radical, and the New Negro was international, before the New Negro Renaissance became identified primarily as a cultural movement in 1920s Harlem.[14] Furthermore, the New Negro was modern before American modernism became identified with cities such as New York and Chicago. As James Smethurst has lucidly argued in *The African American Roots of Modernism*, African American literature of the Jim Crow era, like African American music, also had a profound (if rarely acknowledged) impact on U.S. literary modernism.

As literary and cultural historians have reconsidered the historical and geographical scope of the New Negro Renaissance, the relationship of Afro-modernism to Afro-modernity has become the subject of renewed debate. The very question that preoccupied New Negro writers such as Countee Cullen—"What is Africa to me?"—becomes more complicated when asked in an explicitly international diasporic framework. Before considering the implications of this question for the history of jazz and jazz literature, I will briefly discuss three influential theoretical models of black internationalism that have reconceptualized how Afro-modernism relates to Afro-modernity: black Atlantic, Marxist, and diasporic. Each of these models, which inform my approach to "jazz internationalism" in the subsequent chapters of this book, has implications for Afro-modernist music as well as literature.

Of the theorists who have questioned and rethought the modernity of the African diaspora, none has been more influential than Paul Gilroy, whose conceptualization of the black Atlantic as a counterculture of modernity continues to inform Africana studies. Gilroy critiques the equation of nationality with culture in black studies and emphasizes instead the "stereophonic, bilingual, or bifocal cultural forms" of people of African descent dispersed in the black Atlantic world (*Black Atlantic* 3). Gilroy's transnational, intercultural formulation of the black Atlantic underscores how patterns of cultural and political exchange that have been associated with creolization or mestizage are significant not only for peoples of the Caribbean but also for those of Europe, Africa, and North America. This transnational concept of Afro-modernity compels us to rethink such movements as Garveyism, Pan-Africanism, and Black Power as global movements, but Gilroy also accentuates the importance of black music in the West, and black vernacular cultures more generally, for coming to terms with intraracial differences. It is black musical expression that is most important for asserting an African diasporic "counterculture of modernity," as it defies essentialist identifications with specific nations.[15] Gilroy defines black musical forms as modern and modernist because, like other black cultural forms, "they are marked by their hybrid, creole origins in the West, because they have struggled to escape their status as commodities and the position within the culture industries it specifies," and because they are produced by artists whose practice is understood "as an autonomous domain either reluctantly or happily divorced from the everyday lifeworld." Black musical forms are thus Western and modern, but "their special power derives from a doubleness, their unsteady location simultaneously inside and outside the conventions, assumptions, and aesthetic rules which distinguish and periodise modernity" (73). More importantly, black music also plays a utopian role that exceeds either its practical purposes or its formal qualities: "The power of music in developing black struggles by communicating information, organising consciousness, and testing out or deploying the forms of subjectivity which are required by political agency, whether individual or collective, defensive or transformational, demands attention to both the formal attributes of this expressive culture and its distinctive *moral* basis" (36). While music provides inspiration for living in the present, despite racial subordination and violence, it also projects better social conditions for the future. Black music enacts "the politics of transfiguration," the projections of "qualitatively new desires, social relations, and modes of association within the racial community of interpretation and resistance *and* between that group and its erstwhile oppressors" (37).

Gilroy's black Atlantic conceptualization of Afro-modernity and Afro-modernism has had its greatest impact on early twentieth-century African diaspora studies. As I will suggest in subsequent chapters, his book *The Black Atlantic* has important implications for the routes of jazz and jazz musicians throughout the twentieth century, even though Gilroy does not discuss jazz extensively. Critical responses to *The Black Atlantic* have concentrated on questions that are also important for jazz literature, most notably the differentiation of "black Atlantic" transnationalism from other modes of black internationalism, especially socialist internationalism, and other sites of black internationalism. Gilroy differentiates the social philosophy of the black Atlantic "counterculture of modernity" from Marxism by noting that (1) Marxism privileges systematic crisis rather than lived crisis, and (2) Marxism emphasizes labor rather than the history of slavery, in which work consists of servitude and subordination (39–40). Because of the history of slavery, "artistic expression, expanded beyond recognition from the grudging gifts offered by the masters as a token substitute for freedom from bondage, therefore becomes the means toward both individual self-fashioning and communal liberation" (40). In his important study of interwar black internationalism, *New Negro, Old Left*, William Maxwell has noted that the opposition of the vernacular arts of the African diaspora with Marxism is limiting if not misleading, citing Marxist black musicians such as Andy Razaf as examples of "the possibility of black self-creation through labor" (208, note 24). While Maxwell documents the reciprocal interaction of communism and radical African American writing in *New Negro, Old Left* and elsewhere,[16] Kate Baldwin more directly addresses Gilroy's omission of the Soviet Union's impact on African American conceptualizations of black internationalism. In *Beyond the Color Line and the Iron Curtain* she notes that while Gilroy's idea of black transnationalism is based on a mobility that diminished national boundaries, the communist idea of black internationalism emphasizes "linkages between peoples of the African diaspora and their nonblack allies—those bound together by a shared sense of exclusion from the nation-state, from citizenship" (4). Concentrating on the transformative travels to the Soviet Union by Claude McKay, Langston Hughes, W.E.B. Du Bois, and Paul Robeson, Baldwin asserts that Soviet internationalism, with its professed "antiracism, anticolonialism, social democracy, and international socialism" (2), both influenced and was influenced by these Afro-modernist writers. In contrast to Gilroy's identification of Afro-modernism with the black Atlantic, Baldwin asserts that "black internationalists, from McKay to Robeson, used Marxism to focus on the worlding of capitalism" (10). Baldwin's argument, like that of other cultural and literary studies that have documented and theorized Marxist modes of black internationalism, including Maxwell, Barbara Foley, Winston James, Robin Kelley, Cedric Robinson, James Smethurst, and Michelle Stephens, reminds us that communism and Afro-modernism are not the mutually exclusive categories that they were presumed to be in the Cold War.[17]

Black Atlantic and Marxist formulations of black internationalism have transformed New Negro studies especially, as recent scholarship has increasingly emphasized the "New Negro Renaissance beyond Harlem."[18] Diasporic approaches to Afro-modernism have likewise refigured the internationality of writers such as McKay and Hughes. The most influential diasporic study of Afro-modernist internationalism has been Brent Hayes Edwards's *The Practice of Diaspora*, which expands the scope of the New Negro Renaissance by "not only tracking the transnational contours of black expression between the world wars, but also accounting for the ways that expression was molded through attempts to appropriate and transform the discourses of internationalism" that took on such urgency after World War I (3). These discourses include those of international civil society that were codified in the League of Nations, the Communist Internationale, and European colonialism. Edwards concentrates on Paris as a cosmopolitan site that brought together African Americans, Antilleans, and Africans, a site for cultural interaction that did not exist in the United States or the French colonies. If Paris was understood by African Americans as a "special space for black transnational interaction, exchange, and dialogue" (5), this idealistic vision of internationalism based on presumed French universalist principles of equal rights was contradicted by the experience of French racism, as McKay's fiction so vividly dramatizes. It was also complicated by the differences and misunderstandings between blacks of different cultures. As Edwards argues, black internationalist cultures can be understood only "in translation," and *The Practice of Diaspora* articulates how internationalist discourses "*travel*, the ways they are translated, disseminated, reformulated, and debated by transnational contexts marked by difference" (7). The notion of the African diaspora, then, is not a unifying concept; it is a concept comprised of differences, of changes that have resulted from the "complex past of forced migrations and racialization" (12–13). Edwards contests principles of continuity that have informed conceptualizations of the African diaspora, including alternative abstractions such as Gilroy's black Atlantic. In analyzing the literary and cultural manifestations of the differences within the African diaspora, Edwards accentuates the concept of "décalage," literally a gap in time or in space, or "that which cannot be transferred or exchanged, the received biases that refuse to pass over when one crosses the water" (14). This concept provides "a model for what resists or escapes translation through the African diaspora" (15). It also provides a model for Edwards's precise analysis of the interculturalism of jazz and jazz literature by writers such as Hughes and McKay.

The influential theories of black internationalism that I have summarized have also affected jazz studies, including studies of Afro-modernist jazz literature. I will discuss briefly the implications of black internationalism and Afro-modernism for conceptualizing jazz history before turning specifically to the writers that *Jazz Internationalism* will emphasize. The musicologist Travis Jackson writes that jazz has not been studied much as an African diasporic music, because it has been seen as "one of the most 'European' and least 'African' of all African-derived musics in the Americas" (23). He argues, however, that jazz, like other African music, "privileges interaction, participation, and formal flexibility in the service of transcendence and communication of normative value and cultural identity." Jazz does not simply reproduce social hierarchies, then; it also explores how to transcend them through "metaphoric encodings of deeply held values and strategies for survival" (71). These attributes of jazz as African American music have been theorized for several generations by African American cultural (and music) critics such as Ralph Ellison, Albert Murray, and Amiri Baraka and musicologists such as Christopher Small and Samuel Floyd.[19] Recognizing the internationalist implications of jazz, however, expands its significance as Afro-modernist music. Ingrid Monson reminds us, for example, that jazz musicians themselves have a distinct perspective on modernity, as world travelers who often spend more time on the road than at home, who are thus less identified with a specific place than others, and whose understanding of the international development of black music is informed by their own intercultural experience as well as their musical practice (Introduction 7–8).

The most prominent early formulation of jazz in a literary context, James Weldon Johnson's preface to *The Book of American Negro Poetry* (1921), exemplifies such a worldly awareness as Monson describes. Johnson, who had been a songwriter and diplomat in Latin America as well as the author of the first novel that featured a jazz (or ragtime) musician as a protagonist, *The Autobiography of an Ex-Colored Man* (1912), situates his theory of the origins of jazz within his cosmopolitan experience: "The earliest Ragtime songs, like Topsy, 'jes' grew.' . . . I was, about that time, writing words to music for the music show stage in New York. . . . I remember that we appropriated about the last one of the old 'jes' grew' songs. It was a song which had been sung for years all through the South. The words were unprintable, but the tune was irresistible, and belonged to nobody" (Preface 12–13). Like W.E.B. Du Bois in *The Souls of Black Folk*, Johnson underscores the African American—and African—folk roots of modern black music. And also following the lead of Du Bois's affirmation of the spirituals, Johnson asserts that "the Negro" was "the creator of the only things artistic that have yet sprung from American soil and been universally acknowledged as distinctive American products" (10). However, Johnson was less ambivalent about African American folk materials than Du Bois. While Du Bois insists that African American artists should adapt but elevate folk materials to higher artistic forms of expression, Johnson affirmed the inherent value of African American folk traditions such as folklore, the spirituals, the cakewalk, and ragtime, which he identifies as the "one artistic production by which America is known the world over" (11). Johnson argues insistently that ragtime should be recognized as black music, in its vernacular lyrics as well as its musical and performative elements, but that its appeal had become "national rather than racial" (12) and increasingly popular worldwide. He attributes this international popularity to the "adaptability," or "transfusive quality," of black music, writing that African Americans have demonstrated the capability "to suck up the national spirit from the soil and create something artistic and original, which, at the same time, possesses the note of universal appeal" (20). Johnson proposes that this "transfusive quality" is not limited to the United States or the New World; it is also evident in Europe and other locations where people of African descent have lived. Johnson's formulation of black creativity, while emphasizing the impact of African American folk culture on U.S. national culture, is at once African diasporic in its development and international in its impact.

Johnson's preface to *The Book of American Negro Poetry* was also influential in that his conceptualization of ragtime informs such New Negro Renaissance considerations of jazz as J. A. Rogers's "Jazz at Home" (1925) and Langston Hughes's "The Negro Artist and the Racial Mountain" (1927). "Jazz at Home," the only essay on jazz in Locke's anthology *The New Negro*, asserts that jazz is a "marvel of paradox," but Rogers also calculates that jazz is "one part American and three parts American Negro, and was originally the nobody's child of the levee and the city slum" (216). Like Johnson, Rogers emphasizes the international appeal of jazz, which he attributes to its adaptability and revolt against "convention, custom, authority, boredom, even sorrow—from everything that would confine the soul of man and hinder its riding free on the air" (217). "Jazz at Home" is contradictory in its invocation of popular conceptions—and misconceptions—of the history of jazz, but Rogers's definition of the political significance of jazz anticipates Hughes's "The Negro Artist and the Racial Mountain": "Jazz with its mocking disregard for formality is a leveller and makes for democracy" (Rogers 223). For Hughes, the social democratic implications of jazz can be found specifically in black, working-class entertainment districts such as "Seventh Street in Washington or State Street in Chicago," where "the low-down folks . . . do not particularly care whether they are like white folks or anybody else." These "common people are not afraid of spirituals, as for a long time their more intellectual brethren were, and jazz is their child. They furnish a wealth of colorful, distinctive material for any artist because they still hold their own individuality in the face of American standardizations" ("Negro Artist" 56). Jazz for Hughes is inherently democratic as working-class music, and it is both inherently African as an expression of "the eternal tom-tom beating in the Negro soul" (58), and, as a music of resistance to "American standardizations," it is also distinctively African American.

Johnson's emphasis on the "adaptability" or "transfusive quality" of jazz also anticipates the traveling jazz of early jazz autobiographies, including the first autobiography by a jazz musician, Louis Armstrong's *Swing That Music* (1936). There are a number of reasons that travel plays an important role in jazz autobiographies, whether figuratively or more literally as an account of the jazz life. Travel is, of course, figuratively and literally important throughout African American social and cultural history. This importance is most evident in the blues, where the road takes on such a dramatic resonance. Travel also informs early jazz history, as the experience of musicians such as Armstrong coincided with the movement of jazz from New Orleans to points north and west, especially on the Mississippi River boats that Armstrong writes about. Jazz autobiographies that originate in New Orleans also emphasize the importance of the city's diverse musical cultures on the music's sensibility. While *Swing That Music* is extraordinary in its introductory claim that "Jazz and I Get Born Together" (1), it also typifies jazz life stories in emphasizing the musician's international travels. "I guess I have played almost all over the world," Armstrong begins. "I have swung my bands in Paris and Copenhagen and Brussels and Geneva and Vienna and New York and Chicago and Hollywood and many other places" (1–2). In arguing for the precedence and endurance of the polyphonic style of New Orleans jazz instead of the popular, more rigidly scored dance music known as "swing" in the 1930s, Armstrong underscores the folk origins of jazz in New Orleans and its development into a more dynamic art form than commercial swing. Jazz, Armstrong writes in the opening chapter of *Swing That Music*, emerged from "the soil" of the lower Mississippi, but it also presumably "went back to the tom-toms of our people in Africa" (9). It then followed the routes that Armstrong took as a professional musician, from the Mississippi River boats to cities such as Chicago and New York. Jazz eventually traveled to Europe, where the collectively improvised "hot" music that Armstrong played was validated by its popularity among discerning European jazz fans. Like James Reese Europe, Armstrong confirms the value of African American musical practices through the international affirmation of jazz. As rhetorically complex as the narrative of *Swing That Music* is, with its multiple co-authors and agendas, it accentuates the African American—and African—roots of New Orleans jazz as well as its international "adaptability."

Jazz in the 1920s and '30s was most often considered popular dance music rather than folk music or art music. Writers such as Johnson, Hughes, and McKay were unusual among black intellectuals in their serious attention to the aesthetics as well as social implications of jazz during this period. Writing about jazz by African American intellectuals was actually quite limited during the Jazz Age largely because of the prevailing belief in a modernist aesthetic sensibility that privileged folk art more than commercialized modes of expression as a source for high art. While black nationalist and internationalist organizations such as the United Negro Improvement Association and the African Blood Brotherhood recognized the power of black music to inspire racial solidarity, and thus sponsored jazz performances to generate support for their causes, black intellectuals were more likely to notice how black jazz musicians were marketed as commodities by the music industry, often in racially demeaning terms. If jazz was an international phenomenon that also gained the support of the Communist Party by the 1930s, it was not routinely associated with international modernism. Duke Ellington exemplified the contradictory response to jazz: his compositions were compared to classical music by some critics, but because of his long association with the Cotton Club, his music was more likely to be stereotyped as "jungle jazz." His own attitude toward his music was consistent with the dominant aesthetic politics of the New Negro Renaissance, with his social conscience, his use of vernacular sources for his compositions, and his pride in his African American heritage. He emphasized the international sources and appeal of his music, but he also saw his music as an original form of racial expression that defied the standardization of dance music perpetuated by the music industry. His music was traditional in its consciousness of African American history and folk expression but modern in its embrace of black urban life. Ellington, like Armstrong, challenged conventional distinctions between African American and European music while valorizing music making that had roots in Africa.[20]

Jazz became more widely accepted by left intellectuals during the 1930s, especially with the emergence of the Popular Front. Indeed, "swing era" jazz has been widely understood as a populist if not progressive form of music during this period, with its synthesis of high and popular culture and the increasing racial egalitarianism suggested by integrated dance halls and other jazz performance venues.[21] Jazz became less specifically identified with African American culture, however, which partly explains why there is now considerably less attention to jazz as an Afro-modernist literary medium than there was in the 1920s. Frank Marshall Davis, the primary African American jazz poet of the 1930s, is a notable exception because he translated the swing rhythms of Armstrong, Ellington, and Count Basie into formally inventive, socially conscious poetry. The popularity of jazz in the 1930s in fact benefited white big bands more than African American musicians, who continued to face segregation and discrimination, especially in radio programming and the recording industry. As Ann Petry's *The Street* so powerfully dramatizes, "swing" was seen as much as a sign of increasing control over black music by the commercial music industry as a sign of African American musical success. The same debates about the cultural status of jazz that preoccupied New Negro Renaissance critics reemerged with the greater socioeconomic awareness of the recording industry's power. It is somewhat ironic, then, that the cultural critic who most prominently exemplified 1920s "New Negro" skepticism about jazz, Alain Locke, wrote a compelling account of jazz as Afro-modernist music in his book *The Negro and His Music* (1936). Locke celebrates the folk sources of jazz, noting especially the African rhythmic principles that inform the Latin American and Caribbean music that affected early jazz. He also underscores the precedent of improvisation in both secular and sacred forms of black music: "Such feeling in and compounding of the basic rhythm are characteristic of Negro music everywhere, from deepest Africa to the streets of Charleston, from the unaccompanied hand-clapping of the corner 'hoe-down' to the interpolation of shouts, amens, and exclamations in Negro church revivals" (78). Although still wary of the commercialization of jazz, Locke insists on an African diasporic scope to African American music and a continuity between folk forms of expression. Despite the threat of commercialization to the folk bases of jazz, jazz exemplified the communal power of African diasporic performative traditions as it appealed to urban audiences worldwide.

Jazz studies of Afro-modernism most often identify bebop as the first overtly modern jazz music. As Amiri Baraka argues in *Blues People* (1963), bebop musicians such as Charlie Parker, Dizzy Gillespie, and Thelonious Monk are identified as "the moderns" because they thought of themselves as "serious musicians, even artists, and not performers." And bebop is modern precisely because it is *Afro*-modernist; it is an "anti-assimilationist" sound, in contrast with swing, because it restores jazz to its "original separateness" outside of mainstream American culture (188). The idea of bebop as a "modern" jazz movement also informs more recent conceptualizations of Afro-modernism as a response to twentieth-century Afro-modernity, to the urbanization of African American society, black social and political progress, and conflicting ideas about the social roles of art. More specifically, studies that have defined bebop as a subculture have emphasized how it challenged what jazz historian Eric Porter summarizes as the "banality of swing music, the complacency of older musicians, and a system of economic exploitation and cultural expropriation by whites in the music business" (55–56).²² There was indeed a growing oppositional consciousness among blacks in the 1940s, and thus an increased degree of militancy associated with the sound of bebop, a militancy expressed as well in such bebop poetry as Hughes's *Montage of a Dream Deferred* and the subsequent Beat poems of Bob Kaufman and Ted Joans. This consciousness emerged especially during the World War II years, when support for the war became linked with the demand of black activists and musicians for African American civil rights. This oppositional consciousness, then, was explicitly internationalist in correlating the war against fascism in Europe with the war against racism in the United States. Bebop was also internationalist in its exploration of Afro-Cuban and African music, evident in Gillespie's Afro-Cuban recordings with Chano Pozo in the mid-1940s and Art Blakey's recordings after his 1948–1949 trip to Africa, in which he incorporates African rhythms and drumming styles. Another result of this growing internationalism in 1940s jazz was what Porter characterizes as a growing "critical ecumenicalism," in which bebop musicians rejected the primitivist notions that had long informed jazz discourse but also rejected reductive cultural boundaries, whether based on race, nationality, or definitions of art (61).

Afro-modernism, then, became more overtly internationalist with the evolution of bebop and its subsequent "post-bop" permutations, especially as post–World War II jazz became more consciously allied with the civil rights movement and anticolonialism. As black jazz musicians were increasingly defining themselves as modern artists, they also appealed to "modernity's promise of equality and justice for all." Like civil rights activists, bebop musicians "mobilized the language of merit, universal justice, and transcendence" to demand their recognition in U.S. society (Monson, *Freedom* 70). At the same time, jazz also became a weapon of the Cold War. Ingrid Monson notes the paradoxical Afro-modernism of jazz in this period—namely, that when musicians were increasingly "perfecting their relationship to modernism" and declaring the autonomy of their art, they were also "buffeted by the political forces around them, both domestic and international" (6). These political forces included Cold War pressure to counteract negative perceptions of Jim Crow practices that were being contested in the civil rights movement. In the attempt to dissuade postcolonial alliances with the Soviet Union in Africa and elsewhere, the U.S. State Department sponsored numerous international jazz tours that included renowned musicians such as Armstrong, Ellington, and Gillespie. This is one of the many paradoxes about Cold War jazz that Hughes invokes in his 1961 jazz sequence, *Ask Your Mama: 12 Moods for Jazz.*

As Penny Von Eschen and Monson have noted, the promotion of jazz as the embodiment of the free world was full of ironic contradictions. The correlation of jazz with freedom during the Cold War, for example, tended to reinforce racial stereotypes associated with black performative modes; jazz expression was equated with spontaneity rather than skill, discipline, or the musical conversation implicit in improvisation (Von Eschen, *Satchmo* 11). Such distinctions exemplify broader tensions among critics and musicians in the 1950s about the definition of jazz, as art, popular culture, or a hybrid form that resisted such distinctions. Part of the confusion informing such debates was that the concept of modernism, which black musicians had ascribed especially to bebop, was otherwise rarely associated with African American culture. Furthermore, the nationalist promotion of jazz as a modernist form of American democratic expression contrasted with black musicians' experience of jazz as "deeply embedded in African American history and cultural practices," including the experience of segregation. Black musicians' perceptions of modernity were associated with "mobility and freedom, a cosmopolitan future where the tremendous constrictions of race in America would be transcended" (20). This was indeed a vision that corresponded more closely with the postcolonial aspirations of African freedom fighters than with the U.S. strategy of containment. While U.S. commentators were likely to see the African jazz tours as evidence of the universality of jazz, Africans saw the accomplishments of black musicians more specifically as evidence of African progress (Monson, *Freedom* 130).[23]

In discussing the interaction of jazz musicians with audiences worldwide in the U.S. State Department jazz tours, Von Eschen, Monson, and Robin Kelley accentuate how these tours were not simply acts of cultural imperialism. Noting how the experience of the tours affected how black musicians understood the internationalism of jazz, Von Eschen concludes, "For these musicians, jazz was an international and hybrid music combining not just African and European forms, but forms that had developed out of an earlier mode of cultural exchange, through the circuitous routes of the Atlantic slave trade and the 'overlapping diasporas' created by migrations through the Americas" (*Satchmo* 250). The tours in fact had a lasting but unintended effect on jazz history: the fostering of international African diasporic musical relationships. The interaction between African American and African musicians was mutually beneficial in that African American exposure to African music would transform jazz, and African exposure to jazz would impact "the formation of a modern African identity," as Kelley writes (*Africa Speaks* 5). African American musicians had been involved with anticolonialist activism in Africa since Paul Robeson's involvement with the Council on African Affairs in the 1940s, which inspired numerous jazz musicians as well. By the later 1950s there was growing interest among musicians in African anticolonial movements, most notably in Ghana, which achieved its independence in 1957. The correlation of the African American civil rights movement with the anticolonial liberation movements in Africa manifested itself in several important recordings that combine African musical forms (and musicians) with jazz, including Max Roach's *We Insist!: Freedom Now Suite* (1960), Randy Weston's *Uhuru Africa* (1960), and Art Blakey's *African Beat* (1962). There was also considerable interaction between African American, Afro-Caribbean, and African musicians in U.S. African diasporic neighborhoods such as Harlem and Brooklyn's Bedford-Stuyvesant. Roach and Weston, for example, both grew up in "Bed-Stuy" and developed their distinctive Afro-modernist diasporic jazz partly because of their formative musical experience as children. It is precisely this African diasporic mix that informs Paule Marshall's jazz novel, *The Fisher King*, which takes place in Paris and New York and looks toward the African diaspora of the twenty-first century as much as the postwar period, when jazz was still the most prominent and popular mode of black music.

Jazz Internationalism follows a trajectory that begins with the transatlantic New Negro movement of Claude McKay and concludes with Paule Marshall's retrospective account of the twentieth-century diasporic routes of jazz. In between the international travels of their fiction, this book revisits prominent Afro-modernist sites of jazz history, from Chicago, New York City, and San Francisco to the multiple African diasporic sites of *Ask Your Mama*. I begin with a chapter on the fiction of McKay, which explicitly locates jazz expression within intellectual debates about black internationalism. McKay, who was born in Jamaica but lived in the United States, the Soviet Union, Europe, and North Africa as an adult, represents jazz as a medium of cultural exchange in his best-known novels, *Home to Harlem* (1928) and *Banjo* (1929). Both of these novels relate the figure of the radical black literary intellectual to jazz expression, and although they have been increasingly studied as prototypical explorations of black transnationalism, the significance of jazz for McKay's internationalist vision has received less attention than one might expect. The first novel by a black writer to be so widely identified with jazz as an artistic, social, and commercial phenomenon, *Home to Harlem* initiated debates about black music and narrative form that continue to reverberate in the critical reception of jazz fiction. It also anticipated discussions of the political implications of jazz and its reception that would recur in subsequent decades. Thus it is especially important to rethink how and why McKay represents jazz within a black internationalist framework. Beginning with consideration of McKay's Marxist theorizing of black music, chapter 1 concentrates most intensively on the cultural politics of McKay's first novel, which represents Jazz Age Harlem as a site of African diasporic interculturalism. *Banjo*, which had an enormous influence on the Francophone négritude movement in West Africa and the Caribbean, similarly defines Marseilles as an international site of displaced black migrant workers whose common language is the blues and jazz. As novels that reconsider the cultural politics of the New Negro Renaissance from a radical black internationalist perspective, *Home to Harlem* and *Banjo* interrogate the commercialization of black cultural expression while they explore the critical possibilities of jazz for the marginalized perspectives of black workers, including cultural workers. Featuring an unlikely alliance between an African American working-class World War I deserter and a Haitian intellectual in exile from the U.S. military occupation of his country, *Home to Harlem* enacts a subtle critique of Western imperialist hegemony through its narrative form as well as its more explicit content. Although jazz is more overtly identified with black internationalism in *Banjo*, I emphasize how *Home to Harlem* enacts the uncertainty and possibility of jazz as an intercultural mode of expression.

That is, it enacts the contradictions of how jazz is perceived as well as the role of jazz for improvising social relations that transgress cultural boundaries.

The second and third chapters of *Jazz Internationalism* address how jazz figures in Popular Front African American writing. Jazz was not only immensely popular during the 1930s and 1940s; it was also celebrated by many left intellectuals as a "people's music," a populist form of expression that unified the international and interracial alliances of the Popular Front. Given the increased visibility of radical African American writing in the 1930s, it is surprising that jazz does not figure more centrally in the literary history of this period. One important exception, however, is Frank Marshall Davis, whose jazz poetry and criticism I examine in the second chapter. Davis, who was a journalist and jazz critic as well as a poet, was considered one of the most important poets of his time with the publication of his books in the 1930s and '40s. His first collection of poetry, *Black Man's Verse* (1935), was widely recognized for its innovative adaptations of African American vernacular forms, including the blues and jazz. Because he published little poetry after moving from Chicago to Hawaii during the early Cold War years, however, Davis was largely forgotten until a revival of interest in his work among radical black writers in the 1960s and '70s. He is now better known as an important mentor figure for the young Barack Obama, as Obama suggests in his 1995 memoir, *Dreams from My Father*. This chapter situates Davis's writing within the current scholarly reconsideration of the Black Chicago Renaissance. The Black Chicago Renaissance has long been identified with Chicago's role as a destination for Southern migrants as well as with its prominence as an industrial center. As recent research has emphasized, however, the Black Chicago Renaissance was also a black internationalist movement that was engaged with global questions of race and labor. Chicago was a site of black modernity as important as Harlem, and the Black Chicago Renaissance played an equally formative role as the Harlem Renaissance in conceptualizing and promoting new African American and Pan-African cultural formations. This chapter demonstrates how Davis's jazz writing as a journalist, critic, and poet exemplifies the global orientation of the Black Chicago Renaissance that is becoming increasingly recognized. His jazz poetry is especially important, for the Black Arts generation as well as for his Popular Front contemporaries, not only because of its inventive vernacular forms but also because of his insistence on the African roots of jazz. In articulating how African musical principles inform jazz, Davis also underscored the international and interracial importance of jazz for black and working-class social progress.

The third chapter examines the Popular Front fiction of Ann Petry, which is gaining increasing attention for its historical importance during the 1940s and early 1950s as well as for its influence on subsequent generations of black feminist writers. This chapter concentrates most intensively on her 1946 novel, *The Street*, which was a best seller and highly acclaimed when it was first published. Like Richard Wright's *Native Son*, it was read as an important protest novel in its naturalist account of black working-class life in Harlem. It has since been recognized as an important feminist novel because it underscores the sexual as well as racial ideologies that limit urban black working-class women such as its protagonist, Lutie Johnson. *The Street*, like several of Petry's short stories and her 1953 novel, *The Narrows*, also draws upon the blues and jazz for its characterization of Lutie as well as for its dramatic structure. This chapter investigates Petry's critical engagement with the racial and gender politics of jazz during the World War II years, initially as a radical journalist with the Harlem *People's Voice* and then as a novelist. The "Double V" campaign that linked the fight against fascism abroad with the struggle to overthrow Jim Crow practices in the United States attracted wide Popular Front support. The war years saw intensified efforts by the left, the black press, and black musicians to contest racial inequality, including economic inequality in the music world. If music was understood in the Popular Front as a vehicle for racial uplift and cultural change, for a democratic vision in which "blacks would be recognized and appreciated as culturally distinctive, yet quintessentially American" (Erenberg 135), segregationist and discriminatory practices by managers, booking agents, record companies, and radio networks represented the betrayal of democratic ideals. *The Street* concentrates specifically on the exploitation of women in the jazz business, including performing artists such as Lutie. Petry represents jazz as a vital African American musical form and a presumed vehicle for black upward mobility, but it is also a commercial form subject to the economic and racial politics that the novel's female protagonist does not fully understand. While Frank Marshall Davis's writing suggests the utopian dimensions of jazz as an Africanist mode of internationalism, Petry emphasizes how the nationalist ideology of "the American dream" obscures the recognition of a meaningful African heritage as well as any internationalist vision of working-class, and especially women's working-class, solidarity.

The fourth and fifth chapters of *Jazz Internationalism* emphasize the significance of bebop and hard bop in postwar African American literature. Bebop transformed jazz in a number of ways; because of its innovative approach to jazz composition and improvisation, it brought renewed attention to jazz as a form of art music, but it also brought attention to jazz as a music of social and cultural resistance. Bebop's emergence coincided with a growing political awareness and militancy among young African Americans in the 1940s as well as an increasingly internationalist perspective, partly because of World War II and partly because of anticolonialist movements in Africa and elsewhere. While few of the musicians associated with bebop and hard bop were themselves activists, we can see a correspondence with this growing militancy and internationalism; these musicians asserted a black identity more forcefully while maintaining a cosmopolitan understanding of their art, which was especially evident in the growing interest in African and Caribbean music during the 1940s and '50s. Langston Hughes was aware of the political implications of bebop before any other poet, as his 1951 *Montage of a Dream Deferred* so dramatically exemplifies. The fourth chapter emphasizes, however, his more ambitious but less well known long poem, *Ask Your Mama: 12 Moods for Jazz* (1961). The chapter asserts that *Ask Your Mama* expresses a continuity between Hughes's 1930s Marxist aesthetics and the African diasporic consciousness of his later years through its inventive and challenging post-bop jazz form. *Ask Your Mama* dramatically renders Hughes's dual commitment to a progressive black transnationalist public and an innovative African diasporic jazz poetics. It is comparable to Hughes's earlier jazz poetry, particularly *Montage*, in its range of vernacular expressions, its sharp tonal variations, and its approximation of the improvisatory aspects of jazz interaction. With a formal basis in the black oral tradition of "the dozens," however, *Ask Your Mama* exemplifies Hughes's turn toward a more aggressive posture, politically and aesthetically, at a time when the civil rights movement was becoming increasingly divided between the nonviolent philosophy of civil disobedience advocated by Martin Luther King Jr. and the more militant stance of Malcolm X. More than Hughes's earlier poetry, *Ask Your Mama* dramatizes the interaction of African diasporic cultures in the Americas and in Africa, with its evocation of Afro-Caribbean as well as African American music and its movement between different sites of black revolutionary struggle. In this context, jazz plays an explicitly political role in expressing the revolutionary desire for black liberation in the United States, Africa, and the Caribbean.

No writer exemplifies the importance of bebop for African American poetry more than Bob Kaufman, the subject of chapter 5. And no writer aside from Hughes had a greater impact on subsequent jazz poetry than Kaufman. Because Kaufman is identified primarily with the Beat movement, it is easy to overlook his early affiliation with the Popular Front, which is manifested in his left internationalist historical consciousness and in his hybrid poetic forms, which allude as much to popular culture as to international modernism. Kaufman differs from his better-known Beat peers not only in his "creole" family background (he was born and raised in New Orleans, his mother was a Caribbean–African American Catholic, and his father was an African American with Jewish ancestry) but also in the stylistic hybridity of his poetry, which combines Buddhist philosophy, surrealism, and jazz improvisation. The chapter emphasizes his influential jazz poems, especially poems that translate the performance and legendary significance of Charlie Parker, known as "Bird," into explorations of black internationalism. Kaufman is associated with bebop largely because of his poetry's engagement with the music, life, and legend of Parker. Kaufman's consideration of bebop, though, as well as of Parker specifically, is retrospective, mindful of the lasting power of bebop's revolutionary sound, but also aware of the diminishment of this power through bebop's assimilation into the mainstream of jazz by the mid-1950s. Kaufman's creative restlessness as a jazz poet is comparable to hard bop musicians such as Thelonious Monk or Charles Mingus, subjects of Kaufman poems who extended the possibilities for bebop composition.

The elegiac tone of Kaufman's Parker poems is not atypical of other portraits of Parker in the 1950s and early 1960s, which routinely invoke the tragedy of his painfully brief life. What distinguishes Kaufman's Parker from the Parker who is celebrated by white Beat poets such as Jack Kerouac, however, is his specific attention to the racial dimensions of Parker's life and music. Parker's intense but abbreviated life, and the emergence of bebop in the 1940s more generally, evokes the "dream deferred" so insistently invoked by Hughes's *Montage*. The moment of bebop's emergence as a revolutionary jazz sound coincides with the wartime sense of hope among African Americans for progressive social change. And the rapid ascendancy of "Bird" and his equally rapid decline likewise convey how this hope led so soon to disappointment. Parker's trajectory as a bebop musician also corresponds with the rise and fall of the left during the early Cold War years, a trajectory that Kaufman knew firsthand and that informs the disillusionment with political activism that is so commonly associated with the Beats. Kaufman's rendering of jazz history, however, from his invocation of earlier musicians such as Duke Ellington through his poetic enactment of bop and hard bop performance, insists on the power of jazz as an internationalist discourse of radical resistance.

The conclusion of *Jazz Internationalism* examines the fiction of Paule Marshall, specifically her 2000 novel, *The Fisher King*. A daughter of Barbadian immigrants who grew up in Brooklyn, Marshall has emphasized the distinctive duality of her experience as a Caribbean and African American writer. From her first novel, *Brown Girl, Brownstones* (1959), to her 2009 memoir, *Triangular Road*, her writing has underscored the intercultural conflicts that divide African diasporic communities while asserting the importance of a Pan-Africanist consciousness for resolving these conflicts. The chapter considers how jazz functions as both a source of intercultural and generational conflict and a mode of resolution in *The Fisher King*. Like Marshall's previous novels, *The Fisher King* represents a black Atlantic geography of migration. It traces several different routes of migration, however, from the U.S. South and the Caribbean to New York in the early twentieth century, and from New York to Paris in the postwar years. Narrating the ascent and decline of a Barbadian American jazz musician who leaves his disapproving family in New York to find temporary fulfillment in Paris, *The Fisher King* complexly signifies on previous narratives of African American and West Indian migration. Furthermore, in portraying postwar Paris as a site of refuge for African Americans, *The Fisher King* reconsiders the foremost site of twentieth-century black internationalism. Jazz also figures prominently in the improvisation of the novel's most unlikely and harmonious family, that of the jazz pianist Sonny-Rett Payne; his wife, Cherisse; and her closest friend, Hattie, who also becomes Sonny-Rett's manager and lover and the guardian of Sonny-Rett and Cherisse's grandson. With the dramatic focus on the eventually tragic figure of Hattie, *The Fisher King* also evokes classic blues narratives: Hattie's characterization, as an orphan who has endured hardship since her childhood, recalls the experience of female jazz-blues singers such as Billie Holiday. *The Fisher King* is distinctive among Afro-modernist jazz novels in its simultaneous exploration of the intercultural significance of jazz and the social implications of improvisation. In interweaving narratives of African American and Caribbean migration with mythic narratives of jazz, Marshall not only rewrites Western myths of the Fisher King, but she also suggests a more complexly gendered and international jazz history for the twenty-first century.

1 "Harlem Jazzing"

Claude McKay, Home to Harlem, and Jazz Internationalism

Why did Occupation & Uplift come in? As a capitalistic empire, we needed surplus markets; and Haiti lay at our side entrance. Moreover, it fell within the allotted sphere of influence of the National City Bank of New York. The history of Haiti during the first quarter of the twentieth century is a footnote to the annals of that bank.
—Clement Wood, "The American Uplift in Haiti"

"Home to Harlem" . . . for the most part nauseates me, and after the dirtier parts of its filth I feel distinctly like taking a bath.
—W.E.B. Du Bois, "Two Novels: Nella Larsen, *Quicksand* and Claude McKay, *Home to Harlem*"

The June 1928 issue of *The Crisis* featured the second installment of Clement Wood's exposé of United States policy in occupied Haiti. Wood, a white socialist poet who was perhaps best known for his 1926 jazz sequence titled *Greenwich Village Blues*, was uncompromising in his indictment of the financial motives underlying the occupation: "Once Americans were sensitive about taxation without representation. Now they force this upon a neighboring republic, at the dictate of affected American financial interests" (189). His article reflected a renewed African American interest in the brutal hypocrisy of an occupation that had already lasted more than a decade. After years of decreasing attention to Haiti, articles denouncing U.S. States policy had begun to reappear with greater frequency in journals such as *The Nation*, *Opportunity*, *The Messenger*, and *The Crisis*, anticipating the resurgence of widespread strikes and uprisings that would take place in Haiti the following year. So it is ironic that the same 1928 issue of *The Crisis* that criticized the United States' imperial policy in Haiti also included what has become the most notorious book review of Claude McKay's popular first novel, *Home to Harlem*. One would hardly suspect in reading this review by W.E.B. Du Bois that McKay's fiction would have such an important impact on anti-imperialist black intellectuals in the Caribbean, West Africa, and Europe. Du Bois castigates McKay for catering to "that prurient demand on the part of white folk for a portrayal in Negroes of that utter licentiousness which conventional civilization holds white folk back from enjoying" ("Two Novels" 202). The scenes of "drunkenness, fighting, lascivious sexual promiscuity, and utter absence of restraint" that Du Bois criticizes are, of course, the cabaret, dance hall, and house party scenes that are most associated with jazz in the 1920s. Du Bois acknowledges, though, that McKay is "too great a poet" to write a book that is totally worthless. "The chief character, Jake," he writes, "has something appealing, and the glimpses of the Haitian, Ray, have all the materials of a great piece of fiction" (202). Yet nothing more is said in this review about the Haitian intellectual whose narrative illustrates the destructive impact of an imperial policy that the same issue of *The Crisis* protests. Despite such renewed criticism of the United States' occupation of Haiti in the later 1920s, the story of a Haitian migrant appears to have little place in a novel about Harlem.

Given Du Bois's advocacy of Pan-Africanism during the 1920s, his exclusive attention to the African American context of *Home to Harlem* might seem surprising. His review of the novel, however, represented the response of many African American intellectuals, especially of his generation, who ignored McKay's Haitian protagonist and instead questioned his motivation for a book that bore a disturbing resemblance to Carl Van Vechten's controversial *Nigger Heaven* (1926).[1] Until recently, most readers of *Home to Harlem* have followed its initial reception by Harlem Renaissance critics, concentrating on McKay's primitivist portrayal of Jake, debating the racial politics of the novel's gritty but romantic depiction of his Harlem "semi-underworld," particularly the world of nightclubs and cabarets, where jazz figures so prominently.[2] The first novel by a black writer to be so specifically identified with jazz, *Home to Harlem* provoked debates about black music and narrative form that continue to preoccupy scholars of jazz fiction. It is therefore important to consider the black internationalist framework of *Home to Harlem* and its sequel, *Banjo*. As Timothy Brennan has written, McKay was one of the few writers associated with the New Negro Renaissance who understood the importance of the Caribbean and Latin America for the development of early jazz. And perhaps more than any of his contemporaries in the United States, McKay understood the imperialist presumptions of defining jazz as the musical expression of American democratic values.[3] The black internationalist implications of jazz are especially evident in *Banjo*, but McKay's first novel enacts a more subtle critique of Western imperialist hegemony through its forms as well as its more explicit content. Why, then, did the jazz world of Harlem nightlife seem so disconnected from the African diasporic internationalism of *Home to Harlem* when the novel was first published? And why has the aporia in Du Bois's review—between jazz and imperialism, between cultural politics and international relations—continued to inform the reception of *Home to Harlem*? One answer to these questions is that the novel's structure separates the world of Harlem nightlife frequented by Jake in parts 1 and 3 from the intercultural dialogue between Jake and Ray in part 2. The realm of entertainment is separate from the realm of international politics; the distance between these realms seems as vast as the distance between the worldviews of Jake and Ray.

I will argue, however, that McKay's representation of an international black Harlem is more politically complex than most accounts of him as a "Harlem Renaissance" writer have indicated, and the presumed mutual exclusivity of jazz and international politics is itself a problem that the novel reflexively accentuates.[4] I will discuss specifically how McKay's representation of African American music figures in the cross-cultural dynamic of *Home to Harlem*'s two migrant narratives. The first is Jake's African American migrant narrative, which assumes a rural South–urban North geographical trajectory that is familiar to Harlem Renaissance fiction. Significantly, though, Jake's narrative journey to Harlem begins not in his native Virginia but on a transatlantic freighter from London, shortly after he had left the U.S. Army in France, frustrated by the demeaning treatment of black soldiers who had enlisted to fight in the "white folks' war" (McKay, *Home to Harlem* 8). Accompanying Jake's travels is the sound of the blues and early jazz, and his itinerary recalls the history of jazz, with its origins in the African American South and its renewed international popularity, especially in France, in the aftermath of World War I. The second narrative is Ray's African Caribbean migrant narrative, whose geography of exile evokes later postcolonialist narratives rather than U.S. immigrant narratives.

Home to Harlem represents the uneasy intersection of its two migrant narratives, celebrating the unlikely friendship between the African American working-class war deserter and the young Haitian intellectual who had fled from the U.S. military occupation of his country. Ray's narrative of exile is structurally contained within Jake's picaresque narrative, as it does not begin until the second part of the three-part novel, when we encounter him waiting tables in a railroad dining car where Jake is a cook. And his narrative concludes as abruptly as it begins, at the end of part 2, with his seemingly impulsive departure from Harlem aboard a European-bound freighter. Nonetheless, the friendship that evolves between Ray and Jake transforms both of them as they each confront the mutual prejudice—based on national and class differences—that makes their comradeship so unlikely. The incongruity of the novel's two open-ended narratives represents less of a structural failure on McKay's part, as has been argued by most critics of the novel, than a failure of his readers to conceptualize the political significance of its incongruity. In revealing how African diasporic divisions, particularly in Harlem, were based more on social prejudice than on competing national interests, McKay's novel also suggests its American readers' failure to relate these divisions to a hegemonic imperialist ideology. The Haitian nationality of the novel's African Caribbean protagonist is thus especially important. While Haitians comprised a small minority of Caribbean immigrants to the United States, and Harlem specifically, McKay's exposure of the devastating impact of the American invasion of Haiti underscored the necessity for a renewed counter-hegemonic black internationalist solidarity.

Jazz plays a significant role within the black transnationalist narrative imaginary of *Home to Harlem*. Critics who have discussed the significance of black music in McKay's fiction associate jazz with his critique of dominant Western values, whether that critique is predominantly Marxist, Pan-Africanist, cosmopolitan, or queer.[5] While jazz is more overtly identified with black internationalism in *Banjo*, I will emphasize how *Home to Harlem* enacts the utopian potential of jazz as an intercultural mode of expression. However, the question of what jazz signifies in *Home to Harlem* is complicated by the novel's time frame; although the novel was written during the ascent of jazz as a mass cultural phenomenon in the mid-1920s, it represents the earlier postwar period in which the definition of jazz itself was uncertain. Jazz is associated with the blues, ragtime, and other forms of popular music in *Home to Harlem*, and its aesthetic hybridity raises social questions that preoccupied African American critics throughout the 1920s. Was jazz distinctively African American, given its identification with black musicians but also its wider popularity in the United States and Europe, not to mention the influence of Latin American and Caribbean music on its impact? How was the popularity of jazz a source of pride for African Americans? Conversely, how did jazz reinforce racist stereotypes associated with the tradition of minstrelsy in the United States? How was jazz a mode of mass culture, of folk culture, or of high culture? To what extent should jazz be identified with modernity or with its roots in African modes of performance? As jazz historian Eric Porter has written, by the 1920s jazz had become increasingly recognized as a form of "syncopated, instrumental dance music," but it had also become "a business enterprise and a set of institutional relationships, a focal point for political and social debate, a vehicle for individual and communal identity formation, and, eventually, an idea" (6). *Home to Harlem* explores these multiple dimensions of jazz, and its international framework for understanding black music complicates as it elucidates the social significance of musical improvisation.

Part 1: Harlem

Claude McKay's 1937 autobiography, *A Long Way from Home*, begins with a return trip "to the city that was home," New York, and goes on to tell the tale of a vagabond, but a "vagabond with a purpose . . . determined to find expression in writing" (4). It's fair to say that McKay's reputation has since traveled a long way from "a long way from home." Whether his literary "home" is identified with Jamaica or Harlem depends on the critical geographies in which he has been located, whether Caribbean or African American, postcolonial or post-Americanist. Indeed, the concept of "home" has become as complicated as the legend of the "troubadour wanderer" that McKay cultivated. Understandings of McKay in the twenty-first century have been transformed especially by Marxist studies, African diaspora studies, and queer studies, by critics such as Kate Baldwin, Brent Hayes Edwards, Gary Holcomb, William Maxwell, and Michelle Stephens, all of whom have challenged the disciplinary parameters of modernist and Harlem Renaissance studies.[6] Thus, it is interesting that McKay's fiction is not routinely associated with African American popular music, even though *Home to Harlem* (1928) and *Banjo* (1929) are among the earliest novels to feature jazz performance settings as transformative social sites.[7] Both of these novels relate the figure of the radical black literary intellectual to jazz performance, and although they have been celebrated as prototypical explorations of black internationalism, McKay's literary representations of jazz and the blues have most often been characterized as "primitivist" rather than "modernist." As I will suggest, *Home to Harlem* is an especially appropriate place to examine McKay's response not only to the contested reception of jazz in the 1920s but also to the international significance of jazz as an Afro-modernist form of expression.

As McKay's biographers have noted, there are elements of the author in both protagonists of *Home to Harlem*.[8] Like Jake, McKay had experienced the exhausting work and intense nightlife of migrant laborers living in Harlem, and like Ray, he was disaffected with African American intellectual life and American society more generally. However, given McKay's insistent critique of American and European imperialism throughout his career, it is surprising how few readers have addressed the significance of Ray's nationality to McKay's Harlem novel. Ray reappears as a protagonist of McKay's second novel, *Banjo*, which revisits the young writer's quest for literary expression in Marseilles, amid the vibrantly international milieu of African, Caribbean, and North American black workers. Whereas *Home to Harlem* is usually cited as a flawed but important novel of the Harlem Renaissance, *Banjo* is credited as one of the founding texts of the Pan-Africanist négritude movement, which was also inspired by Haitian nationalist response to American imperialism. If McKay is best known in the United States as the protest poet who wrote "If We Must Die" and other poems of black pride and resistance after World War I, his international reputation rests more on the impact of his prose fiction on postcolonial Caribbean and West African writers such as Aimé Césaire and Léopold Sédar Senghor.[9] This bifurcated reception of McKay's writing exemplifies the central problem that Paul Gilroy investigates in *The Black Atlantic: Modernity and Double Consciousness*: "the fatal junction of the concept of nationality with the concept of culture and the affinities and affiliations which link the blacks of the West to one of their adoptive, parental cultures" (2). The alternative concept of a transnational, intercultural "black Atlantic" is, of course, especially appropriate for a writer like McKay, who spent much of his life quite literally as well as intellectually traversing the Atlantic, just as it is appropriate for the study of events, such as the Haitian Revolution, or movements, such as Garveyism, Pan-Africanism, or négritude, that have had global implications.[10]

In his response to critics of his fiction, particularly *Home to Harlem*, McKay himself underscores the significance of his cross-cultural experience. For example, in a retrospective essay titled "A Negro Writer to His Critics" (1932), he emphasizes the continuity of his earlier Jamaican dialect verse with his novelistic representation of African American working-class speech. In doing so he asserts his own literary cosmopolitanism while questioning the narrow provincialism of his African American critics: "If my brethren had taken the trouble to look a little into my obscure life they would have discovered that years before I had recaptured the spirit of the Jamaican peasants in verse, rendering their primitive joys, their loves and hates, their work and play, their dialect. And what I did in prose for Harlem was very similar to what I had done for Jamaica in verse" (135). Writing from the experience of having lived for many years in Europe and North Africa after he had lived in Jamaica and the United States, McKay suggests that his internationalist perspective was especially attuned to the multiracial development of American urban centers. His conclusion to "A Negro Writer and His Critics" is especially appropriate for understanding the importance of the cross-cultural camaraderie of characters like Jake and Ray in *Home to Harlem*: "The time when a writer will stick only to the safe old ground of his own class of people is undoubtedly passing. Especially in America, where all the peoples of the world are scrambling side by side and modern machines and the ramifications of international commerce are steadily breaking down the ethnological barriers that separate the peoples of the world" (139).

More recently, comparative cultural and literary studies of American modernism have been "steadily breaking down the ethnological barriers" that have defined the parameters of the Harlem Renaissance, arguing that its formation was more intercultural—and more international—than its most influential historians have suggested. By the turn of the century, influential studies began to appear, such as George Hutchinson's interracial formulation of "the Harlem Renaissance in black and white," Ann Douglass's extensive overview of 1920s "mongrel Manhattan," Michael North's comparative analysis of "the dialect of modernism," and Michael Denning's panoramic account of "the laboring of American culture," all of which underscore the interrelations of African American and immigrant cultural forms within the United States.[11] Perhaps the most significant commonality was the rhetorical appeal to cultural pluralism that characterizes African American and immigrant American cultural nationalisms. Liberal proponents of African American cultural nationalism emphasized Harlem's multinational dimension, affirming a model of cultural pluralism that paralleled immigrant claims for a "trans-national" American culture.[12] Such a model of cultural pluralism is most familiarly found in *The New Negro* anthology, which, despite its limited coverage of the Garvey movement and of radical socialist politics, is still considered the canonical text of African American modernism.[13]

Alain Locke's introduction to *The New Negro*, published only a year after the passage of the 1924 Immigration Act, describes Harlem as a cosmopolitan cultural capital whose importance for "Aframerican" nationalism resembles that of the newly emergent national capitals of Europe:

> Here in Manhattan is not merely the largest Negro community in the world, but the first concentration in history of so many diverse elements of Negro life. It has attracted the African, the West Indian, the Negro American; has brought together the Negro of the North and the Negro of the South. . . . In Harlem, Negro life is seizing upon its first chances for group expression and self-determination. It is—or promises at least to be—a race capital. . . . Without pretense to their political significance, Harlem has the same role to play for the New Negro as Dublin has had for the New Ireland or Prague for the New Czechoslovakia. ("New Negro" 6–7)

Locke's claims for Harlem's role as the international cultural center for peoples of African descent—the "home of the Negro's 'Zionism'" (14), as he writes—are echoed elsewhere in the anthology. For example, James Weldon Johnson writes in the essay that would become the introduction to his important 1930 history, *Black Manhattan*: "Throughout coloured America Harlem is the recognized Negro capital. Indeed, it is Mecca for the sightseer, the pleasure-seeker, the curious, the adventurous, the enterprising, the ambitious, and the talented of the entire Negro world; for the lure of it has reached down to every island of the Carib Sea and penetrated even into Africa" ("Harlem" 301). Johnson himself was born shortly after his parents had migrated to the United States from the Bahamas.[14] The large number of prominent African American intellectuals whose families had migrated from the Caribbean also included Du Bois, whose grandfather was from the Bahamas and whose father was born in Haiti. More important to this vision of Harlem as a multinational center of black culture are the contributors to the anthology who themselves had migrated from the Caribbean. In addition to McKay, these would include the short story writer Eric Walrond (born in British Guyana), the scholar of African and African American history Arthur Schomburg (born in Puerto Rico), the journalist and historian Joel Rogers (born in Jamaica), and the journalist and radical political activist W. A. Domingo (also from Jamaica).[15]

In his retrospective account of post–World War I Harlem, *Harlem: Negro Metropolis* (1940), McKay concurred with the New Negro celebration of Harlem as a cosmopolitan "Negro Capital." He wrote that Harlem was "more than the Negro capital of the nation. It is the Negro capital of the world. And as New York is the most glorious experiment on earth of different races and divers [*sic*] groups of humanity struggling and scrambling to live together, so Harlem is the most interesting sample of black humanity marching along with white humanity" (16). Unlike Locke, however, McKay identified this emergent "cultural center" in the post–World War I years with Marcus Garvey, the leader of "African Zionism" (20), who brought worldwide attention to Harlem. Harlem was indeed distinctive in its mix of Caribbean and African immigrants as well as blacks from the United States, and Garvey was the figure who most embodied the transnational implications of the "New Negro": "The flowering of Harlem's creative life came in the Garvey era. The anthology, THE NEW NEGRO, which oriented the debut of the Renaissance writers, was printed in 1925. If Marcus Garvey did not originate the phrase, New Negro, he at least made it popular" (177). While McKay's retrospective celebration of Garvey is informed by his disdain for communism in the 1930s as well as by his commitment to Pan-Africanism, he identifies "New Negro" Harlem with working-class blacks. And his consideration of black popular entertainment, or "the business of amusements" (117–20), likewise focuses on the exploitation of black workers, including performing artists, as well as the working-class pursuit of pleasure in cabarets. Indeed, his distinction between black-owned cabarets before Prohibition and their successors is especially important for *Home to Harlem*, which takes place immediately before Prohibition:

> The Negro cabaratier made a special instrument of the cabaret to attract and hold the restive customers of his race. He created an intimate theatre of relaxation for colored boy and girl, in which the respectable family man could spend an evening away from home and where bachelors were beguiled by darkly singing damsels, to the chinking of glasses, the erotic suggestiveness of Negro music and wailing "blues" of the entertainer. (117)

The success of the "Negro cabaratier" was short-lived, however. With the growing control of entertainment venues by organized crime during and after Prohibition, black cabaret workers were subject to more abusive working conditions: "Behind the exciting Baroque fantasy of Negro entertainment lies the grim reality of ruthless jobbery." This "ruthless jobbery" included the exploitation of black entertainers by white managers. As McKay underscores, jazz bands were routinely subject to "a remuneration on a lower scale than white jazz bands, even though they may perform in the same houses" (119).

McKay did not write extensively about African American music, but his early commentary on the performing arts also emphasizes both the cultural politics of popular music and the professional challenges faced by African American artists. He defined musicians and dancers as artists and as laborers, as cultural workers not unlike himself. Whether writing about popular music such as jazz or about his own novels, he was as skeptical about the response of the African American intelligentsia as he was about white racist criticism. His 1921 *Liberator* review of the immensely successful Broadway musical *Shuffle Along*, which featured African American music, lyrics, choreography, cast, and production, is a good example. McKay defends and applauds the art of burlesque in "A Negro Extravaganza," contesting critics whose aesthetic and moral values blinded them to the social significance of *Shuffle Along*: "And the metropolitan notational critics who have damned 'Shuffle Along' for not fulfilling the role of an Italian light opera are as filmy-sighted as the convention-ridden and head-ossified Negro intelligentsia, who censure colored actors for portraying the inimitable comic characteristics of Negro life, because they make white people laugh!" McKay not only affirms the social value of comedy; he also asserts the potentially transformative social power of black music and dance: "Negro artists will be doing a fine service to the world, maybe greater than the combined action of all the white and black radicals yelling revolution together, if by their efforts they can spirit the whites away from lynching and inbred prejudice, to the realm of laughter and syncopated motion." Suggesting that laughter is more revolutionary than "white and black radicals yelling revolution" in the *Liberator* is itself comic, but McKay is certainly serious when he subsequently recalls an example of the power of black music to heal violent racial conflict. Reflecting on the postwar race riots in London, he recalls the dramatic impact of a performance by the "American Southern Orchestra": "And soon all of the slums of London, forgetting the riots, were echoing with syncopated songs" (24).

The primary target of his criticism in "A Negro Extravaganza" is the African American intelligentsia; in supporting only art that is "dignified and respectable," African American critics implicitly accept the dominant white culture's condescending and judgmental misperceptions of African American popular forms of expression. McKay's critique of such "high" cultural standards sides with the urban black folk, whose popular cultural expression persists "in Harlem, along Fifth and Lenox avenues, in Marcus Garvey's Hall with its extravagant paraphernalia, in his churches and cabarets" (24). However, his concluding affirmation of African American popular culture acknowledges the complications arising from white expectations of "primitive" expression: "Negroes of America, who by an acquired language and suffering, are closer knit together than all the many tribes of Africa . . . cannot satisfy the desire of the hyper-critical whites for the Congo wriggle, the tribal war jig, and the jungle whoop. The chastisement of civilization has sobered and robbed them of these unique manifestations." McKay mocks the very terms for what is presumably primitive about African American culture, emphasizing that whites project their own "Savagedom" onto African American performing artists. In ultimately asserting the Africanness of African American performance, he also enacts the intercultural tension inherent in African American popular culture: "The conventions of 'Shuffle Along' are those of Broadway, but the voice is nevertheless indubitably African expatriate. It is this basic African element which makes Negro imitations so delightfully humorous and enjoyable" (25). In answering critics who dismissed *Shuffle Along* as a cheap imitation of Broadway, McKay celebrates both the creative power of African diasporic musical expression and the critical potential for "Negro imitations" of established cultural forms.

McKay's antipathy to African American "talented tenth" elitism is well documented, and his early cultural criticism displays both an assertive class consciousness and a subtle appreciation of the challenges faced by the "indubitably African expatriate" performing artist. The most extensive example of McKay's social analysis of African American music in the early 1920s extends this awareness to the international stage of the Fourth Congress of the Communist International, in 1922. His book *The Negroes in America*, which was commissioned by the Soviet State Publishing House after McKay's report on the "Negro Question" at the Fourth Congress, includes a chapter titled "Negroes in Art and Music." While McKay begins with a discussion of African visual arts, he asserts that blacks in the United States are largely limited to the performing arts: "The ruling classes of America are reconciled to the fact that the distinctive syncopated music of the American people has a Negro origin and that Negroes excel in singing, dancing, and acting as natural artists. But that is all. It would be sacrilege to the primacy of whites to encourage the artistic aspirations of blacks" (59). McKay emphasizes how African American performing artists were largely excluded from major roles in the theater and opera in the United States. And in the one arena where African American performing artists were accepted, musical theater, they were limited to the performance of "traditional songs or eccentric dances" (60). In addition, black artists were subjected to the timidity of the African American intelligentsia, which resisted realist portrayals of African American working-class life that might appear offensive, including "genuine Negro folk songs and jazz songs" (61). It is thus remarkable that African American artists were successful in the musical and theatrical world, given that they were caught "between two fires—the unjust white criticism and the criticism of the Negro intelligentsia" (62). Even more remarkable is McKay's conclusion, which defiantly asserts that black artistic expression represented nothing less than an international vanguard:

> Our age is the age of the Negro in art. The slogan of the aesthetic art world is "Return to the Primitive." The Futurists and Impressionists are agreed in turning everything upside down in an attempt to achieve the wisdom of the primitive Negro. . . . It is often strange to see how an ultracivilized public sits at the feet of a simple savage teacher and gleans so little from him because he is too civilized to learn. (63)

This language is uncompromising in its celebration of the "primitive" arts of the African diaspora. But by identifying the "primitive" with "wisdom," with education, with progress, McKay, here as well as elsewhere, reclaims the categories most often invoked to denigrate African and African diasporic cultures.

If jazz is identified with the "primitive," then in McKay's fiction it is done so to question the very terms by which jazz was characterized as either modern or African. International modernism, McKay suggests, was inseparable from

Afro-modernism. Like James Weldon Johnson and Alain Locke, McKay celebrated the African origins of jazz as well as the distinctively African American participatory dynamic of jazz performance. However, his embrace of jazz as an urban working-class expressive form was closer in spirit to the younger generation of Langston Hughes, who challenged the aesthetic biases of critics who dismissed the blues and jazz. For McKay, like Hughes, jazz represents "the low-down folks, the so-called common element," whose "joy runs bang! into ecstasy. Their religion roars to a shout. Play awhile. Sing awhile. O, let's dance!" (Hughes, "Negro Artist" 56). As in Hughes's writing about jazz, jazz performance figures not only dramatically but also stylistically in *Home to Harlem*. When Jake returns home in the first chapter, the first place he goes is a cabaret called "the Baltimore," where he meets and falls in love with a prostitute named Felice. When he is reunited with Felice and departs from Harlem with her in the final chapter, he departs from this same cabaret. For Jake, Harlem is the nightlife world of cabarets, where "all night long, ragtime and 'blues' playing somewhere, . . . singing somewhere, dancing somewhere!" (15). The cabarets that Jake frequents are sites of unpredictable sexual possibility, where musicians and dancers interact intimately, and where Jake is as likely to mix with "dandies" and "pansies" as with the "chocolate-brown and walnut-brown girls" (8) he identifies with Harlem. Such social improvisation is further suggested through the narrative enactment of jazz performance, through "red moods, black moods, golden moods. Curious, syncopated slipping-over into one mood, back-sliding back to the first mood. Humming in harmony, barbaric harmony, joy-drunk, chasing out the shadow of the moment before" (54).

The cabarets of *Home to Harlem* represent the potential for interracial working-class camaraderie that Chandler Owen celebrated in his 1922 *Messenger* article, "The Cabaret—A Useful Social Institution." He characterizes the cabaret as "one of the most democratic institutions in America. It is breaking down the color line. It is destroying the psychology of caste. It is disseminating joy to the most humble and the most high. It is the dynamic agent of social equality." This socialist vision of the "black-and-tan" cabaret underscores the social power of music and dance, the capacity of jazz to counteract the destructiveness of racial antagonism where civic institutions have failed to do so. Accentuating the power of "the so-called common people, white and black," to interact congenially despite the incendiary race baiting of "lying newspapers, screens, and demagogues," Owen asserts, "The cabaret is an institution. It is doing in many cities what the church, school and family have failed to do. It is destroying the hydra-headed monster of race-prejudice" (461). Owen's claim that the cabaret is a "useful institution" for fostering interracial understanding and cooperation was not uncontested on the African American left, as Sterling Brown's more skeptical portrayal of a black-and-tan in his poem "Cabaret" most dramatically exemplifies. However, Owen's argument corresponds with McKay's understanding of the power of black music to heal racial divisions. *Home to Harlem* extends Owen's claims in suggesting how the social space of the cabaret also destabilizes normative expectations of gender and sexuality. As Shane Vogel writes, the cabaret is a site of "utopian potential" in *Home to Harlem*, a site for imagining alternative understandings of race and sex, a site that fosters "nonnormative intimacies."[16] As the syncopated sound for improvising new social relations, jazz functions paradoxically as a simultaneously "modern" and "primitive" mode of expression, the expression of a "strange un-American world where colored meets and mingles freely and naturally with white" (106), extending to "Paris and Cairo, Shanghai, Honolulu, and Java" (107), but also the distinctively African American expression of abandonment to "pure voluptuous jazzing" (108).

Of all of the cabarets and dance halls in *Home to Harlem*, the club known as the Congo stands out as a refuge from the racial and class tensions that make Harlem nightlife so precarious. McKay introduces the Congo as "a real throbbing little African in New York. It was an amusement place entirely for the unwashed of the Black Belt. . . . Pot-wrestlers, third cooks, W.C. attendants, scrub maids, dish-washers, stevedores" (29). Unlike "the veneer of Seventh Avenue, and Goldgraben's Afro-Oriental garishness," the Congo was "African in spirit and color" (30). As a black establishment that caters to the service workers and laborers of New York, the Congo suggests the potential for black working-class camaraderie. It also suggests the creative power of black music to transgress social boundaries that might otherwise divide these workers. While *Home to Harlem* is not as explicit as *Banjo* in mixing songs that represent the multiple traditions of the African diaspora, its quotation and juxtaposition of blues and jazz songs underscores the unifying potential of black popular music. McKay quotes liberally from songs that were circulating during and after World War I, and he dramatizes the creative ability of performing artists to adapt and translate popular songs for the specific social institutions in which they are performed. This improvisational ability to transform popular songs often involves the disruption of gendered expectations, as when the cabaret singer at the Baltimore, "a shiny coffee-colored girl in a green frock and Indian-waved hair," sings in "a man's bass voice . . . 'I'm crazy, plum crazy / About a man, mah man'" (31). A different form of improvisation occurs at the Congo, when Congo Rose begins an immensely popular song, "Hesitation Blues," and segues into Bessie Smith's more risqué "Foolish Man Blues":

And it is ashes to ashes and dust to dust,
Can you show me a woman that a man can trust?
　　　Oh baby, how are you?
　　　Oh baby, what are you?
　　　Oh, can I have you now,
　　　Or have I got to wait?
　　　Oh, let me have a date,
　　　Why do you hesitate?
And there is two things in Harlem I don't understan'
It is a bulldycking woman and a fagotty man. (37)

"Hesitation Blues" was already a classic song by 1919, not only as a popular African American folk song, but also as a song that was published as early as 1915 by Billy Smythe. It was also published in 1915 by W. C. Handy, as "Hesitating Blues," with lyrics that featured separated lovers trying (unsuccessfully) to reach each other by telephone. "Hesitation Blues" was first recorded by the Victor Military Band in 1916 and was made internationally famous by James Reese Europe's 369th U.S. Infantry "Hellfighters Marching Band." To transform this traditional song, with its renowned history of interpretation, into a "drag 'blues' that was the favorite of all the low-down dance halls" (McKay, *Home to Harlem* 36) is at once an implicit critique of how African diasporic music becomes "respectable" and a celebration of iconoclastic performers like Bessie Smith. In his creative adaptation of popular lyrics, here and elsewhere in *Home to Harlem*, McKay acknowledges the poetry of African American popular music, poetry that depends as much on the power of performative improvisation as on linguistic skill. By quoting songs without attribution and instead emphasizing the call-and-response social dynamic of their performance, McKay appeals to the communal identification with African diasporic songs rather than their status as commodities. And by situating such a familiar song as "Hesitation Blues" in the "low-down" mix of Congo Rose's performance, McKay anticipates Hughes's adaptation of this song for more explicit social commentary in *Ask Your Mama*.

As improvisational and convivial as the scenes of dancing appear in *Home to Harlem*, McKay does not idealize the nightlife of cabarets. The most ecstatic scenes are repeatedly disrupted by violent conflict, if not the intrusion of the police. When the dancers at the Baltimore reach a "high point of excitement" in chapter 4, for example, this excitement is suddenly interrupted: "A crash cut through the music. A table went jazzing into the drum. The cabaret singer lay sprawling on the floor" (32–33). "Jazz" is a verb that is identified with emotional volatility as well as release from everyday pressures, with violence as well as sexual desire. Such volatility is not limited to black-

and-tan nightclubs. Even in the Congo, as well as in the clubs that catered to a wealthier and often whiter clientele, the social tensions between black workers are never far from erupting. The scene when Congo Rose dances with the "boy who was a striking advertisement of the Ambrozine Palace of Beauty" (91) is as ecstatic as any scene in the novel. As the pianist begins playing "When Luty Dances," he "seemed in a state of swaying excitement . . . his eyes toward the ceiling in a sort of savage ecstatic dream" (92), "lean, smart fingers beating barbaric beauty out of a white frame" (94). As excitedly syncopated as the prose rendering of the piano becomes, the enactment of the "exercise of rhythmical exactness for two" (93), of Rose and the boy, is equally propulsive. Yet this scene of joyful release is brief, as it is interrupted by the entrance of Susy and her subsequent dismissal of Zeddy and, more violently, a raucous fight between two West Indian women. The African refuge of the Congo is disrupted by an ugly exchange between West Indians, between West Indians and American blacks, and between men and women, all of whom resort to the most common, and most demeaning, stereotypes about each other's otherness. This scene, like other cabaret scenes that move suddenly from dance-floor harmony to intraracial—but often intercultural—conflict, suggests how fragile the camaraderie of cabaret life is in *Home to Harlem*.

The interracial harmony of Madame Suarez's buffet flat speakeasy in chapter 8 is likewise only temporary, if not illusory, because it is subject to the surveillance and intrusion of undercover as well as uniformed police. Here Jake can "luxuriate with charmingly painted pansies" while admiring women so eloquent that "they resembled the wonderfully beautiful pictures of women of ancient Egypt" (104–105). With its interracial mix, this buffet flat exemplifies the "strange un-American world where colored meets and mingles freely with and naturally with white" (106). But not for long! On a Saturday night when everyone is immersed in "pure voluptuous jazzing," the "five young men unmasked as the Vice Squad and killed the thing" (108). These men had "posed as good fellows, regular guys, looking for a good time only in the Black Belt. They were wearied of the pleasures of the big white world, wanted something new—the primitive joy of Harlem" (109). These apparently "regular guys" betray not only Jake's trust in their goodwill, their presumed willingness to interact with blacks as social equals; they also betray the very stereotype of white patrons of Harlem nightlife, familiar to popular accounts of Harlem nightlife such as *Nigger Heaven*, leaving the "big white world" for the "primitive joy of Harlem." This scene also reminds Jake, and reminds readers who might otherwise seek such "primitive joy," of the harshness of the racial order that is quickly restored. Madame Suarez is sent to Blackwell's Island to serve a six-month sentence. In contrast the white girls who were

arrested in the raid are not imprisoned. They are, however, reprimanded by
the judge, who says that "it was a pity that he had no power to order them
whipped. For whipping was the only punishment he considered suitable for
white women who dishonored their race by associating with colored persons"
(*Home to Harlem* 110).

In addition to revealing the power of the state to enforce the racial and
sexual order that the social space of cabarets disrupts, McKay also underscores the difficult labor conditions of cabaret musicians and service workers.
If the Congo represents a "thick, dark-colorful, and fascinating" (36) refuge
from the racial tensions of the streets outside, the life of the singer Congo
Rose is precarious at best. The fact that McKay represents her everyday life, as
well as her every-night life, with social and psychological specificity exemplifies how *Home to Harlem* demystifies the "primitive" allure of jazz and jazz
women specifically. The chapter titled "Congo Rose" represents contrasting
versions of her persona. The first is her role as the cabaret singer, with her
commanding authority on the dance floor. The second is the after-hours
Rose, who seems utterly dependent on men for protection and self-esteem.
As strong as she seems as a performer, her economic success depends on
her sexual appeal to men, and this extends to her domestic life as well: she
is either singing for tips or "singing" for the protection of a man. Although
the novel takes Rose's plight seriously, she also functions as a character who
reveals Jake's ethical consciousness. There is an important parallel between
the two events that distinguish Jake's integrity from the more questionable
values of characters such as Zeddy: (1) his refusal to work as a scab during
a longshoremen's union strike, and (2) his refusal to accept payment from
Rose to be her "sweet man." In both cases, he refuses to compromise his
principles for the pursuit of financial gain—that is, he refuses to sell himself
or to demean others. The fact that Rose insists that he hit her to demonstrate
his love for her is what compels him to leave Harlem. The fact that her insistence seems normative, if not definitive of the professional and domestic
life she exemplifies, suggests that the "utopian potential" of the cabaret does
not extend to the female workers whom the cabaret proprietors depend on
for their profits.

Part 2: Haiti

Because *Home to Harlem* identifies Jake with a predominantly African American Harlem, it is easy to overlook the worldliness of his character as well as
the international dimensions of Harlem. In his initial return home, Jake is
introduced as part of a multinational, multiracial crew on a transatlantic

freighter. From the beginning, McKay foregrounds how national identity is subjected to a transnational logic of racial and class hierarchy. The novel's opening two sentences suggest that racial categories are self-explanatory: "All that Jake knew about the freighter on which he stoked was that it stank between sea and sky. He was working with a dirty Arab crew" (1). Yet such an apparently self-evident equation of "Arab" with "dirty" is complicated by the narrative's subsequent racial contradictions. Within the racial hierarchy of this ship, which relegates "the Arabs" to the lowest level of "filth," Jake is elevated to a higher status than his fellow stokers. Yet he is not deceived when a white sailor says to him, "'You're the same like us chaps. You ain't like them dirty jabbering coolies'" (2–3). Jake's unstated response suggests an experienced consciousness of how the interrelated hierarchies of race and class render such "flattery" suspect: "But Jake smiled and shook his head in a non-committal way. He knew that if he was just like the white sailors, he might have signed on as a deckhand and not as a stoker" (3). The material consequences of racist ideology supersede any spurious attempts to bridge racial divides, as the subsequent narration of Jake's earlier wartime experience reinforces. Like other African American soldiers who had enlisted to fight, Jake is limited to manual labor at the army base camp. Frustrated, he makes a seemingly impulsive decision to leave the army and travel to England, a decision whose potential consequences eventually follow him home to Harlem. Significantly, Jake leaves France because he is seduced by the kindness of an English sailor who calls him "darky" rather than "nigger" (5). He is seduced despite the admitted knowledge that "back home" such language would signify "friendly contempt." Although he "thought how strange it was to hear the Englishman say 'darky' without being offended" (5), Jake settles in London's increasingly racially mixed East End and even lives with a white woman. When postwar race riots disrupt his temporary complacency in London, however, Jake realizes that England is hardly exempt from the racial hatred he had identified with the United States. His initial lapse of judgment, the moment of trust "colored" by his comparison of white American and English treatment of blacks, becomes painfully evident to him. He has no choice but to leave the "white folks' war" (8) as far behind as he can, so he embarks for Harlem on the freighter.

Because Jake is a deserter, albeit from a military that had deserted him in his desire to fight for his nation, he cannot leave the war entirely behind him. As casual as his picaresque migrant life appears to be, as confident as he is that he can always find another job or another lover, he is an outlaw throughout the novel. Yet his status as a war deserter does not seem unusual in Harlem, and the possibility of arrest for desertion is only vaguely threatening until the end of the book. While his friend and fellow veteran Zeddy warns him as soon as he returns that the "'gov'mant still smoking out deserters and draft dodgers'" (22), even offering rewards to those who turn them in, this specific threat becomes submerged within the more general threat of random arrest that black men take for granted in McKay's Harlem. Nonetheless, Jake's outlaw status is given significant structural weight in the novel. Not only does he come home to Harlem as a war deserter, but he also eventually leaves Harlem as a result of being publicly exposed as such. The novel's primary narrative weight is given to Jake's quest for Felice, the "sweet brown" prostitute with whom he falls in love his first night back in Harlem, only to lose her until the novel's conclusion, when they are reunited and eventually depart for Chicago. The geography of this quest is not informed by a mythic pull of Harlem as a black mecca, however, even though Felice herself embodies this myth with her attractiveness, her generosity, and her elusiveness.[17] It is defined instead by the more pragmatic need to escape the "white folks' business," to find refuge among black migrants like himself.

Jake's final decision to leave Harlem is impelled by his exposure as an outlaw by the same friend, Zeddy, who had warned him to keep quiet about his desertion. In the climactic barroom conflict over "whose woman" Felice is, Zeddy's final defense is to shout at Jake, "'You come gunning at me, but you didn't go gunning after the Germans. Nosah! You was scared and runned away from the army.'" As hurt as Jake is by Zeddy's desperate accusation, he is even more disturbed by the absurd truth of his final words: "'I ain't got no reason to worry sence youse down in the white folks' books'" (327). In the aftermath of this fight, Jake is disgusted that he has succumbed to the level of violence and hatred he had experienced in Europe:

> He was caught in the thing that he despised so thoroughly . . . Brest, London, and his America. Their vivid brutality tortured his imagination. Oh, he was infinitely disgusted with himself to think that he had just been moved by the same savage emotions as those vile, vicious, villainous white men who, like hyenas and rattlers, had fought, murdered, and clawed the entrails out of black men over the common, commercial flesh of women. (328)

Interestingly, the very woman whose "commercial flesh" had initially signified Harlem's immense appeal to Jake reminds him not only of the masculinist absurdity of his regret for not fighting in the war but also of the real threat he faces as a known war deserter. "'What right have niggers got to shoot down a whole lot of Germans for?'" she asks. "'Is they worse than Americans or any other nation a white people? You done do the right thing, honey . . . but all the same, we can't stay in Harlem no longer, for the bulls will sure get you'" (331–32). While Jake's immediate impulse is to "go on off to sea again," Felice's pragmatic solution to his dilemma depends on a clear distinction between "his America" and a "country" less rigidly inscribed by the rule of law: "'This heah is you' country, daddy. . . . This heah country is good and big enough for us to git lost in. You know Chicago? . . . I hear it's a mahvelous place foh niggers'" (332–33). They leave for Chicago that night. If Jake is an outlaw from a nation that has denied him his rights as a citizen, he can still lay claim to a country within but apart from this nation, even if its primary appeal is that it is "'big enough . . . to git lost in.'"

In contrast with Jake, the only "country" that Ray can claim as "home" is occupied by the U.S. Marines. The introduction of Ray in part 2 parallels the novel's introduction of Jake on the transatlantic freighter as he first appears in the highly stratified, class-conscious milieu of a railroad dining car crossing Pennsylvania. Whereas Jake is at first part of a multinational crew on the freighter, however, Ray is presumably the only "foreigner" among the African American Pullman porters and waiters. Ray's exile is accentuated not only by his outsider status among his co-workers—as a Haitian and as an intellectual—but also by the delayed appearance of his narrative within the novel. While Jake's opening journey home to Harlem initiates the novel's overarching narrative pattern of movement, with Harlem as its (sometimes) centrifugal and (sometimes) centripetal center, Ray's narrative journey initially appears to have neither a "home" nor any other destination. As he is exiled from his native Haiti, his narrative likewise appears out of place within Jake's African American migrant narrative. This initially anonymous waiter is at first an anomaly to the incredulous Jake, who presumably has never heard a black man speak French nor has even heard of Haiti.[18] Although we see Ray primarily through Jake's eyes, the novel reminds us that "Jake was very American in spirit and shared a little of that comfortable Yankee contempt for poor foreigners. And as an American Negro he looked askew at foreign niggers. Africa was jungle, and Africans bush niggers, cannibals. And West Indians were monkey-chasers" (134). When Jake asks where Haiti is, Ray's answer assumes an imperial American geopolitical frame of reference: "'An island in the Caribbean—near the Panama Canal'" (131). Nonetheless, Jake is captivated by Ray's discourse on "the romance of Hayti" (136). He asks him how a student of literature and history like himself could end up working on an American railroad dining car. When Ray responds, "'Uncle Sam put me here,'" Jake's impulsive reaction is defensive: "'Whadye mean Uncle Sam? . . . Don't hand me that bull'" (136). Ray explains:

> "Maybe you don't know that during the World War Uncle Sam grabbed Hayti. My father was an official down there. He didn't want Uncle Sam in Hayti and he said so and said it loud. They told him to shut up and he wouldn't, so they

shut him up in jail. My brother also made a noise and American marines killed
him in the street. I had nobody to pay for me at the university, so I had to get
out and work. Voilá!" (136–37)

If an educated, French-speaking citizen of an independent black nation is
almost inconceivable to him, Jake proves to be a receptive student of Ray's
lecture on Haiti's proud but tragic history.

Ray, on the other hand, is initially far less receptive to Jake's more practical
lessons of migrant work life, as his contempt for American imperial arrogance
eclipses any recognition of commonality he shares with his black co-workers.
He is both repulsed by the thought of any kinship with them and disturbed
by this repulsion as he reflects on his racial identity during the crew's layover
in Pittsburgh: "These men claimed kinship with him. They were black like
him. Man and nature had put them in the same race. He ought to love them
. . . if he had a shred of social morality in him." But instead he questions
the very grounds for this "social morality": "Why should he have and love
a race?" (153). While Ray sees racial and national idealizations as similarly
problematic responses to white supremacist ideology, the troubling question of his own national identity supersedes any thoughts of cross-cultural
racial commonalities: "He remembered when little Hayti was floundering
uncontrolled, how proud he was to be the son of a free nation. He used to
feel condescendingly sorry for those poor African natives; superior to ten
millions of suppressed Yankee 'coons.' Now he was just one of them and he
hated them for being one of them" (155). Like Jake, Ray's vision is initially
limited by the very nationalism he decries. Any transnational alliance with
the African American working class is difficult to imagine, even though he
is now "one of them." Because Haiti is no longer a "free nation," he can only
imagine "home" in his delirious nightmares as a refuge from "the clutches
of that magnificent monster of civilization" (155), a fantastic "paradise" that
blends childhood memory with primitivist fantasy of an exotic tropical landscape where "taboos and terrors and penalties were transformed into new
pagan delights" (158).

During the early years of the Harlem Renaissance, the one concern that
most unified African American and Caribbean intellectuals was the demand
for Haitian self-determination. As editor of *The Crisis*, Du Bois himself had
appealed to his readers to oppose the occupation of Haiti as early as 1915.
Probably the most prominent African American critic of United States policy
was James Weldon Johnson, who reported injustices in occupied Haiti in 1920
for *The Crisis* and *The Nation*. Drawing attention to both the unconstitutional-
ity of the United States intervention and the commercial motivation behind

it, Johnson set the tone for future reports on occupied Haiti.[19] During the long period of occupation (1915–1934), Haiti's revolutionary history also became an important point of reference for both black nationalist and communist radicals. *Home to Harlem* anticipates the appeal to Haiti's revolutionary past in 1930s proletarian fiction as well as in C.L.R. James's landmark history, *The Black Jacobins*.[20] But, as McKay suggests in *Home to Harlem*, awareness of Haiti's national history—including its recent history—was far removed from the proletarian consciousness of a character like Jake, even during the years of most intense conflict. In fact, such awareness of Haiti had also become far removed from American public consciousness by the mid-1920s, years of apparent calm following the consolidation of American military control. This decreased American attention to Haiti's ongoing ordeal—so dramatically different from the awareness of anti-imperialist Haitian nationalism that McKay encountered living in Paris at this time—is the unstated political subtext of *Home to Harlem*.

Opposition to the American military occupation of Haiti within the United States was strongest during the election year of 1920, following the military response to the massive uprising that took place in 1919. By 1919, U.S. policy makers had drastically revised the Haitian constitution. The new constitution blatantly served American economic and military interests and denied democratic rights to Haitians. Most notably, it legalized alien land ownership, suspended the elected Haitian legislature, and legalized all acts of the military occupation. In addition to the introduction of such antidemocratic policies, the United States also implemented plantation agriculture that was financed by private American investments, which destroyed the existing land-tenure system of peasant freeholders. While there had been popular resistance to U.S. economic and military policy since the occupation, the most intense guerilla warfare took place during the uprising of 1919. The marines responded with their superior weaponry, killing more than three thousand Haitians. Criticism of the occupation intensified in the United States when military documents about "the indiscriminate killing of natives" were publicized.[21]

The investigative articles that James Weldon Johnson wrote for *The Nation* and *The Crisis* had the greatest impact on African American public awareness of Haiti. After visiting Haiti on behalf of the NAACP, Johnson wrote bluntly about the economic reasons why the United States had chosen to occupy that country. While revealing the racist hypocrisy of antidemocratic policy undertaken on behalf of American political ideals, the examples of political injustices and military atrocities he cites in the *Nation* article belie the very claims for respecting national sovereignty that informed the Wilson administration's World War I policy:

The Administration . . . with less justification of Austria's invasion of Serbia, or
Germany's rape of Belgium, without warrant other than the doctrine that "might
makes right," has conquered Haiti. It has done this through the very period
when, in the words of its chief spokesman, our sons were laying down their
lives overseas "for democracy, for the rights of those who submit to authority
to have a voice in their own government, for the rights and liberties of small
nations." (Johnson, "Self-Determining Haiti" 238)

Johnson's reference to the most obvious World War I European examples of
violated national sovereignty not only reveals the duplicity of Wilson's foreign
policy; it also echoes more radical claims for Haiti's political significance as
a victim of imperial aggression. After the 1919 revolt, Haiti was often compared to the emerging nations seeking independence from British colonial
rule. According to the socialist *Messenger*, for example, the United States
had no credibility in arguing for "the self-determination of smaller nationalities," for "Santo Domingo and Haiti are the Ireland of America" ("Santo
Domingo Protests" 226). Underscoring the systematically imperialist design
of the United States' foreign policy in the Caribbean, *The Messenger* argues
elsewhere that "Haiti is America's India. . . . Sentiment, homilies on justice
and morality have no weight in a world of imperialism. Only profits count.
No other reason can be assigned for Great Britain in Egypt, Japan in Corea
and Siberia, or America in Haiti" ("America's India" 418). *The Crisis* likewise
emphasized the parallels of Haitian claims for self-determination with the
claims of India, Egypt, and Ireland, especially in Du Bois's reports on the
initial Pan-African congresses.[22] Johnson's investigative article in *The Crisis*,
while covering much of the same ground as his *Nation* series, also appeals
directly to the interests of his African American readers in considering the
plight of Haiti, "for Haiti is the one best chance that the Negro has in the world
to prove that he is capable of the highest self-government. If Haiti should
ultimately lose her independence, that one best chance will be lost" ("The
Truth about Haiti" 224). Johnson reminds his readers that the United States
was the "last of all the strong nations to recognize [Haitian] independence"
(218) and the first to violate Haiti's national sovereignty. In emphasizing
that the Haitian people were now subject to the same racial "prejudice" of
"southern white men" that had long oppressed African Americans, Johnson
appeals to the democratic ideals that link Haitian self-determination with
the interests of African peoples worldwide.

Given how strong such protests against the American occupation of Haiti
were, it is remarkable how quickly the cause of Haitian nationalism disappeared from the headlines of the major African American journals. By 1927,

however, there was a resurgence of African American interest in the Haitian response to the occupation, already over a decade long. The African American journal that devoted the most attention to Haitian cultural politics in the late 1920s was *Opportunity*, the National Urban League publication then edited by Charles S. Johnson. The *Opportunity* articles on Haiti include Rayford W. Logan's critique of supposed United States accomplishments in Haiti, "The New Haiti" (April 1927); John Vandercook's account of his travels to Haiti, "Whitewash" (October 1927); and the Haitian writer Dantès Bellegarde's "Haiti under the Rule of the United States" (December 1927), translated by Logan. Not surprisingly, Bellegarde's article is especially passionate in decrying the ongoing U.S. "'civil occupation' whose evident aim is to absorb or destroy all the moral and economic forces of the Haitian people" (354). Reiterating some of the same points made by James Weldon Johnson (whom he cites), his thorough indictment of U.S. economic and political policy in Haiti reveals the absurd disjunction between American propaganda and the realities of everyday life for Haitians. The American policy, Bellegarde writes, serves nobody's long-term interests, especially those of the American imperialists: "The American action in Haiti is in bankruptcy" (357).

Given that *Home to Harlem* itself reveals how the "bankruptcy" of the "American action" had everything to do with the white supremacist ideology through which it was justified, it is remarkable that so many reviewers of McKay's novel felt that it had "struck a deadly blow" at the whole black race. Paradoxically, the critical objection to McKay's representation of Harlem relates to desires—and anxieties—that similarly have informed American cultural mythologies of Haiti. As Michael Dash has written, American representations of Haiti since its independence most often have been projections of fantasy or insecurity; Haiti has been "the extreme case, whether it was virgin terrain, a garden of earthly delights where the black race could begin again or the closest and most histrionic examples of Africa's continental darkness" (2–3). During the occupation, these dichotomous representations of Haiti intensified. Such projections also characterized popular perceptions of Harlem in the 1920s, as McKay's novel itself exemplifies. Like the sensationalist vision of Haiti, Harlem nightclubs offered the exotic appeal of unrestrained sensuality. As Dash writes, Harlem nightlife provided "a safe safari into the world of the primitive . . . a plunge into the unknown, a salutary disorientation for those who were willing to indulge their wildest fantasies" (46). *Home to Harlem*'s commercial success attests to the popular desire for such "disorientation," and the polarized critical response to the novel among black American reviewers suggests how politically charged primitivist representations of black life still were in the late 1920s. But if the more conspicuous narrative of Jake's amorous adventures provoked the controversy that dominated critical discussion of the novel, it also seemed to deflect its readers' attention from the embedded narrative of the historically conscious Haitian exile.[23] Ray's narrative in fact underscores the hegemonic power of primitivist stereotyping, as it appeals to a Pan-Africanist vision that can embrace such divergent experiences as those of Jake and Ray, of the African American and the African Caribbean, of the proletarian and the intellectual. And while Ray's narrative does not feature raucous cabaret scenes as in part 1, African American music—and jazz specifically—plays a significant role in resolving Ray's quandary as a writer to reclaim the "primitive" for a progressive conceptualization of black internationalism.

If Jake is challenged to imagine a world of black self-determination, a world that he identifies with the rhetorical power of intellectual discourse, Ray is challenged as a writer to render the poetic power of Jake's black proletarian speech.[24] As affectionate and mutually supportive as Jake's friendship with Ray becomes, their distance from each other remains. However, this distance becomes less one of cultural difference than of social class, of education, of Jake's awareness that because he is not "proper-speaking" like Ray his future is limited (273), and of Ray's awareness that his education has failed to provide him a language to represent Jake's working-class world: "The sudden upset of affairs in his home country had landed him in the quivering heart of a naked world whose reality was hitherto unimaginable. It was what they called in print and polite conversation 'the underworld'" (224). While Ray's literary vision is limited by the proprietary codes of "print and polite conversation," his distance from Jake's "underworld" is also a problem of translation: "The compound world baffled him, as some English words did sometimes. Why *under*world he could never understand. It was very much upon the surface as were the other divisions of human life" (224–25). Ray recognizes that the problem of representing Jake's working-class world is less a problem of absolute social stratification, given his own involvement with this world, than of his literary education. Though he had been taught to value the social vision of nineteenth-century novelists such as Hugo, Stowe, Dickens, Zola, and especially the Russian realists, he realizes that with the "great mass carnage in Europe and the great mass revolution in Russia . . . he had lived over the end of an era" (225–26).

As betrayed by his education as Ray feels within the African American working-class world that he has adopted, paradoxically, it is his experience of social upheaval in his own country that has given him the insight to recognize the challenge of representing Jake's world: "Thank God and Uncle Sam that the old dreams were shattered. Nevertheless, he still felt more than ever the utter blinding nakedness and violent coloring of life. But what of it? Could he create out of the fertile reality around him? Of Jake nosing through life, a handsome hound, quick to snap up any tempting morsel of poisoned meat thrown carelessly on the pavement?" (228–29). As bitterly ironic as Ray's "thanks" to "Uncle Sam" are, and as brutally pessimistic as his portrayal of Jake is, Ray's meandering reflections suggest a link, however unconscious at this point, between Haiti and Harlem. But it is only when he decides to leave Harlem that Ray can conceive of this connection in more affectionate terms. In the final chapter of part 2, "A Farewell Feed," Ray tries to reconcile his contempt for the self-satisfaction and limited aspirations of the Harlem bourgeoisie, personified by his girlfriend, Agatha, with his respect for the African American working-class resourcefulness and joie de vivre that he associates with Jake. Yet he recognizes his distance from Jake as well: "Life burned in Ray perhaps more intensely than in Jake. Ray felt more and his range was wider and he could not be satisfied with the easy, simple things that sufficed for Jake" (265). He identifies this sensitivity, and this restlessness, with his need to write, a need that he articulates in racial terms:

> He was a reservoir of that intense emotional energy so peculiar to his race. Life touched him emotionally in a thousand vivid ways. Maybe his own being was something of a touchstone of the general emotions of his race. And upset—a terror-breathing, Negro-baiting headline in a metropolitan newspaper or the news of a human bonfire in Dixie—could make him miserable and despairingly despondent like an injured child. While any flash of beauty or wonder might life him happier than a god. (265–66)

As presumptuous as Ray's vision of the writer might seem, the example he cites for his sensitivity suggests a transnationalist antidote to his alienation. He remembers "the melancholy-comic notes of a 'Blues' rising out of a Harlem basement before dawn," and the emotional power of this memory provides nothing less than "the key to himself and his race. That strange, child-like capacity for wistfulness and laughter" (266). Ray's description of the blues is indeed primitivist—"strange, child-like"—but it also expresses the capacity of the blues to move listeners who are not African American (but who are aware of the history that informs the blues). As the "key to himself and his race," the blues answers Ray's quest for a mode of expression that is at once emotionally resonant and distinctively African. The blues suggests a language for a self-consciously modern writer who does not want to lose the "strange, child-like" power of African American folk music, a language powerful enough to transcend cultural differences and thus suggest a "key" to a black internationalist formulation of African diasporic music.

Ray's blues epiphany is not so simple, of course, and when he reconsiders what Harlem has meant to him, he remains ambivalent about working-class

African American life. But there is no question about his lasting appreciation of African American music. In departing Harlem, he recognizes jazz, as well as the blues, as a source of joy, as the inspiring sound of the black metropolis, and, significantly, as a reminder of his childhood in Haiti:

> Going away from Harlem. . . . Harlem! How terribly Ray could hate it some-times. Its brutality, gang rowdyism, promiscuous thickness. Its hot desires. But, oh, the rich blood-red color of it! The warm accent of its composite voice, the fruitiness of its laughter, the trailing rhythm of its "blues" and the improvised surprises of its jazz. He had known happiness, too, in Harlem, joy that glowed gloriously upon him like the high-noon sunlight of his tropic island home. (267)

Ray has hardly solved the problem of reconciling his condescending disdain for "Harlem niggers" (264) with his attraction to the "warm accent" of Harlem's "composite voice." This romantically nostalgic vision instead converts Harlem into a primitivist paradise like his own "tropic island home." Anticipating his departure for Europe, Ray can only identify Harlem with "home" within the retrospective realm of the exile's memory. At the same time, however, the insinuation that the "improvised surprises of its jazz" invoke a correspondence between African diasporic sites, between Harlem and Haiti specifically, suggests an understated hope for the future as well as a melancholic sense of the past.

Ray's problem with representing Jake's proletarian "underworld" is ultimately the novel's socio-aesthetic problem as well, but this problem is obliquely mirrored by Jake's difficulty in imagining Haiti as either an independent black nation or a nation subject to U.S. military rule. Significantly, the childhood home that had filled Ray with such longing during the dreadful layover in Pittsburgh, the moment of his most intense estrangement that also begins his friendship with Jake, reappears much more casually at the conclusion of his narrative. The mere mention of the home from which Ray remains exiled reminds us that occupied Haiti has virtually disappeared from the novel's narrative surface until this point, just as the occupation had practically disappeared from public discourse during the years when McKay was composing *Home to Harlem*. If this Haitian past is temporarily relegated to the narrative underworld of *Home to Harlem*, displaced by the very questions about representing African American working-class life that obsess Ray, the reemergence of his Haitian past suggests how the novel's political unconscious is more complex than his vision of the childhood tropical paradise. The translation of his exile into the "composite voice" of Harlem blues and jazz underscores how the systematic source of his dislocation is not unrelated to that of the African American migrant, a dislocation from home that even Jake cannot entirely repress. Ray's professed admiration for Jake in their concluding conversation is not without an ironic reminder of the African American's politically naive worldview: "'If I was famous as Jack Johnson and rich as Madame Walker I'd prefer to have you as my friend than—President Wilson'" (273). But as oblivious as Jake seems to Ray's Haitian vision of Wilson's hypocritical imperial policy, his desire to "understand things better and be proper-speaking" (273) poignantly reveals a class consciousness that makes Ray's "constant dreaming" (274) seem self-indulgent. "'Ef I was edjucated,'" says Jake, "'I mighta helped mah li'l sister to get edjucated, too (she must be a l'il woman, now), and she would be nice-speaking like you' sweet brown, good enough foh you to hitch up with'" (273). While Jake reminds us of the class divide that prevents such a union of the proletarian and the intellectual, the parenthetical reflection on his sister reminds us of his sense of homelessness. As Ray's memory of occupied Haiti is repressed for many chapters only to recur as a reminder of the American repression of its imperial policy, Jake's memory of the "little sister down home in Petersburg" (210) whom he had not seen for nine years is likewise repressed until this moment when the differences between the two comrades seem most acute. Significantly, the "surface" resemblance of Ray's "edjucated" African American girlfriend, Agatha, to Jake's dimly remembered sister underscores the class difference that separates them and suggests the racial commonality that underlies their shared sense of dislocation. Ray rejects Jake's bourgeois aspirations for education, but his romantic fantasy of losing himself "in some savage culture in the jungles of Africa" is hardly a viable alternative (274). This self-defined "misfit" (274), severed from the roots of his native Haiti, is only beginning his education as a writer as the novel returns full circle to its opening. Emulating Jake despite his warnings, Ray departs from Harlem just as Jake had initially returned: as a laborer on an international freighter. Ray's journey, though, extends the black Atlantic geography of Jake's journey to a more global trajectory, "across the Pacific to Australia and from there to Europe" (263). Before this long journey begins, Jake and Billy Biasse insist that they complete their "farewell feed" with "a li'l sweet jazzing." After all, as Jake says to Ray, "'there ain't no jazzing like Harlem jazzing over the other side'" (275). While jazz has become a language that resonates across African diasporic cultures, Harlem is no less the site of its "composite voice."

Part 3: Jazz Internationalism

There may be "no jazzing like Harlem jazzing over the other side," but there is plenty of "jazzing . . . over the other side" in *Banjo*. McKay's sequel to

Home to Harlem, published a year later, features an itinerant jazz musician as its protagonist, Lincoln Agrippa Daily, better known as "Banjo," an African American who resembles Jake as a "great vagabond of lowly life" (11). *Banjo* also features dramatic scenes of jazz performance and considerable dialogue about African diasporic music by the international cast of black "vagabonds" who temporarily inhabit the Vieux Port of Marseilles. This cast includes Ray, who, as in *Home to Harlem*, first appears in the second part of the novels, after we are introduced to Banjo and his proletarian cohort of black drifters. As in *Home to Harlem*, Ray functions as the intellectual writer figure, who reflects on the socio-aesthetic challenge of representing the vagabond world that the novel itself represents. As Brent Hayes Edwards has written, the "vagabond internationalism" of *Banjo* represents a "global community of the dispossessed," a temporary, improvised male community that so thoroughly rejects the claims of "civilization" that it defies Marxist formulations of the proletariat (*Practice* 199). This vagabond "community" hardly fulfills utopian or even pragmatic claims for black internationalism, as the novel accentuates the linguistic, cultural, and political differences that divide the characters. As in *Home to Harlem*, these differences provoke productive discussion and debate, but also conflict, with McKay underscoring how nationalism functions divisively and destructively, among characters whose national affiliations are tenuous, whether by choice or by default. Banjo's disavowal of his nationality is extraordinary, even among expatriate "race men" such as Goosey, who vows never to return to "those United Snakes" (117). Banjo was born in the American "Cotton Belt," and "everything about him—accent, attitude, and movement—shouted Dixie" (11–12). Yet, he enlists in the Canadian army during World War I, and after returning from Europe upon completion of his service, he persuades U.S. immigration officials to deport him in order to ensure overseas passage to Marseilles. Like Ray at the end of *Home to Harlem*, he embarks on a circuitous global journey to "the other side," through "the Panama Canal to New Zealand and Australia, cruising cargo around the island continent and up along the coast of Africa," before finally reaching the port of Marseilles (12).[25] Other characters have less choice, or less resourcefulness, than Banjo and are instead "deportees from America for violation of the United States immigration laws—afraid and ashamed to go back to their own lands" (6), or unable to return for political reasons.[26]

Ray's sense of exile is less pronounced in *Banjo* than in *Home to Harlem* in that he identifies himself by his travels as much as his country of origin. His identification of Haiti with Harlem is more explicit, though, if less prominent, in *Banjo*. In the African diasporic working-class arena of the Marseilles waterfront, Ray's nationality is less important than his skill as a translator and intercultural mediator. He also takes pride in his ability to mimic different nationalities, to pose as American, British, French or West Indian, in order to reveal the blindness of nationalist pride. The transformation he had experienced since his time in Harlem is explicitly stated: he "had undergone a decided change since he had left America. He enjoyed his role of a wandering black without patriotic or family ties" (*Banjo* 136). The antinationalist impulse of the "wandering black" in *Home to Harlem* has grown into a firm resolve, a commitment to expose and resist the "spiritual meannesses" of imperialist European and American patriotism (137). His home country is hardly even mentioned, and when his background is mentioned, it has been transformed to resemble McKay's own experience more closely. We find out that he had lived in Jamaica after his family's exile from Haiti. He says, "'I was there for two years when I was a kid. We had a little revolution and the President that was ousted was exiled to Jamaica with his entourage. My father was among them and that was how I happened to go'" (159–60).

While Ray's childhood experience is now less rooted than it had seemed in *Home to Harlem*, he cannot totally repress the distant memory of the Caribbean he had identified with Haiti earlier. When he falls asleep late in *Banjo* to "scenes of tropical shores sifted through hectic years," he ultimately dreams not of Haiti but "instead of Harlem . . . the fascinating forms of Harlem. The thick, sweaty, syrup-sweet jazzing of Sheba Palace" (284). If the erotic exoticism of Harlem nightlife displaces Haiti in Ray's unconscious, his dream also foreshadows the unexpected appearance the next day of none other than *Home to Harlem's* Jake, who we find out has named his child after Ray. Like Ray, however, Jake too has left his wife and child (but not the responsibility of support) for a life "a broad" (291–93). As voluntary as Jake's life as a sailor "a broad" appears to be, and as voluntary as Ray's self-defined "proletarian" existence as a writer, "'rolling along, stopping anywhere I'm put off or thrown off'" (306), also appears to be, the figure in *Banjo* who most explicitly embodies the tentativeness of black migrant life is ultimately Taloufa, the native of Nigeria whose subsequent residence in Great Britain and the United States had left him vulnerable to immigration restriction policies in both countries. Like so many "colored seamen . . . West Africans, East Africans, South Africans, West Indians, Arabs, and Indians," Taloufa had become a "'Nationality Doubtful' man with no place to go" (312–13). Taloufa's "Nationality Doubtful" status epitomizes the cruelty of a colonial legacy that had "gone out among these native, earthy people, had despoiled them of their primitive soil, had uprooted, enchained, transported, and transformed them to labor under its laws, and yet lacked the spirit to tolerate them within its walls" (313–14).

His example underscores not only the shared legacy of "the colored man" worldwide but the need for international solidarity as well.

The closest approximation to such black internationalist collectivity in *Banjo* is the jazz "orchestra" that Banjo assembles early in the novel. While there are many moments of intercultural dialogue through and about popular music in the novel, Banjo's quest to form and then sustain a band is also the closest approximation to a narrative "plot" in this "Story without a Plot." The temporary success of the band underscores how the musical practice of jazz improvisation figures as a model for the social practice of improvising communities. The band is international, including the West Indian Malty, the "Senegalese" Taloufa, the African American Goosey, as well as the African American "Canadian" Banjo. While they perform only sporadically, and while they attain what Banjo sees as the "aesthetic realization of his orchestra" (97) only once in the novel, music plays a critical role in expressing both the potential and the limitations of black internationalism in *Banjo*. There are more specific references to the 1920s jazz and blues repertoire in *Banjo* than in *Home to Harlem*. When we are introduced to Banjo as "an artist" in the novel's opening pages, he plays the popular 1925 song "Yes, Sir, That's My Baby," with Ginger and Bugsy dancing a "strenuous movement of the 'Black Bottom'" in response (7–8). Other popular songs that are mentioned suggest the African diasporic range of black popular music in *Banjo*, from the West African "Stay, Carolina, Stay" (95), to "The West Indies Blues" (81), to "The Garvey Blues" and "all the 'blues' that Banjo's memory could rake up" (108). The song that is most identified with Banjo, however, is "Shake That Thing," his preferred version of Jelly Roll Morton's famous composition "Jelly Roll Blues." It is no coincidence that this song is introduced with the opening of the first black-owned café in Marseilles, the Café Africaine, as its dance floor epitomizes the power of African diasporic music to transcend cultural differences: "Jungle jazzing, Orient wriggling, civilized stepping. Shake that thing! Sweet dancing thing of primitive joy, perverse pleasure, prostitute ways, many-colored variations of the rhythm, savage, barbaric, refined—eternal rhythm of the mysterious, magical, magnificent—the dance divine of life . . . Oh, Shake That Thing!" (57). If this exuberant language that concludes part 1 of *Banjo* is unabashedly primitivist, it also approximates the rhythmic intensity that it celebrates. This moment of release is of course temporary, but it is not simply a temporary reprieve from everyday struggle; it is also an antidote to the deadly violence that immediately precedes the scene and an affirmation of the intrinsic potential for a more harmonious mode of collectivity.

The performance that enacts Banjo's "aesthetic realization of his orchestra" is preceded by a contentious discussion of black music between Banjo and Goosey. Goosey asserts that the "banjo is bondage . . . the instrument of slavery. . . . We colored folks have got to get away from all that in these enlightened progressive days" (90). Banjo defends his right to play the banjo, and indeed to make money playing "coon stuff," despite the legacy of minstrelsy: "'But wha' you call coon stuff is the money stuff today. That saxophone-jazzing is sure coon stuff and the American darky sure knows how to makem wheedle-whine them "blues." He's sure-enough the one go-getting musical fool today, yaller, and demanded all ovah the wul'" (91). This debate between two African American characters about the politics and economics of black popular music becomes a more international discussion of Garvey and the Back to Africa movement. By situating a debate about music in a more open-ended discussion of black nationalism and internationalism, McKay underscores the cultural politics of black music—and jazz specifically. When the orchestra performs, then, immediately after this discussion, it seems appropriate that the song that is played most extensively is the "rollicking West African song" "Stay, Carolina, Stay" (95). The African "Nationality Doubtful" Taloufa sings this song, and the intensity of his expression evokes the history of slavery as well as the ongoing experience of displacement that had brought him to Marseilles. The tune is not complicated, based on the simple refrain of the title and the repetition with minimal variations of the initial verse. However, the emotional power of Taloufa's performance is transformative; the same characters who disagreed about Garvey in the previous chapter are now united in their joyous interaction as musicians. While this scene, like other nightclub performance scenes in *Home to Harlem* and *Banjo*, is brief, and soon interrupted by violence, it temporarily fulfills Banjo's "aesthetic realization of his orchestra." This multinational group of musicians furthermore suggests the fulfillment of a black internationalist collectivity that seems so unlikely elsewhere in the novel. African diasporic musical forms have the potential to cross borders because of their shared roots in African musical practices and the shared communal ethos that informs these practices. As the narrator of *Banjo* concludes after the successful performance of Banjo's "orchestra": "'Beguin,' 'jelly-roll,' 'burru,' 'bombé,' no matter what the name may be, Negroes are never so beautiful and magical as when they do that gorgeous sublimation of the primitive African sex feeling. In its thousand varied patterns, depending so much on individual rhythm, so little on formal movement, this dance is the key to the African rhythm of life" (105).

McKay's affirmation of the "primitive" power of black music has divided his readership for several generations; his fiction both ironically stages demeaning Western concepts of the primitive and attempts to reclaim the primitive for his radical black internationalist social vision. Ray's role, in both *Home to Harlem* and *Banjo*, is especially important, then: in his role as a participant-observer in the black proletarian communities of these novels, he functions as an intermediary between these communities and more "edjucated" readers.

No moment is more telling about his role than in the chapter of *Banjo* called "Storytelling," when the Senegalese characters on "the Ditch" become suspicious of his motives as a writer, fearing "that he would write something funny or caustic of their life that would make them appear 'uncivilized' or inferior to American Negroes" (114). As the politically astute Goosey says more directly, "'But the crackers will use what you write against the race!'" (115). As much as Goosey resembles Du Bois in his review of *Home to Harlem*, Ray is not simply a stand-in for McKay, whether in *Banjo* or *Home to Harlem*. Indeed, by making Ray's West Indian immigrant narrative a tale of Haitian exile, McKay suggests a common ground for cross-cultural dialogue among African diasporic critics of American imperialism. While *Home to Harlem* discloses a racist ideology that linked U.S. imperial foreign policy to domestic policies of segregation and discrimination, McKay also draws attention to the African Caribbean response to the United States' occupation of Haiti. At the same time that African American intellectuals were debating the political implications of *Home to Harlem*'s primitivist portrayal of Jake, Haitian artists and intellectuals were answering Ray's call for a new literature, inspired as much by *Banjo* as any other novel. The invisibility of "the Haitian, Ray" to American readers of *Home to Harlem* may ultimately tell us more about the novel's lasting significance than Jake's controversial visibility. Likewise, the postcolonial future that Ray can barely imagine, rather than the 1920s Harlem that disturbed so many readers, may tell us more about the lasting legacy not only of McKay but also of the New Negro Renaissance as an international movement.

2 "Black Man's Verse"

The Black Chicago Renaissance and the Popular Front Jazz Poetics of Frank Marshall Davis

"Jest le's beat it away from Harlem, daddy. This heah country
is good enough and big enough for us to git lost in. You know
Chicago?"
—Claude McKay, *Home to Harlem*

Do that thing jazz band! . . .
Let the jazz stuff fall like hail on king and truck driver, queen and
    laundress, lord and laborer, banker and bum
Let it fall in London, Moscow, Paris, Hong King, Cairo, Buenos
    Aires, Chicago, Sydney
—Frank Marshall Davis, "Jazz Band"

When Jake proposes to "go on off to sea again" in order to escape from New York at the conclusion of Claude McKay's *Home to Harlem*, Felice asks him bluntly, "'What you wanta go knocking around them foreign countries again for like swallow come and swallow go from year to year and nevah settling down no place? This heah is you' country, daddy. What you gwine away from it for?'" (332). The alternative that she offers to Jake's proposed overseas flight is Chicago. Not a foreign country, but also not Harlem, Chicago is at once a distinctively American city and a city where Jake and Felice can "git lost in" as African Americans seeking refuge. So it is interesting that Frank Marshall Davis, who likewise saw Chicago as an attractive destination to reinvent himself as a young man, portrays the city in a global continuum of legendary cities in his poem "Jazz Band." Chicago, for Davis, occupies a position that is usually reserved for New York in the world's imagination of metropolitan migrant destinations, largely because its jazz scene was the most dynamic and magnetic of any city in the world during the interwar years. Musicians such as Louis Armstrong, Jelly Roll Morton, and Joe "King" Oliver, who were themselves migrants from New Orleans, had established Chicago as a jazz mecca in the 1920s.[1] While the Harlem Renaissance is routinely associated with the international appeal of jazz during the Jazz Age, the Black Chicago Renaissance has been less frequently identified with either internationalism or jazz. The Black Chicago Renaissance is now more widely recognized, however, as both a local African American movement that emerged through the development of South Side Chicago cultural institutions and a black internationalist movement committed to global questions of race and labor. As Darlene Clark Hine has written, not only did Chicago become increasingly cosmopolitan through the movement of migrants back and forth from the city, but it also became "an important site, incubator, and exporter of a modern black culture across the nation and globally."[2] The role of labor organization was especially important for the Black Chicago Renaissance, particularly in the 1930s and '40s, and the black cultural institutions that emerged in Chicago were aligned with the Popular Front commitment to both black and interracial cultural radicalism. These institutions included the Associated Negro Press, the first African American news agency; the *Chicago Defender*, the leading black newspaper of the time; *Negro Digest*, the nationally successful magazine about African American life; the South Side Community Arts Center; and the South Side Writers Group. Among the many writers who emerged and became prominent through the Black Chicago Renaissance were Richard Wright, Margaret Walker, Gwendolyn Brooks, and the writer who happened to be the most celebrated jazz poet of the 1930s, Frank Marshall Davis.

It is surprising that jazz does not play a more important role in African American writing of the 1930s and '40s. Jazz was not only immensely popular; it was also celebrated by many leftist intellectuals as a "people's music," a populist form of expression that unified the international and interracial alliances of the Popular Front. Given the increased visibility of radical African American writing in the 1930s, it seems unlikely that jazz does not figure more prominently in the literary history of this period. One important exception, however, was Frank Marshall Davis, whose first collection of poetry, *Black Man's Verse* (1935), was widely recognized for its innovative adaptations of African American vernacular forms, including the blues and jazz. Davis, who was also a journalist and jazz critic, was considered one of the most important poets of his time with the publication of his books in the 1930s and '40s. Because he did not publish much poetry after moving from Chicago to Hawaii during the early Cold War years, Davis was largely forgotten until a revival of interest in his work among radical black writers came about in the 1960s and '70s. He is now better known as an important mentor figure for the young Barack Obama, as Obama writes in *Dreams from My Father*. This chapter situates Davis's writing within Popular Front debates about the social significance of jazz, especially in early jazz autobiographies and histories. I argue that Davis's jazz poetry is worthy of greater consideration, not only because of its influential vernacular forms but also because of his knowledge of jazz history. In emphasizing how African musical principles inform jazz, Davis also demonstrated the international significance of jazz for black and working-class social progress.

Davis is known primarily as a social realist, a "chronicler and documentary observer of his time and place" (Bone and Courage 211), a poet whose appeal is not altogether different from his appeal as a journalist. Literary historians have recognized his modernist qualities, particularly the inventiveness of his figurative language and the energy of his free verse lines, but even these poetic elements are usually correlated with attention to social reality.[3] And because his poems are rhetorically and formally similar to the poetry of Carl Sandburg, Edgar Lee Masters, and Vachel Lindsay, who have been widely discredited by the New Criticism and subsequent formalist approaches to modern poetry, whatever claims that can be made for his modernism are inevitably qualified by this Midwestern lineage. The most pertinent questions about Davis's reputation as a poet, of course, have to do with the overtly political rhetoric of his poetry. If he is a "chronicler and documentary observer of his time and place," he is also documenting the social conditions that need to be transformed. As a poet who is identified with the radicalism of the 1930s, Davis has been largely dismissed because he was a political poet, a poet whose literary concerns were too much of their time and place. Like the majority of 1930s "proletarian poets," Davis is considered to be limited by the instrumentalist rhetoric of his poetry and by the historical fact that he published his best-known poetry in the presumably exceptional 1930s. It did not help, of course, that he was blacklisted during the early years of the Cold War and published hardly any poetry again until the 1970s.

If there is any attribute of Davis's poetry that has been most praised by subsequent poets and scholars, if not his contemporaries, it is his engagement with jazz and African American music more generally. According to Eugene Redmond, for example, Davis's jazz poetry "anticipates the work of literally dozens of poets of the sixties" (234). He is routinely anthologized in collections of jazz poetry and is perhaps best known currently for his poems that enact jazz performance. Even in the rather specialized realm of jazz poetry, however, his presence is still limited by his reputation as a 1930s poet. For example, he is mentioned only briefly in the most comprehensive study of jazz poetry, Sascha Feinstein's *Jazz Poetry: From the 1920s to the Present*.[4]

Davis is in fact an exception among African American writers in publishing jazz poetry in the 1930s. Langston Hughes established his reputation as a jazz poet in the 1920s, but he did not publish jazz poems in the 1930s. Sterling Brown's groundbreaking *Southern Road* was published in 1932, but his poetry was published infrequently afterward. Davis stands out as the one African American poet whose poetry takes up the social and cultural significance of jazz in the 1930s. If his poetic enactment of jazz performance was noticed at the time when swing was reaching its peak of popularity, however, it was soon eclipsed by the ascendance of bebop, which attracted a new generation of poets as well as accomplished poets such as Hughes.

As a political poet who writes about African American music, Davis defies expectations of both proletarian and jazz poetry. James Smethurst has written that Davis addresses the same questions about folk and mass culture that Hughes and Brown deal with in their poetry. If, as Smethurst writes, Hughes's poetry can be defined by its "urban internationalist and popular culture aesthetic," while Brown's poetry is "rural, local, and folkloric," Davis complicates this dichotomy. His poetry was folkloric in "creating 'realistic' portrayals of the urban . . . folk and expressive culture that is often opposed to mass culture" (*New Red Negro* 118). Davis, along with Hughes and Kenneth Fearing, was one of the first poets on the left to engage seriously with mass culture, even as he questioned the extent to which mass culture could be useful for progressive political purposes. Through points of view that modulate between objective description and identification with the folk, Davis's poetry makes a "simultaneous critique and reclamation of mass culture" (*New Red Negro* 140). This is especially true about his jazz poetry. This poetry is formally continuous with the modernist free verse Davis read in college, which included not only Sandburg, Masters, and Lindsay but also the poets who were featured in the New York avant-garde journal *Others*.[5] As John Edgar Tidwell asserts, Davis saw free verse and improvised music as similarly "unconventional and iconoclastic" (Introduction to *Livin' the Blues* xxvi). As jazz improvisation represented a rebellion against the Western musical tradition, free verse "improvisation" similarly broke from metric regularity. As formally rebellious as Davis's jazz poems are, it is worth emphasizing that these poems can also be characterized as social realism in that they explore both the impact of mass culture on the African American masses and the social milieus of jazz performers, as workers as well as artists. In his collections that feature dramatic scenes, imagery, and sounds of jazz, especially his first book, *Black Man's Verse*, jazz is inseparable from the dynamic but often bleak social reality of urban African America that Davis documents. Finally, his jazz poetry is also engaged with previous African American literary interpretations of the blues and jazz, such as those of Hughes and Brown. Even though Davis did not write a manifesto or make specific claims for the generic definition of jazz poetry, he did write extensively about jazz and the blues. Before looking at his jazz poetry more specifically, I will discuss how his memoir, *Livin' the Blues*, reenacts his lifelong engagement with African American music.[6]

Few African American writers have identified their writing with the history of jazz as precisely as Davis does. As he reflects on his life story in *Livin' the Blues*, he writes:

> I have lived on the periphery of jazz and the blues since I was eight. I watched and listened as this revolutionary new music developed through New Orleans, Dixieland, swing, bop, progressive, and the avant garde of today. I felt with them the frustration of black musicians and bands, who originated the art, as they received only a fraction of the adulation they deserved while honky musicians received the lion's share of the glory and money. (331)

In recollecting his long experience with jazz, Davis identifies jazz not only with music history but also with the long history of African American struggle. He defines himself as a witness of jazz history, who "watched and listened" as jazz evolved. More importantly, though, he underscores his participation in this history, as a writer who "felt . . . the frustration of black musicians and bands" who had "originated the art" but were not adequately recognized or rewarded. Jazz history, then, is much more than a series of formal changes; it is a social, economic, and political history that exemplifies the African American quest for equal rights. As a participant-observer, Davis relates his own experience as a writer with this social history of jazz.

Davis's social vision of jazz emerged through his experience as a jazz journalist, educator, and disc jockey in Chicago during the 1930s and '40s. Before this period, which was also his most prolific period as a poet, he experienced jazz as a fan and, while in college, as a fledgling jazz saxophonist. *Livin' the Blues* narrates his exposure to jazz, from his boyhood in Kansas through his professional involvement with jazz in Chicago and his subsequent jazz journalism in postwar Hawaii. Although the title of *Livin' the Blues* identifies Davis's life story as a blues narrative of African American struggle, his memoir is very much a jazz history in its correlation of important milestones in his life with developments in jazz. As Davis narrates his maturation, he discusses the music he hears, the musicians he meets, and his growing awareness of the historical importance of jazz. He recalls the earliest live performances of jazz and the blues he attended as a teenager, from W. C. Handy and his Orchestra of Memphis to Ma Rainey in her Georgia Frolics sideshow. And he discusses the impressive collection of jazz records he assembled at the time, working as a record distributor for Black Swan, Okeh, and Paramount. Because his early years coincided with the early development of the blues and jazz, Davis witnesses how jazz was initially experienced—in performance, on the phonograph, and eventually on the radio. By the time he finishes college and makes his way to Chicago, it is clear that Davis is not only a jazz fanatic but also exceptionally knowledgeable about the music. His first impulse when he arrives on Chicago's South Side in 1927 is to check out the most famous black-and-tan cabarets at the time: the Sunset, which was featuring Louis Armstrong, and the Plantation Café, where King Oliver and his Creole Jazz Band were playing. And his first impression of the South Side is itself a jazz impression: "Walking slowly down State Street toward 35th I heard the loud belches of the overstuffed city, but rising above this cacophony was the swooping sound of loudspeakers blaring the new Bix Beiderbecke–Frankie Trumbauer recording, 'Singin the Blues'" (*Livin' the Blues* 104). Jazz is at once a part of the noisy streets of Chicago and an antidote to the city's "cacophony."

As much as Davis identifies jazz with the urban world of Chicago, and specifically with the musicians who had migrated from New Orleans to Chicago, his understanding of jazz is more broadly informed by his study of African American history and cultural anthropology. Through his immersion in African American cultural, social, and political history as a journalist for the black press in Chicago and Atlanta, he became increasingly aware of the social significance of jazz. His "Rating the Records" columns for the Associated Negro Press in the late 1930s demonstrate how jazz was a source of African American cultural pride and a medium of racial integration. Davis's study of African cultures, especially through the anthropological work of Melville Herskovits, was especially important for his understanding of the African sources of jazz. He identified jazz specifically with African musical practices and their adaptation to the experience of slavery in the New World: "Jazz came into existence as a result of our unique status in America. African musical concepts, differing radically from the musical traditions of Europe, were the only ancestral art permitted to survive under slavery." The distinctively West African approach to "rhythm, timing, and tonality" was not only evident in the hymns and work songs of African American slaves, but it was also the basis for the blues and jazz. African American music is by definition "protest music," Davis writes, because it sustains African cultural practices and contests the authority of Western understandings of music. The blues, with "their topical content and protest against untenable conditions," represented a form of "personal protest" against Jim Crow restrictions. Jazz subsequently represented a more "united protest" in its defiance of Western

European musical traditions (*Livin' the Blues* 234). With its "new devices of tone, interval polyrhythms, and innovative use of various instruments along with the revival of improvisation," jazz was a "revolutionary" challenge to European musical concepts. Furthermore, it was a revolutionary social practice, with "the democracy inherent in the jazz band and the equality of all of its members." By the 1930s the appeal of jazz had spread nationally and internationally beyond its origins in African American culture, but even as it was adapted by European composers into symphonic compositions, it was still a "major weapon" against white supremacy in its affirmation of African American creative expression (235).[7]

Davis became increasingly prominent within the Chicago jazz community in the 1940s. In addition to his work as a jazz record reviewer for the Associated Press, he taught "possibly the first regular courses ever given in the History of Jazz at a school," at the socialist Abraham Lincoln School in the Chicago Loop. Drawing from his extensive record collection as well as African field recordings from the Field Museum of Natural History and Herskovits's private collection of recordings, Davis's jazz history course emphasized African as well as African American history in order to "isolate those strong and persistent elements of African culture which survived slavery and were the heart and soul of jazz." The purpose of this class was "to underline the global importance of jazz" and to develop a deeper historical awareness of Africa and African America through the study of jazz (284). One result of the class was the development of the Hot Club of Chicago, the local chapter of the United Hot Clubs of America, with its purpose of promoting and preserving the history of jazz, especially New Orleans and Chicago jazz. Davis became involved in scheduling and emceeing jazz programs that featured local and touring African American musicians who were unlikely to be featured in commercial jazz magazines. As John Gennari has written, in revising and expanding jazz history through their reissue of obscure recordings by black musicians, the Hot Clubs increased interest in black musicians among white fans. In doing so, they increased the consciousness of African American musical accomplishment among jazz fans and enhanced the case for racial integration. Davis made a more explicit case for racial integration in his role as a disc jockey for the Marshall Field radio station WJJD.[8] Beginning in 1945, he hosted a program called "Bronzeville Brevities." He saw his purpose on the radio, like his purpose with the Abraham Lincoln School and the Hot Club, as both educational and political. But while his jazz history and Hot Club experience consisted mostly of white jazz enthusiasts, his "Bronzeville Brevities" show appealed more to African American listeners. For an audience that was more racially diverse, he made a point of featuring at least one recording with "mixed personnel" in order to "propagandize on the democracy of jazz and suggest increased integration in other fields" (Davis, *Livin' the Blues* 286).

Davis became an influential spokesman for swing and its roots in the blues at the time when bebop was emerging. He was initially skeptical about bebop, because he felt that "some of its practitioners admitted they were trying to curve jazz into a form acceptable to traditional white standards." While he resented the attitude of making jazz "'respectable' for use on the concert stage," he did admire the ambitious experiments of composers like Duke Ellington, but largely because "his music remained strongly rooted in the blues and its characteristic tonal scale, as well as in African rhythmic complexity" (288). He eventually admired Charlie Parker and Dizzy Gillespie for the same reason. In questioning the avant-garde status of bebop, Davis appeared to occupy the conservative side of "the modernist-fundamentalist divide" between defenders of bebop and defenders of earlier forms of jazz. As Gennari has written, however, both sides of this debate were politically progressive, and both were modernist, although they understood the cultural role of music differently (*Blowin' Hot and Cool* 109). Unlike jazz musicians and critics who argued that racial equality was meaningful only if African American musicians were free to pursue whatever creative direction they preferred, Davis believed that the struggle for equality was best served by valuing African American folk expression. He understood early jazz in Marxist terms as "an urban, multiracial, working-class achievement, a powerful populist critique" of cultural elitism, a critique rooted in African American experience and creativity (Gennari, *Blowin' Hot and Cool* 108). By the 1960s Davis would expand this understanding of jazz as a form of social protest into an increasingly international arena. He came to appreciate Latin American music "because of its pulse emanating from Africa," and he favored African American musicians such as Art Blakey, John Coltrane, Sonny Rollins, Charles Mingus, and Archie Shepp, who "not only returned to Africa for renewed inspiration but . . . tuned their ears to the sounds of Asia in developing a broader, more encompassing music of dynamic protest derived from non-European sources" (*Livin' the Blues* 288). In looking back on his own evolution as a jazz enthusiast, Davis recognized continuity evident in the resistance to new forms of African American music: "The spiritual descendants of those horrified by the revolutionary protest of jazz in the early part of this century are those today upset by the blazing anger of an Archie Shepp or an Albert Ayler" (288). His later poetic portraits of early jazz luminaries such as Armstrong, Ellington, and Billie Holiday are as much an affirmation of this continuity as they are a challenge to younger listeners who dismissed swing as the popular music of a more accommodationist era of African American history.

Davis's first book, *Black Man's Verse*, established his reputation as a dramatic alternative to the lyric poetry of the Harlem Renaissance. It received considerable attention for a first book of poetry, especially a first book of poetry published by a small press during the Depression. In his 1936 review of the previous year of African American literature for *Opportunity*, Alain Locke noted the transformation of African American literature from the previous decade. The new writing was "prosaic, partisan, and propagandistic, but this time not in behalf of striving, strident racialism, but rather in a protestant and belligerent universalism of social analysis and protest. . . . In a word, our art is going proletarian" ("Deep River" 7). If such emphasis on truth rather than beauty was less conducive to poetry than to narrative prose, Locke identified Davis's *Black Man's Verse* as the book that best exemplified the vigor of 1930s social protest. Davis, along with Richard Wright, was a poet "who really brings fresh talent and creative imagination to this writing field," a poet who had "gone deeper into the substance of Negro folk life" than even Langston Hughes ("Deep River" 10).[9] Two years later, Locke would similarly commend Davis's second book, *I Am the American Negro*, as "the outstanding verse effort of the year" ("Jingo" 11), even if it did not exceed the expectations established by his dynamic debut. It may seem surprising that Locke so valued Davis's poetry, given his reluctance to include overtly political poetry in *The New Negro*.[10] By the mid-1930s, however, Locke saw Davis as the urban counterpart to Sterling Brown in his dramatic rendering of "Negro folk life." He was not alone. Brown himself praised Davis's "ability for strong and vivid revelations of the American scene" ("Literary Scene" 217). Like Locke, Brown valued the "sardonic realism" (217) of Davis's poetry, even as he also criticized his "overfondness for the Lindsay effects" (220), such as the marginal musical cues that accompanied a number of poems in *Black Man's Verse*. Davis's first book was also favorably reviewed in magazines and journals associated with modern poetry more generally. Most notably, Harriett Monroe wrote in *Poetry* that "there is a great deal of swinging strength in this book of a Chicago Negro . . . a good deal of strength, much satirical club-bludgeoning over injustices to his race, some epigrammatic wit, and often touches of imaginative beauty" (293–94). Monroe also noted the similarity of Davis's free verse prosody to that of Sandburg and Lindsay but said his poetry was not derivative: he was a "poet of authentic inspiration" (295).

While such esteemed readers as Locke and Brown agreed that Davis succeeded in dramatizing "Negro folk life," reviewers of *Black Man's Verse* had difficulty reconciling the book's jazz poetry with its radical political criticism.

As the reviews by Locke and Brown suggest, there was considerable uncertainty about the status of jazz in the folk life of Davis's South Side Chicago. Was jazz an urban form of African American folk life? Given its commercial success, not to mention its interracial success, could jazz be considered a form of folk expression? These are questions that Locke and Brown each addressed in writing about African American music, and they were both skeptical, although hardly dismissive, of the idea of jazz as a medium of African American folk culture. As for jazz poetry, the most famous "jazz poets" of the 1920s before Hughes were Sandburg and Lindsay, and their enactments of jazz performance were considered sensationalist by many readers and even offensively primitivist, particularly in the case of Lindsay's "The Congo." The distinction between "poetry" and "propaganda" was also problematic. Monroe makes this distinction clearly and simply ignores the more overtly political poems of *Black Man's Verse*. And while Locke praises the power of testimony in Davis's poetry, he is also wary of poetry that follows the "prosaic, partisan, and propagandistic" spirit of "proletarian" writing. What made *Black Man's Verse* so challenging for reviewers is what made it so original in the 1930s: its dialogue of forms of poetic expression that were considered generically incompatible. Poems that enact jazz performance interact with the more descriptive poems of social realism as well as the more overtly political poems of social criticism. Jazz is indeed a form of urban African American "folk life" in this context, but it is also a working-class form of expression, despite the escapist if not exotic associations of jazz cabarets that Davis represents. What makes *Black Man's Verse* so original is the very questions it raises about commercial mass culture and urban African American folk culture, about jazz as a site for not only social critique but also social empowerment.

Black Man's Verse* is unified thematically by its time and place, Depression-era South Side Chicago, which Davis evokes through the shifting points of view of his poems. In addition to the opening sequence of poems that represent the social life and history of African American Chicago, there are several briefer sequences that demonstrate Davis's expertise in genres beyond "social realism": "Fragments," "Love Cycle," and a series of commemorative portraits titled "Ebony under Granite." The opening sequence that begins with "Chicago's Congo" is especially ambitious in its historical breadth and dramatic complexity, however, as Davis represents African American life through a "crazy quilt" (*Black Moods* 8) of rhetorical modes. The poems move dramatically among descriptive, declamatory, and introspective modes, sometimes mixed within individual poems. *Black Man's Verse* is, as Tidwell has written, like "a Duke Ellington symphony: experimental, cacophonous, yet strangely harmonious. . . . The collection is a virtual collage of lyrical moods, ranging from the tragic to the comic" (Introduction to *Black Moods* xxxvii). Comparing *Black Men's Verse* to an Ellington composition seems particularly apt, given the sonic as well as thematic complexity of Davis's book. Ellington's comment on his 1940 composition "Harlem Air Shaft" could apply to *Black Man's Verse* as well: "So much goes on in a Harlem air shaft. You get the full essence of Harlem in an air shaft. You hear fights, you smell dinner, you hear people making love. You hear intimate gossip floating down. You hear the radio. An airshaft is one great big loudspeaker" (qtd. in Thompson 131). While Davis features the noise of streets and nightclubs more than the intimate sounds of domestic spaces, the interplay of voices, and indeed the interplay of public and private spaces, throughout *Black Man's Verse* enacts a similarly evocative portrait of the South Side. Like Ellington's capacious compositions, Davis's collection suggests the confusion of noise and modern music, of the city and jazz performance, that was so prevalent in the early critical discourse about jazz. He does so, of course, to question and refute the often racist correlation of jazz with urban (black) noise.

While there are only several poems that concentrate specifically on jazz performance in *Black Man's Verse*, the collection is unified by its references to jazz and other forms of African American music. In the opening sequence of poems there are a number of poems that include notes for musical accompaniment—from the first poem, "Chicago's Congo (Sonata for an Orchestra)," to "Lynched (Symphonic Interlude for Twenty-one Selected Instruments)," to "The Slave (For a Bass Viol)," to "Hands of a Brown Woman (For a Quartet of Two Guitars, a Banjo, and a Tom-Tom)," to "Lullaby (Melody for a 'Cello)," to "death (overture for an organ)." Several poems have titles that refer to music, such as "I Sing No New Songs," "Jazz Band," and "Lullaby." And a number of poems figure everyday life through jazz imagery, suggesting that jazz is integral to the consciousness of South Side residents. Significantly, the jazz imagery of *Black Man's Verse* represents a range of moods and emotions, as Davis expands the figurative possibilities of jazz from its stereotypical perceptions in the mass media as well as from its earlier resonance in jazz poetry by Sandburg, Lindsay, and even Hughes. For example, the first poem in *Black Man's Verse* that features jazz imagery, "Rain," figures a rainy day in Chicago in language that is subdued but also suggestive. The poem begins by characterizing the rain as an "old man / in a music store" (17). Following this "gray" figure is an image of "houses" that are themselves composed of "harp strings / in a music store." The third and concluding transformation of the initial image likewise seems meditative, until the final line of the poem abruptly wakes us from the old man's reverie. The "ancient man" plays "a weary jingle / a soft jazz jingle" on the harp, but only for a moment, as he "dodders away / before the boss comes 'round" (18). By interrupting the gentle but "weary" mood of the poem with the concluding reminder that a record store is a commercial establishment, Davis underscores the socioeconomic conditions that inform African American music and delimit its performance and dissemination. Like earlier forms of African American music, jazz is ultimately a fugitive form of collective expression that resists the control of "the boss." In signifying on Hughes's "The Weary Blues," Davis furthermore suggests that jazz poetry, like jazz and blues music, is a collective African American form of expression. Jazz poetry is also a democratic, urban form of expression that Davis identifies especially with Chicago. In "Five Portraits of Chicago at Night," for example, the sky above the city is figured lyrically as "many fingers plucking stars, beating a silent rat-tat on the drumhead of the moon" (27). The portrait of Chicago that concludes this sequence, though, is a more familiarly Sandburgian image of the city that "roars coarse songs to the blaring tune of many freights hauling grain and / cattle and steel, to the indigo jazz of mills and men and sweat" (28). Such imaginative allusions to music, like the musical titles of poems in *Black Man's Verse*, suggest a continuity between the poems that feature jazz performance with the black urban world from which they emerge. They also imply a continuity between jazz and other forms of African American music as well as earlier jazz poetry by poets such as Hughes or Sandburg. Like Ellington's extended compositions, *Black Man's Verse* is at once modern in its sonic allusions to urban Chicago and traditional in its invocation of earlier forms of African American music and poetry.

The opening poem of *Black Man's Verse*, "Chicago's Congo," introduces the dramatic interplay of modes and moods, of voices and visions, that structures the book as a whole. The seemingly antithetical geography of the title recalls such Midwestern precursors as Sandburg's "Chicago" and Lindsay's "The Congo." Unlike Sandburg's masculine proletarian "Hog Butcher of the World / Tool Maker, Stacker of Wheat, / Player with Railroads and the Nation's Freight Handler" (Sandburg 3), the beginning of "Chicago's Congo" is a more fanciful "overgrown woman / wearing her skyscrapers / like a necklace" (Davis, *Black Man's Verse* 5). And in contrast with the "hoo-doo" of Lindsay's notorious "Mumbo-Jumbo, god of the Congo" (Lindsay 257), "Chicago's Congo" imagines "a red warrior moon victorious in a Congo sky" (Davis, *Black Man's Verse* 5). While formally similar to Sandburg's verse, and Whitman's verse before him, with free verse lines that feature syntactic parallelism and dramatic repetition of key words and phrases, "Chicago's Combo" invokes the many musings on African heritage associated with the

New Negro Renaissance. Davis's antithesis of the Congo to Chicago initially suggests the troubled introspection of Countee Cullen's "Heritage":

> From the Congo
> to Chicago
> is a long trek
> —as the crow flies (5)

The wordplay of the final line, with its suggestion of Jim Crow, recalls the uneasy allusion to slavery in "Heritage," but the correlation of colonialism in Africa with segregation in Chicago sets the stage for a more assertive portrait of African American Chicago. The geography of "Chicago's Congo" is closer to that of Hughes's "The Negro Speaks of Rivers" in affirming the continuity of Africa and African America. Its representative if not mythic African American first-person speaker as well as its oratorical style is likewise reminiscent of Hughes's celebrated first poem.

"Chicago's Congo" is distinguished, though, by a rhetorical complexity that is more unpredictable than either "Heritage" or "The Negro Speaks of Rivers." Beginning with the outlandish description of the city as "an over-grown woman," the voice of the poem modulates from assertion ("Sing to me . . . show me . . . tell me") to questioning ("do spears kill quicker than printed words?") (Davis, *Black Man's Verse* 5). At the same time, it progresses from parallelism between images of the Congo and Chicago that suggest incongruity as much as continuity between the jungle and the city. The initial resolution of these contrasting images occurs through the first-person representative male speaker, who is both strong and articulate, street-smart and sensitive. The "song" of this persona is at once a synthesis of the Congo and Chicago and a reflection on its own process of creation:

> A song dashes its rhythms in my face like April rain
> My song is a song of steel and bamboo, of brick flats and reed huts, of
>   steamboats and slim canoes, of murder trials and jackal packs, of con
>   men and pythons
> My tune I get from automobiles and lions roaring, from the rustle of bank-
>   notes in a teller's window and the rustle of leaves in Transvaal trees
> I ask you to find a better song; a louder song, a sweeter song—
> Here's something Wagner couldn't do (6)

The song of "Chicago's Congo," then, is as much a song of Africa as it is a song of urban America, and by invoking Wagner as the antithesis to this song, the poem celebrates what is distinctively African American about its creation. It goes on to portray the South Side in specific documentary terms, through the proper names of religious and commercial institutions as well as descriptive scenes of urban poverty. The song that the poem sings ultimately has "no tune" and "no words." It is a song that "everybody knows, nobody knows" and a "melody of everything and nothing." This song, then, is an anonymous song of the South Side proletariat, unintelligible to outsiders because its social world defies conventional modes of realist representation—"you get it or you don't" (7). At the same time, this anonymous song recalls the African songs that survived slavery, the very songs that were transformed into work songs and hymns and ultimately into the blues and jazz.

At the center of *Black Man's Verse* is a trio of poems that feature jazz performance: "Jazz Band," "Mojo Mike's Beer Garden," and "Cabaret." In dramatizing jazz performance, "Jazz Band" and "Cabaret" are especially important for the social and cultural questions they raise about jazz and its reception. This sequence of jazz poems follows the gritty proletarian portrayal of "Gary, Indiana," with its international cast of workers:

> A hundred thousand people
> Europe in America
> Africa in Indiana
> an extension of Mexico
> The Orient transplanted
> another Babel
> all different
> all alike (19)

This international vision of working-class men and women, who are unified only by the hardness of their labor, is one of Davis's earliest poems (written in 1928), although it anticipates Popular Front images of interracial solidarity a decade later. It also anticipates the international scope of "Jazz Band," which celebrates the power of jazz to transcend cultural differences.

"Jazz Band" is perhaps the most overtly musical of Davis's jazz bands, because it replicates the sounds and rhythms of jazz instruments as well as enacting the performance of musicians. The poem addresses the musicians directly, at first in terms that resonate with the imagery of "Chicago's Congo": "Play that thing, you jazz-mad fools! / Boil a skyscraper with a jungle / Dish it to 'em sweet and hot" (20). While the enthusiastic direct address to musicians suggests a number of early Hughes poems, most notably "Jazz Band in a Parisian Cabaret," the manic energy of their "sweet and hot" swing is invoked through more wildly inventive figurative language. The "plink plank plunk a plunk" of the jazz band subsumes to as it mocks the somberness of European classical music: "Chopin gone screwy, Wagner with the blues . . . Got a date with Satan—ain't no time to lose" (20). And it puts New York in its place as well: "Strut it in Harlem, let Fifth Avenue shake it slow . . . Ain't goin' to heaven nohow—crowd up there's too slow" (21). Most importantly, jazz has the transformative power to cross class, national, and religious boundaries. The international list of cities is truly global: "London, Moscow, Paris, Hong Kong, Cairo, Buenos Aires, Chicago, Sydney." And its sensual effect on dancers has the power to supplant religions worldwide as well: "Make 'em shout a crazy jargon of hot hosannas to a fiddle-faced jazz god / Send Dios, Jehovah, Gott, Allah, Buddha past in a high-stepping cake walk" (21). If "Jazz Band" signifies on the most paranoid fantasies of jazz ("Got a date with Satan") as well as on the minstrel tradition so often associated with jazz, it does so comically, satirically, mocking the very deities whose names are invoked to condemn jazz.

The concluding metaphor for jazz in "Jazz Band" suggests a more professional urgency for jazz musicians, however:

> Your music's been drinking hard liquor
> Got shanghaied and it's fightin' mad
> Stripped to the waist feedin' ocean liner bellies
> Big burly bibulous brute
> Poet hands and bone crusher soldiers
> Black sheep or white? (21)

While the personification of jazz here continues the poem's celebration of the music's raucous improvisatory spirit, it also raises questions of agency and ownership. "Your music" is addressed to the jazz band, but the music is not only drunk; it has been "shanghaied." This term ironically echoes the previous references to international sites for jazz, but its more specific colloquial meaning suggests the practice of forced conscription of sailors through trickery or intimidation, particularly through the use of alcohol. The metaphor of jazz being "shanghaied" and subsequently "fightin' mad" evokes the exploitative practices of the music industry, taking advantage of musicians who may have been granted free access to alcohol but were not adequately compensated or acknowledged for their creative labor. The intensity of African American jazz is fueled by the anger that the music industry has taken and transformed the music, deceiving and diminishing its creators in the process. "Jazz Band" anticipates the more direct claims of Hughes's 1940 "Note on Commercial Theatre"—"You've taken my blues and gone" (Collected Poems 215)—but it does so more forcefully and more angrily. The conscription of jazz, "stripped to the waist feedin' ocean liner bellies," suggests both the forced labor of African slaves and the "wage labor" of the working class.

At the same time, the heavily alliterative "Big burly bibulous brute" underscores the strength and creative capability of African American jazz; while the primary association of "bibulous" here is with alcohol, "bibulous" also suggests the absorbency of jazz, the ingenuous ability of African American musicians to absorb, transform, and claim or reclaim musical forms, whether "black" or "white." The concluding appeal to "Step on it, black boy" (22) is thus double-edged: it affirms the "blackness" of jazz while it underscores the demeaning relationship of black musicians to their white employers and to the commercial market for jazz more generally.

"Jazz Band" and the subsequent "Mojo Mike's Beer Garden" echo earlier sounds and images of *Black Man's Verse*, especially sounds and images associated with jazz. While "Jazz Band" is an explicitly musical performance of the black internationalist potential of jazz, "Mojo Mike's Beer Garden" figures jazz implicitly in that the location the poem depicts, along with the poem itself, is "an unscored symphony / of colors and sounds" (22). The juxtaposed images and portraits that comprise "Mojo Mike's Beer Garden" are comparable to a Romare Bearden collage; music is figured visually rather than aurally: "Sharp scissors of a radio / snip fancy cutouts in the thick noise" (22). This vision of music as a creative shaping force manifests itself throughout *Black Man's Verse*, but nowhere more dramatically than in the poem that follows "Mojo Mike's Beer Garden," "Cabaret." "Cabaret" is dramatically different in tone from Sterling Brown's celebrated poem of the same name. Like Davis's poem, Brown's "Cabaret" takes place in Chicago, in a 1927 black-and-tan cabaret. And like Davis's poem, Brown's "Cabaret" contrasts jazz with the spirituals as well as with the more "authentic" folk expression of the blues in the rural South. Unlike Brown's "Cabaret," though, which is both mournful and acerbic in its representation of jazz as a commodified form of expression, Davis's "Cabaret" celebrates jazz as a raucously sustaining life force. The poem explicitly blends the secular and religious African American musical forms that Brown juxtaposes to accentuate what is lost with the mass migration of African Americans to northern urban centers like Chicago. Davis celebrates jazz sacrilegiously, challenging moralistic judgments of jazz and cabaret life more generally. He initially does so by personifying the jazz instruments as religious figures:

> O the big bassoon leads the members in prayer
> The sax sings hymns, cornet hums the air
> The banjo's conscientious, begs the viol to reform
> The piano titters lightly, goo-goo eyes the trombone horn
> And the solemn bass drum takes up collection

And the solemn bass drum takes up collection. (23)

Even more pointedly, the poem goes on to identify a "dirt-brown woman" who has "a voice for hymns or blues," whose blues lyrics are comparable in tone to "All God's Chillen's Got Wings." The blues and the spirituals are similarly soulful, prompting the question "Where do blues leave off and hymns begin?" (23).

As explicit as this opening conflation of jazz, blues, and spirituals as African American "soul" music is, Davis's "Cabaret" complicates this vision of black music by introducing and synthesizing additional contrasting perceptions of black music. Jazz is identified with bodily movement that can be identified with the cabaret or the black church: "Grotesque gyrations / Rhythmic contortions." But jazz also challenges oppositions of the bodily and the aesthetic, of "Ambulatory mammals" and "Unconscious aesthetes." Jazz is ultimately identified with rhetorical as well as physical dexterity, with the linguistic power to seduce dancers: "Irrefragably urged . . . By importuning inhibitions / The jazz band conjures." When Davis refers parenthetically to the "dancing dozens" in these lines, he speaks as much to the defiant, and here flamboyant, rhetorical movement of the poem as to the comparable movement of dancers. He also personifies the instruments in terms that accentuate their urban individuality, comically, until the final instrument, the banjo: "But I don't think I'd talk to the banjo. We both suckled at Sorrow's breast and I have no more time for pain" (24). Jazz, then, does not simply provide a means of release from everyday troubles. The most traditionally African instrument, the banjo, reminds the speaker of the shared suffering, and the shared heritage, that unites people of African descent. It also reminds readers that jazz is as fundamentally African in its roots as it is hybrid in its ability to creatively respond to new locations and social conditions. The implicit argument here is that jazz, the blues, and the spirituals serve similar communal needs for African Americans, but jazz is most able to blend creatively the different forms of expression that constitute African American music.

Black Man's Verse underscores how jazz is related to the continuum of African American music through allusions to jazz in poems that follow "Cabaret." These poems address questions that are usually associated with religion, questions of individual life and death, and questions of African American spirituality, but they do so through allusions to jazz in dialogue with other forms of African American music. The poem immediately following "Cabaret," "Returned," presents a speaker imagining his death and afterlife. The series of possibilities are at times comic and at times poignant, but jazz and the blues are central to the speaker's wishes for his final moment: "Let Death come to me at a cabaret while a jazz band prays to its god . . . let the jazz heart miss a beat . . . then let a trumpet cry, a saxophone sob out Handy's hymn of the St. Louis Blues . . . Life's a ragtime da-de-da, da-de-da . . . you stay in tune or quit the band" (25). This irreverent extension of the jazz mood of "Cabaret" is an unlikely segue to the more somber poem that follows, "The Slave," with its allusions to the Negro spiritual "Go Down Moses" and its "sadness . . . / carved on a black man's soul" (26). Jazz is similarly related to the spirituality of "Hands of a Brown Woman," with its musical cue, "For a Quartet of Two Guitars, a Banjo and a Tom-Tom." This heroic portrait of an archetypal black woman explicitly relates African American music to Africa as her hands "chant . . . whole histories / of the sensuous African jungle" (28). Through this mythic figure of Mandy Lou, Davis suggests a deep continuity between Africa and the New World, evoked in the instrumentation of the poem's musical cue as well as the expressive hands of Mandy Lou. Finally, jazz figures prominently in the poem that follows "Hands of a Brown Woman," "Creation," which evokes the original creation of the world as well as the poet's creation of his world. While irreverent in its tone, "Creation" asks questions that accentuate the political as well as musical possibilities raised by *Black Man's Verse* more generally:

> I haven't decided about my world.
> I would like to use a ball of gray mud
> and paint my people every conceivable color
> in order to give variety.
> But then—
> Why not a square of red flannel
> with all of the people black?
> Black against red
> red setting off black—
> but would that be a symphony
> or a jazz band? (30–31)

Should the speaker create a multiracial world, a world of "variety," or a black world? Does *Black Man's Verse* speak for a democratic ideal of pluralistic harmony or a more definitive ideal of black solidarity? And what is the significance of the distinction between a symphony and a jazz band? Neither "Creation" nor *Black Man's Verse* ultimately resolves these political questions, which concern the social purpose of poetry and jazz as much as the social ideals the speaker here imagines. The fact that these questions are not resolved is itself significant, though, as this poem, like the volume as whole, engages readers in the process of constructing meaning, a presumably social process of dialogue that could itself be compared to the call-and-response dynamic of jazz and other African American cultural forms. *Black Man's Verse* blurs the distinctions between "a symphony / or a jazz band" as Ellington's compositions do, absorbing the sounds of African American urban life and imagining new possibilities for "creation" in the process.

As *Black Man's Verse* demonstrates, jazz functions thematically and dramatically, figuratively and aurally, as a mode of African American creativity and a mode of social criticism in Davis's poetry. While jazz is identified with African American urban life and African American history, it also enacts possibilities for intercultural and interracial dialogue. The capacity of jazz to raise questions and foster intercultural dialogue is perhaps most evident in "Dancing Gal," a poem that was published in Davis's second book, *I Am the American Negro*. Like the jazz poems of *Black Man's Verse*, especially "Jazz Band," "Dancing Gal" underscores the social conditions of jazz performance as it figures jazz internationally. In contrasting the performance of a "dancing gal" in a black-and-tan with perceptions of her exoticized sensuality, "Dancing Gal" revisits the dramatic scenario of McKay's "The Harlem Dancer," Hughes's "Nude Young Dancer," and Brown's "Cabaret." Written from the first-person point of view of an observer who both participates in and distances himself from the crowd's fascination with the dancer, "Dancing Gal" resembles McKay's 1917 sonnet, with the poet's concluding identification with the dancer's alienation: "But looking at her falsely-smiling face, / I knew her self was not in that strange place" (McKay, *Complete Poems* 172). "Dancing Gal" is more open-ended, however, even as it acknowledges the distance between the spell of "Africa's madness, India's sadness" cast by the dancer and the more mundane social reality of "a Midwest gal / in a Jew's café" (64–65). "Dancing Gal" is actually more comparable to Hughes' poems such as "Nude Young Dancer" in asking questions about jazz performance rather than asserting conclusions.

Like the other patrons of the black-and-tan, the speaker in "Dancing Gal" is enchanted by the performance of the dancer and the musicians even as he questions his own perceptions. The poem begins with a question directed generally to the black-and-tan patrons: "Black and tan—yeah, black and tan / Spewing the moans of a jigtime band / What does your belly crave?" The description of the dancer that follows highlights the colors of the black-and-tan club, including the skin color of the dancer, "brown-sugar brown," who is dancing seductively "Beneath a yellow thumb / Of steel-stiff light." The line break after "thumb" suggests that the dancer, with all of her creative ability to enchant the audience, is under the "thumb" of her employer, if not overdetermined by the social, economic, and racial dynamic of the black-and-tan establishment more generally. She is described nonetheless in passionately sensual terms, although the descriptive language here also suggests the economic conditions of her performance: "Young girl breasts in gold encased / Scant gold around her lower waist." This "gold encased" image of the dancer inspires a reverie that takes the speaker, and the poem, far from this Chicago café as the "drab and muted human shapes" of the café become "a long lean god" in Tanganyika and a "frozen idol" in Hindustan (64). This vision of "Africa's madness, India's sadness" is a creative adaptation of the jazz dancer's movement, a poetic vision of the transformative impact of jazz performance, and an interpretive rendering of the spiritual as well as sensual dimensions of jazz. Tanganyika (Tanzania) and Hindustan (India) also evoke their ancient cultural histories and their resistance to colonial rule, and the enjambment and lack of punctuation in these lines suggests the continuity of African and Indian resistance movements. As much as this poem may imagine an "Afro-Asian" vision of jazz, it is also admittedly primitivist in exoticizing the performance of a "Midwest girl / In a Jew's café." The variation of the opening question that concludes the poem is as much a commentary on the poem itself as on popular perceptions of jazz: "Black and tan—yeah, black and tan / Drenched in the jazz of a swingtime band / Is this what your belly craves?"(65). The question is self-reflexive in that Davis implicitly addresses the audience for jazz poetry, including his own poetry, as he addresses the patrons of the black-and-tan. What are the conventions and expectations of poetry that enacts jazz performance? Is it possible to escape the primitivist associations of jazz when positing a conti-nuity between African and African American music and spirituality? How can a poet realistically represent the transformative power of jazz without representing the popular conceptions—and misconceptions—associated with the music's sensual allure? "Dancing Gal" enacts the primitivist associations of jazz performance that it also critiques, even as the poem's mythic projec-tions celebrate the spirituality as well as the sensuality of jazz. By implicitly addressing the reader as well as the black-and-tan audience, Davis makes readers more aware of the sensual power of jazz—and the rhetorical power of jazz poetry—as he questions the very conventions that inform that power.

Davis reached the peak of his popularity as a poet with his first two books in the 1930s. During the late 1930s and the 1940s he became increasingly active as a journalist and columnist for the Associated Negro Press. As a political commentator he became more assertive in denouncing racism, domestically and in the military during the war, most notably in his war-time column, "Passing Parade." He also became more involved with radical interracial literary and political organizations, and his commitment to the

Communist Party in the mid-1940s suggests how his advocacy for racial equality became inseparable from his socialist vision of democracy. As he became better known as a writer, Davis also became a more prominent figure in the jazz community, nationally and locally in Chicago, where he played an increasingly public role as a jazz educator. Given this active involvement with jazz, it is surprising that he did not write any jazz poetry after the publication of *I Am the American Negro* until 1974, when he wrote a series of jazz portraits that were published in the journal *Black World* and later collected into a chapbook titled *Jazz Interludes: Seven Musical Poems* (1975). *I Am the American Negro* and his third collection of poetry, *47th Street* (1948), feature poems of social realism and social commentary on African American Chicago, but jazz figures less prominently in these books than in *Black Man's Verse*.

Davis's public life as a Chicago poet basically ended after World War II when he became increasingly subject to anticommunist persecution. Partly in response to anticommunist pressure, and partly in pursuit of a refuge where his interracial marriage with Helen Canfield Davis would not be so controversial, Davis and his wife decided to spend some time in Hawaii in the winter of 1948 (*Livin' the Blues* 311). This visit lasted the rest of his life; he settled in Honolulu and did not even visit the mainland United States again until 1973. As Tidwell asserts, Davis can be counted among the many radical exiles who sought refuge from Cold War persecution; his decision to leave Chicago for Hawaii was undoubtedly informed by his desire to evade harassment by the FBI and the House Un-American Activities Committee.[11] However, Davis's move to "Paradise" did not conclude his activism as a journalist. He wrote a series of columns for the Associated Negro Press titled "Democracy: Hawaiian Style" in 1949 and a weekly column for the pro-labor weekly newspaper, the *Honolulu Record*, titled "Frank-ly Speaking." This column included a 1955 series on the history of black music. Davis's first impression of Hawaii was that "he had been suddenly freed from the chains of white oppression," that he now "had a sense of human dignity" that he did not have in the mainland United States (312). As a journalist who wrote about labor issues for the *Record*, he was not naive about the racial prejudice and discrimination that existed in Hawaii, especially in the wake of World War II. Nonetheless, Davis wrote that Hawaii was "the only area in the United States which has successfully shown the possibility of integration with integrity. Here various ethnic groups have been able not only to maintain group identity and pride but work together with other peoples of vastly different traditions and live side by side without noticeable tension" (318). This discovery of the ethnic pluralism that distinguished Hawaii transformed Davis's understanding of jazz somewhat as well. While he emphasized the African roots of jazz and the distinctively African American social contexts in which jazz emerged, he also noted the cosmopolitanism of early jazz, especially the mix of musical cultures that informed the development of jazz in New Orleans. New Orleans was distinctive for its Spanish and French cultural and musical influences, but, most importantly, "it was the one place in America where African music and dancing was permitted to survive" ("Jazz in New Orleans" 20). This recognition of African music in New Orleans was the definitive factor in the development of jazz, as Davis writes. He found a comparable interest in African American culture in Honolulu, especially among young people, and his account of his later years as an elder figure in the multiracial Honolulu neighborhood known as "the Jungle" attests to his appreciation of the city's cosmopolitanism.[12]

In 1972 Davis was invited by his friend and comrade Margaret Burroughs, whom he had known since 1940, to return to Chicago to read his poetry. Given the many years since he had established his reputation as a poet, Davis was skeptical about potential interest in his writing. Burroughs convinced him, though, that the younger generation of African American writers associated with the Black Aesthetic movement would be especially interested in his poetry. Before too long, Stephen Henderson, Dudley Randall, and other prominent writers had contacted him, and the following year he embarked on a reading tour that took him to Chicago, Washington, D.C., Atlanta, San Francisco, and Berkeley. Davis read much of his early poetry on this tour, including the jazz poems that were receiving renewed attention by younger writers, but he also introduced a series of new jazz portraits that were published in the journal *Black World* in 1974: "Duke Ellington," "Louis Armstrong," "Billie Holiday," and "Charlie Parker" ("Poems by Frank Marshall Davis").[13] *Black World*, published in the 1960s as *Negro Digest*, was perhaps the most important journal for the Chicago Black Arts movement, because it combined literature and cultural commentary with social and political analysis. Under the editorship of Hoyt Fuller, *Negro Digest* published younger African American poets such as Haki Madhubuti and Carolyn Rogers, who would become identified with the new Black Aesthetic, along with more established Chicago poets such as Gwendolyn Brooks and Margaret Danner. By the time that Davis's poetry appeared in *Black World*, the journal had become more internationalist in its exploration of African and African diaspora issues. This is especially evident in the February 1974 issue, which included Davis's poetry. While this issue included essays on African American literature and history by younger writers, including a review essay by George Kent of *Understanding the New Black Poetry* and an essay by Toni Morrison on the making of *The Black Book*, it featured as many articles on African issues as on African American topics. It seems especially fitting, then, that Davis's poems were preceded by a long historical study by John Henrik Clarke titled "The Afro-American Image of Africa" and followed by an essay by Sterling Brown, "Portrait of a Jazz Giant: 'Jelly Roll' Morton." In addressing the long history of African American perceptions of Africa, Clarke made the case for the continuity of African American consciousness in the New World, a continuity that had been distorted by representations of Africa in the mass media and educational system in the United States. The result of such distortion was a "rejection of Africa and a deep longing for the Africa of our imagination" (6), a topic that Davis had addressed in his jazz writing as well as his poetry since the 1930s. Brown's biographical essay on Jelly Roll Morton likewise connected with Davis's musical and literary interests; it is as much an act of recovery of this musician who was "frustrated and neglected in his lifetime" (47) as it is a historical study of his music and its significance. Like Davis, Brown had a deep appreciation for early jazz, and his essay on Morton and his legacy is not unlike Davis's poetic portraits of Ellington, Armstrong, Holiday, and Parker. Brown, like Clarke and Davis, also had the historical experience that spanned the initial publication of *Negro Digest* in 1942, as a general interest African American magazine, and the more politically radical *Black World* in the early 1970s.[14]

The jazz portraits that Davis published in *Black World* depicted figures who were associated with the swing era, including Parker, whose early big band years in Kansas City were overshadowed by his legendary success as a bebop saxophonist. These free verse poems evoke distinctive musical features of each musician while celebrating the lasting power and beauty of swing more generally. Davis revisits the musicians who were most prominent during the Popular Front years when he was most active as a poet and jazz journalist, dramatizing their ongoing significance. His portrait of Louis Armstrong, for example, presents the legendary "Zulu King" through patterns of repetition, of alliteration and unexpected rhyme, that enact both the syncopated rhythm of Armstrong's swing and the improvisatory brilliance of his playing. Beginning and ending with the court of the New Orleans Zulu King, with "twenty-six / Of the craziest chicks / Shaking that thing," the poem dramatizes at once the regality and playfulness of Armstrong's musical persona. The poetic language of Armstrong's biography as a musician is black vernacular: "He was a young un' / When he blew himself / Smack dab on the throne." The imagery of Armstrong's creative improvisation is also appropriately inventive: "Notes swing out / Shining like sun-stroked gold / Lithe as contortionists" (*Black Moods* 192). Armstrong's solos move gracefully but also intensely, darting like "stunting jets" and burning like "boiling lava," while his voice sounds like "gravel / Fallin' in a tin bucket / With a melodic beat." The imagery of Armstrong's expressiveness as a musician is by turns electric and earthy, but most importantly, the poem insists on the lasting power of Armstrong's sound. It resonates as powerfully among the "new cool people / Of the jazz jungle" (193) as it does in the memory of the king in his court decades before. "Louis Armstrong" is as much an argument for the revolutionary spirit of swing as it is a commemoration of a musical hero from the early years of jazz. "Duke Ellington" is similarly celebratory in dramatizing the musician's creative versatility and compositional capaciousness. Ellington is a "Conjure man," "Magician," "Inventor," "Crazy painter," and "Mad sculptor," and his music is rendered in heavily alliterative phrases and in surreal imagery that suggests its synaesthetic power (189). Like the Armstrong portrait, "Duke Ellington" also appeals to "hipsters" past and present, suggesting a continuity rather than a contrast between swing and more experimental forms of jazz in the 1960s. Davis even echoes his own earlier jazz poetry in personifying the musical instruments: "Someday someone should give a dance for the band / Let the instruments dress and have a ball" (190). In this reprise of "Cabaret," Davis suggests that his jazz poetry, like Ellington's compositions, has not lost the power to appeal to a younger generation of listeners.

In portraying Armstrong and Ellington as legendary but living figures in language that evokes the swing era but is also assertively contemporary, Davis insists on the lasting relevance of music that many younger listeners would have considered passé. Armstrong and Ellington have been the subjects of literary tribute prior to Davis's portraits, but his poetic performance of their significance also speaks to earlier jazz poetry, such as his own, which, despite its association with the early decades of jazz, resonated with renewed intensity among the New Black poetry. Literary portraits of Billie Holiday and Charlie Parker raised different challenges, however, given the number of poems commemorating each and the elegiac tone of most of these poems. Both Holiday and Parker were conventionally portrayed as tragic figures, self-destructive in their addiction to heroin, but also victims of a postwar authoritarian world that considered influential jazz musicians socially and politically suspect and treated them accordingly. Holiday in particular is portrayed as a sorrowful figure whose subtly expressive voice conveys a lifetime of abusive mistreatment, from her difficult childhood in Baltimore to the postwar bouts with addiction and the law that threatened her professional life as a singer. While she has since been recognized as a blues woman whose songs of desire and disappointment mask a keen awareness of racial and sexual exploitation, she was more often remembered after her death for the fragility of her voice and instability of her professional and personal life.[15] Davis's "Billie Holiday," though, is closer in tone to a poem written about Holiday before her death— Hughes's "Song for Billie Holiday" (1949)—with its opening variations of the question "What can purge my heart / Of the song / And the sadness?" (Hughes, *Collected Poems* 360). Like Hughes, Davis not only addresses the sadness of Holiday's songs; he also invokes the media through which her voice is heard. Unlike "Song for Billie Holiday," however, which concludes, "Bitter television blurred / By sound that shimmers—Where?" (360), Davis's "Billie Holiday" affirms the magical qualities of electronic media to preserve such compelling voices as Holiday's: "By the presto of electronics / I reincarnate Lady Day" (*Black Moods* 188). "Billie Holiday" is elegiac, but its mournfulness is compensated by the inventiveness of Davis's figurative language for her voice and its impact on her listeners. Rather than a tragic victim, Holiday has a commanding artistic agency:

> She pulls
> Notes fall
> Into her molten mold
> Of flaming sound
> Burning
> Bright as a hungry sun (188)

These expressive lyrics suggest a creative presence more familiar to poems addressed to John Coltrane, and the fact that Holiday is imbued with such artistic power distinguishes Davis's "Billie Holiday" from more sorrowful poems about her. Yes, she is a blues singer who will be forever remembered by lyrics like "My man he don't love me / He treats me awful mean" (189), but she is also a blues singer whose voice is magical: "She sings / And her words taste / Of lavender butter / Spread with a unicorn's horn" (190). Furthermore, she is a singer whose presence outlasts the "responsibilities" and "pushers" who compromised her creative life. Davis celebrates not only a singer whose understated assertiveness opened listeners' ears to the sorrows of African American history, but a singer whose expressions of strength and perseverance are timeless. The magic of this poem consists in the wondrous ability to revive a voice from the past and renew its significance: "How easy it is / A switch turns / And the dead breathes again" (188). If this technological power is so easy, perhaps, that it is taken for granted, Davis suggests nonetheless that a singer like Holiday can transform future generations with the intensity and beauty of her testimony. In enacting this possibility, he indicates that a revisionist poem like "Billie Holiday" can have a similarly transformative impact.

By including a portrait of Charlie Parker in this series of swing portraits, and later in *Jazz Interludes* with his 1930s jazz poems, Davis implicitly answers accounts of Parker's genius that underestimate his formative years with dance bands in Kansas City. Parker's first recordings, after all, were with the Jay McShann Orchestra in 1941 in Wichita, not far from Davis's own hometown. While Davis was hesitant to embrace bebop at first, he acknowledged that bebop "mirrored not only the frustration of Negroes in their quest for first-class citizenship but was a vivid portrait of America and a chaotic world" ("Mirror of Jazz" 29). It did not appeal to the African American masses, though, and it was only later that Davis came to appreciate bebop's grounding in the blues. He never questioned Parker's brilliance as a saxophonist, however, which he first encountered with his recordings with the McShann band (*Livin' the Blues* 287). "Charlie Parker" is similar to other poetic Parker tributes in its enactment of "Yard Bird's" imaginative flight as a musician. But his portrait is more subdued in its elegiac mood and thus more poignant than the portrayals of Parker's ascent and fall by poets such as Jack Kerouac, Kenneth Ford, and Howard Hart. As Sascha Feinstein has written, too many poems dedicated to his legendary persona "projected a God-like status on Parker, and in doing so they lost the humanness of the man. The descriptions of the music and of Parker himself became overexposed, whitened-out in adulation" (*Jazz Poetry from the 1920s* 90). Davis signifies on this idolization of Parker, beginning with a question about his nickname, itself the subject of legends: "Who named him Yard Bird?" (*Black Moods* 190). And while Davis's Yard Bird ascends to the heavens and burns his wings like Icarus, he is from beginning to end a "homing pigeon / With no home to fly to" (190). This figure of the "homing pigeon" is surely more common than the figure of the mythic bird in the heavens that follows, but it is a mythic figure in its own right, a blues figure whose migrant journey is both necessary and sorrowful. "Charlie Parker" is at once a poem of flight, in its double sense of departure and ascent, but the impossibility of a return flight home speaks to both Parker's own difficult family life as a child and the representative existential reality of his predicament. Flight becomes a form of escape and escape becomes a motive, and as high as Parker can fly, the fall of this "majestic bird" seems overdetermined. The middle part of this poem, which begins "In the rambling sky," is not unlike other poetic enactments of Parker's sound, with its brief, frenetic free verse lines, its dense alliteration, and its rhythmic unpredictability, and the imagery of "freedom" and "daring" is commonly associated with bebop's defiance of conventional expectations. It is interesting, though, that the depiction of Parker's flight echoes the very same language for Armstrong's improvisations, "Dipping, darting" in the air (191). This repeated figure suggests a creative continuity between Armstrong and Parker, as unlikely as this would seem in the bebop milieu that sharply differentiated Parker's cool demeanor on stage from Armstrong's showmanship. This resonance suggests a common grounding in the blues that links Parker with Armstrong, which is ultimately more important to Davis than their contrasting personae. To portray their improvisations as the songs of birds in flight is not so unusual, but by relating Parker's musical genius to Armstrong's not only recovers a common blues tradition that informs their innovations; it also brings Parker back to earth from more outlandishly legendary accounts of his solitary genius. For Parker, however, there is "no home to fly to," and the tragedy of his intensely creative, or creatively intense, movement as a musician is that he cannot soar forever and is "Helpless / On the ground." Davis's Yard Bird is "trapped / And hooked / And cooked—That's the simple story" (191).

The story of Charlie Parker is of course not so "simple," just as the story of "Charlie Parker" is not simple. The poem also evokes Davis's own life story, with his sense of exile from his own roots in Kansas. By including the story of Yard Bird with the stories of Armstrong, Ellington, and Holiday, Davis creates a new historical context for understanding Parker's significance as a musician. He complicates this story even further when he remixes these portraits with his earlier "Jazz Band," "Cabaret," and "Dancing Gal" in *Jazz Interludes* a few years later. In combining these jazz poems from different eras, Davis initiates a dialogue between swing and later forms of jazz. While he underscores the continuity of jazz, a continuity based on the blues, this remix suggests less a seamless continuity than a creative tension between different experiences of jazz. Davis also projects a new, or newly revived, literary reputation for himself in the process, a reputation that was enhanced by laudatory reconsiderations of his poetry by Stephen Henderson, Dudley Randall, Eugene Redmond, and other historians of African American poetry.[16] He is at once a radical poet of the Popular Front 1930s and a radical poet of the 1970s Black Aesthetic. After years of absence from African American literary life, his persona was not unlike the figure of PaPa LaBas at the end of Ishmael Reed's *Mumbo Jumbo*, the eccentric spokesman for an earlier period of black pride who challenges a younger generation of African Americans, the embodiment of the message Reed adapts from Arna Bontemps's *Black Thunder*: "Time is a pendulum. Not a river. More akin to what goes round comes round" (218). At the same time, however, Davis embodies a 1960s and '70s spirit of rebellion in his identification with the Honolulu counterculture that he celebrates in *Livin' the Blues* and particularly in "That Incredible Waikiki Jungle," a manuscript that he never completed. The excerpt from this manuscript in *Livin' the Blues* narrates his return to the mainland and his surprising recognition as a "'long lost folk hero of black poetry'" (343).

As amazed as he is by the enthusiastic reception of his poetry readings by younger people, the story of his interaction with the "Now Generation" in the Waikiki neighborhood known as "the Jungle" is a story of rejuvenation. Divorced from his wife, Helen, and economically impoverished, Davis took on the persona of a trusted sage, an elder figure who supported the multi-racial young "rebels" of "the Jungle" as he was inspired by them to imagine the possibilities of new democratic social formations.

The most famous young person who sought Davis's advice in Honolulu is none other than President Barack Obama. Obama's reflections on "Frank" in his best-selling memoir, *Dreams from My Father*, have done more to renew interest in Davis's life story, if not his poetry, than any other book. While Obama does not identify "Frank" specifically by his full name, his portrayal of this "poet named Frank" he visits in "a run-down section of Waikiki" with his grandfather describes Davis precisely:

> He had enjoyed some modest notoriety once, was a contemporary of Richard Wright and Langston Hughes during his years in Chicago—Gramps once showed me some of his work anthologized in a book of black poetry. But by the time I met Frank he must have been pushing eighty, with a big, dewlapped face and an ill-kempt gray Afro that made him look like an old shaggy-maned lion. He would read us his poetry whenever we stopped by his house, sharing whiskey with Gramps out of an emptied jelly jar. As the night wore on, the two of them would solicit my help in composing dirty limericks. Eventually, the conversation would turn to laments about women. (76–77)

This initial portrait of the artist as an old man is hardly flattering, as "intrigued by old Frank" as Obama was at this time as an "eleven- or twelve-year-old" (77). Frank is depicted as a somewhat ominous, hard-drinking bluesman whose better days as a poet were far behind him. As a teenager, however, Obama seeks Davis's advice, especially when he is questioning his own racial identity. When Davis tells Obama about his own experience growing up in the same region of Kansas as Obama's (white) grandparents, he underscores the ongoing implications of Jim Crow discrimination and segregation. "I still have to watch myself. I have to be vigilant, for my own survival," he says (90), concluding that "black people have a reason to hate" (91). The memory of Frank recurs at key transitional moments in the life story Obama narrates in *Dreams from My Father*. His lessons are most prominent at times when Obama is questioning his own sense of purpose, as he does in his early years at Occidental College. Appropriately enough, he recalls Davis as he is listening to Billie Holiday, late at night, feeling the blues that she sings. And he remembers how Davis defined college: "An advanced degree in compromise" (97). The "real price of admission," Davis tells Obama, is:

"Leaving your race at the door.... Leaving your people behind.... You're not going to college to get educated. You're going there to get *trained*. They'll train you to want what you don't need. They'll train you to manipulate words so they don't mean anything anymore. They'll train you to forget what it is that you already know. They'll train you so good, you'll start believing what they tell you about equal opportunity and the American way and all that shit. They'll give you a corner office and invite you to fancy dinners, and tell you you're a credit to your race. Until you want to actually start running things, and then they'll yank on your chain and let you know that you may be a well-trained, well-paid nigger, but you're a nigger just the same." (97)

The extent to which Davis's words are prophetic is debatable, as the Oval Office certainly raises more complicated questions about "equal opportunity and the American way" than a "corner office." What is unquestionable, though, is the stunning confluence of Davis's uncompromising social realism, his cutting analysis of race relations at the highest levels of professional accomplishment, with the more subtle sharpness of Holiday's blues. Obama's portrait of Davis recalls the juxtaposition of his radically "proletarian" social poetry with the blues expression of his jazz poetry. In citing Davis's words as a challenge to his own questionable convictions, Obama reenacts the provocative power of Davis's poetry.

Dreams from My Father also portrays Davis as a man of two eras. There is "Frank and his old Black Power, dashiki self . . . certain in his faith, living in the same sixties time warp that Hawaii had created" (98). And there is the imagined younger version of Davis in Chicago: "I imagined Frank in a baggy suit and wide lapels, standing in front of the old Regal Theatre, waiting to see Duke or Ella emerge from a gig" (145–46). These images of the radical "Black Power" figure of the 1960s and the dapper jazz enthusiast of the 1930s seem disconnected and somewhat incongruous. They also seem quite distant from the twenty-first-century world, in which Obama later served as president of the United States. It is amazing, then, that Frank Marshall Davis has now achieved the fame, indeed "notoriety," that eluded him in his years as a writer. On the left, Davis has been cited as a significant influence on the development of Obama's social consciousness. Historian Gerald Horne, for example, discussed Davis's importance in a 2008 speech celebrating the Tamiment Library's acquisition of the Communist Party USA archives. Considering Davis's work as a radical activist and journalist in Hawaii, Horne concludes:

In his best selling memoir "Dreams of my Father," the author speaks warmly of an older black poet, he identifies simply as "Frank" as being a decisive influence in helping him to find his present identity as an African-American, a people who have been the least anticommunist and the most left-leaning of

any constituency in this nation—though you would never know it from reading so-called left journals of opinion. At some point in the future, a teacher
will add to her syllabus Barack's memoir and instruct her students to read it
alongside Frank Marshall Davis' equally affecting memoir, "Living the Blues"
and when that day comes, I'm sure a future student will not only examine
critically the Frankenstein monsters that US imperialism created in order to
subdue Communist parties but will also be moved to come to this historic and
wonderful archive in order to gain insight on what has befallen this complex
and intriguing planet on which we reside.

Not surprisingly, such a characterization of Davis's legacy has drawn the
attention and ire of right-wing critics of Obama's presidency. If success can
be measured by the voracity, if not veracity, of one's critics, then Davis, like
Obama, can now be considered extraordinarily successful. His influence on
the young Barack is routinely cited as evidence of Obama's unfitness for the
presidency. He is indeed the subject of numerous conspiracy theories about
Obama in books with sinister titles like *Obama Nation: Leftist Politics and
the Cult of Personality*; *The Roots of Obama's Rage*; *Radical-in-Chief: Barack
Obama and the Untold Story of American Socialism*; and *The Manchurian
President: Barack Obama's Ties to Communists, Socialists, and Other Anti-
American Extremists*.[17] If Davis was indeed caught in a "sixties time warp,"
as Obama has written, then the president's critics occupy an early Cold War
time warp that demonizes the left as "anti-American," regardless of Obama's
moderate policy decisions. One book, Paul Kengor's *Dupes: How America's
Adversaries Have Manipulated Progressives for a Century*, even dedicates an
entire chapter to Davis and reprints his FBI file. Davis would have laughed
at his current notoriety, not only as a communist but also as a "pervert" (the
author of the pseudonymous "autobiographical" novel *Sex Rebel: Black*), who
was, perhaps, the unacknowledged father of Obama.[18] But he probably also
would have told Obama, "I told you so." As for the Davis who represented
jazz, as an influential poet, journalist, and educator, he would not have been
surprised that a black president would be characterized with such accusa-
tions of communism, anti-Americanism, foreignness, and illegitimacy that
were associated with the early emergence of the commercial blues and jazz,
not to mention the subsequent emergence of swing, bebop, rhythm and
blues, rock-and-roll, hip-hop, and virtually all forms of popular black cultural expression that have appealed to interracial audiences. In the words of
Mumbo Jumbo, "Time is a pendulum. Not a river. More akin to what goes
round comes round" (218).

3 "Do You Sing for a Living?"

Ann Petry, The Street, *and the Gender Politics of World War II Jazz*

"Sometimes tunes play tricks in your head and turn out to be somep'n you heard a long while ago and all the time you think it's one you made up."
—Ann Petry, *The Street*

About one-third into Ann Petry's 1946 novel, *The Street*, after five suffocating chapters of anxiety, frustration, and dread, the novel's protagonist, Lutie Johnson, decides to escape the drudgery of her everyday life and relax for a moment at the local Junto Bar and Grill. An "oasis of warmth" in the winter (141), an "illusion of coolness" in the summer (142), the Junto is a welcoming "social club and meeting place," where you could "pick up all the day's news" (143) or pick up someone to love. Sitting at the bar with a beer, Lutie finds herself singing along to the jukebox sound of a popular "sweet" ballad called "Darlin.'" And, as Petry writes, "Her voice had a thin thread of sadness running through it that made the song important, that made it tell a story that wasn't in the words—a story of despair, of loneliness, of frustration . . . a story that all of them knew by heart" (148). This moment of release, this moment of shared sorrow, this moment when she sings, "'There's no sun, Darlin', There's no fun, Darlin,'" is also the moment of Lutie's "discovery." A man identified only by his flawless hand pays for her drinks and stands behind her. Their eyes meet in the bar's mirror, and he asks, "'Do you sing for a living?'" This is the beginning of Lutie's career as a singer—her opportunity for success, for financial security, for escape from "the street." It is also, of course, the beginning of the end. As she looks up, she sees the owner of the bar, the owner of "the street," "Old Man Junto," "studying her in the mirror" (149).

"Do you sing for a living?" is a feminized variation of a recurring question in *The Street*: "What do you do for a living?" The question of "what you do for a living" provokes suspicion, if not hostility, whether it's addressed to the jazz pianist Boots Smith or the aspiring singer Lutie. It's a question of power, the power of "the man," the white man Junto, to control the lives of black musicians. Yet the suggestiveness of "sing," with its sexual as well as musical connotations, like the suggestiveness of Lutie's name—the musical "lute," the monetary "loot," even the sonic closeness of "lute" to "lewd"—conveys what distinguishes female labor in the business of jazz during the swing era. The jazz woman was expected to "sing," not play an instrument. The jazz woman was also expected to "swing," but not like the jazz men assembled behind her. The jazz woman was expected to fulfill more conventional feminine roles, as contradictory as these roles were. While the men wore uniforms, the jazz woman stood apart from the band in a glamorous gown and sang songs that expressed private, intimate emotions. At the time when *The Street* is set, however, 1944, these gendered divisions of labor, like gendered divisions of labor in industry, were hardly stable. Men were at war, and women assumed positions that were previously unavailable. Men were at war, and women had a greater degree of independence, whether financial, professional, or sexual. Men were at war, and there were new opportunities for female jazz musicians. Such transgression of gendered roles also produced considerable anxiety and considerable resistance, however. As Sherrie Tucker and other scholars of the swing era have shown, the question of women's labor in the 1940s not only provoked new debates but also intensified long-standing debates about the economics and ideological significance of jazz.[1] Such wartime questions of women's labor inform Petry's representations of jazz in *The Street*. They also inform the novel's disruption of conventional expectations of genre as well as gender: *The Street*, after all, is among the earliest jazz novels by women writers and one of the first that features a female jazz musician as its protagonist. Petry's realist portrayal of the business of jazz underscores the exploitation of African American musicians, especially women, but her narrative evocations of jazz improvisation suggest the creative potential for rethinking and transforming expectations of women's writing as well as women's musicianship.[2]

In recent years Petry's writing has received increased attention for its historical importance as well as for its influence on subsequent black feminist writers. Specifically, scholars of the literary left have redefined her significance for African American literary and cultural studies. Alan Wald's *Trinity of Passion: The Literary Left and the Antifascist Crusade* (2007) and the collection of essays edited by Alex Lubin, *Revising the Blueprint: Ann Petry and the Literary Left* (2007), underscore especially the continuity of her 1940s Harlem journalism and activism with the testimony of her best-selling novel, *The Street*. This essay will extend such renewed interest in Petry's involvement with the left to consider the significance of *The Street* as a jazz novel. *The Street*, like several of Petry's earlier short stories, draws upon jazz for its dramatic structure and for the portrayal of its protagonist. While Petry tends to celebrate jazz as a creative mode of African American cultural expression in her short fiction, *The Street* emphasizes how jazz is also a commercial medium subject to economic, racial, and gender politics.[3] In representing jazz singing as labor and as the exploitation of an African American working-class woman, Petry dramatizes the ideological contradictions of jazz, and specifically swing, as a progressive symbol of U.S. democracy. I will suggest, then, that *The Street* enacts a left feminist critique of Popular Front idealizations of jazz during World War II. Petry accentuates the wartime racial inequality that would intensify activism on the African American left and also provoke the more aggressive sound of bebop among younger African American jazz musicians. At the same time, Petry reminds us of the gendered division of labor in jazz, which identified women with glamour and sexuality rather than skilled musicianship, even as the wartime shortage of male workers created more (temporary) opportunities for female jazz musicians.

The Street is widely recognized as a "novel of social criticism," as Petry herself has suggested, and it has been compared most often with Richard Wright's *Native Son*.[4] It is less frequently considered a jazz novel. During the 1940s, however, the realms of social protest and jazz expression often converged. Several critics have associated *The Street* and its protagonist, Lutie Johnson, with the blues tradition, and readers often note the importance of the jazz performance settings for Lutie's characterization, but there has been surprisingly little attention given to the role of jazz for the novel's social criticism.[5] One critic, Jürgen Grandt, has made an especially compelling case that *The Street* should be taken more seriously as a jazz narrative. Jazz is important, most obviously, for Lutie's aspirations for upward mobility, for escaping the entrapment of "the street," as delusional as these aspirations prove to be. As Grandt writes, Lutie's jazz performances hardly result in the liberation that she momentarily experiences when she sings; her jazz dream proves to be an illusion, as the male gaze of Boots and Junto "imprisons [her] at the very moment she sings of liberation" (27–28). Jazz does not play the redemptive role associated with narratives of male jazz musicians, then, as Petry accentuates how women are limited by the demanding labor conditions and masculinist mentality of the jazz world. As Grandt argues, though, Petry also dramatizes Lutie's plight through structural devices that are comparable to jazz. The novel's mix of timelines, its patterns of repetition that interrupt its linear narrative movement, can be compared to the "complex, multilayered manipulation of time, that elusive, mysterious quality called *swing*" (31). There is a dramatic tension between the naturalist movement of events toward an inevitable conclusion and the improvisatory moments that disrupt this movement, particularly the narrative flashbacks that are told from various perspectives. If the "swing time" of narrative movement is itself "accompanied by the deterministic teleology of the street's pernicious forces" (39), this movement between present and past, and between the multiple centers of consciousness, also suggests alternative possibilities that are neither adequately explored nor fully recognized by Lutie. Jazz functions not only as a mode of social criticism but also as a mode of literary criticism in *The Street*. In focusing on the limitations of Lutie's social and political awareness, Petry underscores the ideological constructs that are often confused with naturalist modes of hereditary and environmental determinism.

The Street represents a period of jazz history that was itself full of explosive tensions. On the one hand, jazz was widely associated with U.S. nationalism during World War II. The ideology associated with swing in the 1930s and early 1940s, with its belief in democratic equality, ethnic pluralism, and racial tolerance, made it especially suitable for nationalist goals of fighting fascism. On the other hand, the war underscored the contradictions of such an ideology, given the segregated military and the persistence of racial inequality in the United States. Jazz was valued especially on the Popular Front left for its interracial appeal, as an "organic, democratic art form rooted in black culture" (Erenberg 122). Numerous journals associated with the Popular Front, from *The Nation* and *The New Republic* to the *Daily Worker* and the *New Masses*, featured left jazz writing as did African American newspapers such as the *Amsterdam News*, the *Chicago Defender*, and the *Pittsburgh Courier* (136). The jazz journals that emerged with the popularity of swing, *Down Beat* and *Metronome*, likewise made the case for the central importance of African American jazz musicians by the 1940s. And leftist jazz historians such as Marshall Stearns and Frank Marshall Davis argued not only for the central role of African Americans in jazz but also for the African roots of jazz and of African American popular music more generally. Despite disagreements on the left about what constituted "authentic" jazz by the 1940s, there was certainly agreement about the irony of a racially segregated society fighting white supremacy in Europe.[6] It is not surprising that African American jazz musicians were less likely to perceive swing in idealistic terms of American democracy than Popular Front journalists. Because of their experience with the commercial realities of the music world, "swing" signified increasing control over African American music by the recording industry as much as African American musical success. To identify swing with American democracy in wartime propaganda obscured the inequalities that limited African

American musicians. Thus the contradictions of the war years affected the racial consciousness of African Americans most powerfully, which led to a new racial politics of jazz that would become identified with the bebop movement after the war.[7]

Petry's knowledge of jazz was shaped by her experience living in Harlem from 1938 to 1947 and, specifically, by her experience working as a journalist with the *Amsterdam News* and *People's Voice*.[8] Her involvement with *People's Voice*, which began with its inaugural issue in February 1942, was especially important for developing the social vision of her first novel, *The Street*.[9] She worked for *People's Voice* until 1944 as a reporter, editor, and columnist. She wrote stories about Harlem and national protests and edited the "National Roundup" of news and the women's pages. She was most visible, however, as the writer of a weekly column titled "The Lighter Side," which surveyed Harlem political, social, and cultural events. While her writing in all of these realms demonstrates her commitment to the newspaper's African American leftist vision of democracy, "The Lighter Side" perhaps best exemplifies the ironic wit and feminist consciousness that distinguish her journalistic writing.[10] *People's Voice* was founded by editor in chief Adam Clayton Powell Jr. and publisher Charles P. Buchanan as a "working class paper" that was "non-partisan" and "non-sectarian" ("Editorial Policy" 21). As its initial February 14, 1942, "Editorial Policy" statement asserted, it sought democracy in the United States as the country was presumably fighting for democracy in Europe and Asia: "We firmly believe that this is the people's hour to make democracy real and thereby make it world triumphant. If this is not done, we may lose the war" (21). This "scene of civil liberties, racial equality and human justices" was identified with the very social and economic issues that inform *The Street*, especially housing, education, and jobs. The first issue of *People's Voice* exemplifies how it explicitly linked the struggle against Jim Crow racism with the Allied fight against fascism. The wide range of local and national news stories included several stories about discrimination against African Americans in the military and defense industries. It also included accounts of discriminatory wartime military policy in the United States, such as a story on the New York City Board of Education's policy of requiring teachers to identify their students' race and religion for air raid evacuation plans. The most blatant example of Jim Crow military policy served as the "Most Important Question of the Week" in a section of the paper titled "The People's Town Hall": "You know of the recent decision of the Red Cross to accept blood from Negro donors. This blood is to be processed and used only for Negro soldiers. Do you think this is in keeping with democracy?" Columns by Mary McLeod Bethune, "Along the Battlefronts," and Powell, in his weekly "Soapbox," likewise correlated the struggle for racial justice in the United States with the fight against fascism, as did a brief poem by Andy Razaf, "The Negro Speaks," which begins, "Democracy is threatened from within / By fools who make a fetish of their skin."

People's Voice also offered extensive coverage of popular entertainment, from sports to theater, music, and radio. Its coverage of jazz in particular focused on the economic challenges faced by musicians as much as their accomplishments. For example, the first issue featured a number of announcements and reviews of jazz performances as well as a column by Nell Dodson on Harlem nightlife, "The Owl Patrol," which is similar in its ironically gossipy tone to Petry's "The Lighter Side." The "Radio" section featured reviews of records and radio shows, but it also included articles about the struggles for African American performing artists to make a living in the Jim Crow world of popular entertainment, in New York City and in the United States more generally. For example, Dodson wrote an article about the difficulty that African American bands had in finding jobs in white hotels and clubs. She underscored the social and personal costs for African American musicians who were struggling to find steady work: "In the past year dissatisfaction among Negro musicians has been on the increase. They're tired of constant road work; unstable home life with its double expense, lack of air time; they're tired of taking the knocks of the band profession without getting any of the boosts." Joe Bostic's "Radiograph" column was equally direct in its documentation and criticism of discriminatory policies in the entertainment industry. Explaining how African American entertainers were excluded in radio popularity polls, because "the 'money' programs are produced by the advertising agencies rather than radio station production departments," he recommends nothing less than a consumer boycott against companies that "prosecute such an effective boycott against Negro performers."[11]

The incident related to jazz that received the most coverage in *People's Voice* was the New York City police department's decision to close the legendary Savoy Ballroom in 1943, presumably because white servicemen had contracted sexually transmitted diseases from prostitutes who were allegedly working there. The outrage expressed on the pages of *People's Voice* is hardly surprising, given that the newspaper's publisher, Charles Buchanan, was also the manager of the Savoy. But the city's decision to shut down the ballroom generated widespread anger in Harlem and in the jazz world more generally. The Savoy was world famous in the 1930s and '40s as the largest interracial site for jazz, especially for jazz dancing, in New York City. It was an important cultural center for residents of Harlem, particularly for young people, and it attracted a substantial number of white patrons from New York and visitors to New York who came to listen to the hottest swing bands and watch the renowned Lindy Hoppers dance. While the Savoy was a source of local pride for African Americans who lived in Harlem, it also evoked the democratic ideals associated with swing. According to the Harlem *Amsterdam News* in 1939, "Perhaps no other spot in this great country is so symbolic of the American ideal. The Savoy is truly a melting pot—a cross section of American life. There, every night in the week, every race and nationality under the sun, the high and the low, meet and color lines melt away under the influence of the rhythms of America's foremost sepia swing bands" (qtd. in Erenberg 155). When the city decided to close the Savoy a few years later, there was outrage and suspicion in Harlem about the city's motives. The front-page headline in the 1943 May Day *People's Voice* expressed this suspicion directly: "WHAT'S BEHIND SAVOY CLOSING: Is It Police Move to Bar Whites from Harlem?" According to *People's Voice*, the motive for the city's decision was clear: the closing of the most prominent interracial jazz venue in Harlem would force jazz enthusiasts to patronize Lower Manhattan clubs instead. Not only was this an economic attack on Harlem, but it also was a racist attack on the democratic principle of interracial social relations. "THE CLOSING OF THE SAVOY is one of the most serious setbacks that race relations have received in the City of New York," wrote Powell, and the repercussions of the city's decision were severe: "This is the first step toward segregation. Unless this movement is nipped in the bud NOW it is just a question of time before there will be complete jim-crow in the City of New York. . . . While Negroes are losing their lives abroad, Hitler has scored a jim-crow victory in New York" (Editorial).

Powell's response to the closing of the Savoy may seem overstated, and he certainly was not reluctant to employ hyperbole in his editorial statements, but it was not extreme. Two weeks later, Petry offered her opinion in "An Open Letter to Mayor LaGuardia." Her appeal to the mayor succinctly represents the skepticism and outrage among Harlemites about the city's decision, arguing for the Savoy's importance as a community center as well as a place for entertainment. She explicitly links the Savoy with civic organizations that supported the nation's war effort and concludes: "You see you're depriving Harlemites of a lot of pleasure, and you're depriving Negro organizations of money. That's why I wrote this letter." In linking "pleasure" with "money," entertainment with economics, Petry's letter anticipates the dramatic tensions that would inform *The Street*, which features a dance hall that resembles the Savoy. But her letter also evokes the widespread anger in Harlem about the closing of the Savoy, not only because it symbolized African American creativity and community pride but also because it was the most famous in-

terracial social venue in the city. The Savoy was a democratic symbol for the
left particularly, as a poem by Andy Razaf in the same issue of *People's Voice*
as Petry's letter expresses. If the Savoy was guilty, he writes, it was "Guilty of
syncopation / Of joy and animation." It was guilty, that is, of the democratic
ethos and racial harmony of its dance floor. But it was really guilty, Razaf
concludes, "of its location," Harlem. Several months later, Harlem would be in
flames. And while the 1943 "Harlem Riot" was provoked by a police officer's
shooting of a black serviceman, the closing of the Savoy was an important
catalyst for the anger expressed by young people on the streets of Harlem.[12]

The primary events of *The Street* take place a year after the riot, in Novem-
ber 1944, in the midst of a presidential reelection campaign that seems so
inconsequential that it is not even mentioned. If President Roosevelt earned
the support of African Americans partly for his leadership in improving
urban housing and labor conditions, this is not evident in *The Street*. And
if his support by the Popular Front was also related to the escalating fight
against fascism, "domestic" as well as "foreign," this likewise seems far removed from the everyday battles of the Harlem "street."[13] No one expresses
skepticism about the premises of the "Double V" campaign more succinctly
than the jazz musician Boots Smith in *The Street*, following the scene when
he first hears Lutie sing in the Junto Bar and Grill. Shortly after he asks Lutie
to audition for his band, she asks him why he's not in the army. He laughs
out loud—for a long time—and says: "'Who—me? . . . You don't think I'd get
mixed up in that mess." When she then asks him why he was not drafted, he
responds: "'Something wrong with one ear' . . . and his voice was so unpleas-
ant that she said nothing more about it" (165). This conversation, one of the
few times the war is brought up in the novel, suggests so much about Boots's
assertive but fragile masculinity as a black jazz musician. It occurs after a
harrowing car ride from the Harlem nightclub where Lutie meets Boots to
"the cold, white night" (157) north of the city. Lutie is cautious, and scared,
when Boots answers affirmatively to her question, "'Do you mean that you
think I could earn my living singing?'" When he buys her a beer and asks
her to audition at the Casino, she looks at him and sees that "his eyes on her
face were so knowing, so hard, that she thought instantly of the robins she
had seen on the Chandlers' lawn in Lyme, and the cat, lean, stretched out
full length, drawing itself along on its belly, intent on its prey" (150). But she
also sees the possibility of escape from her dark, dreary apartment on 116th
Street, and she agrees to take a ride with Boots. The naturalistic figure of the
predator and his prey soon gives way to the more exhilarating, but for Lutie
no less frightening, figure of the black man in flight. Traveling north, Lutie
observes that "Boots Smith's relationship to this swiftly moving car was no

ordinary one. He wasn't just a black man driving a car at a pell-mell pace. . . .
The act of driving the car made him feel he was a powerful being who could
conquer the world. . . . It was like playing god and commanding everything
within hearing to awaken and listen to him" (157). This expression of power,
which Lutie conveys in aural terms, is more than an act of self-assertion: it
is the black man's defiance of a racist "world that took pains to make them
feel they didn't belong, that they were inferior" (158). Not surprisingly, this
act of defiance concludes with an encounter with a white policeman on the
return trip to Manhattan. Remarkably, though, Boots handles this threatening encounter smoothly with his explanation that his "'band's playin' at the
Casino tonight'" (165) and a cash payment to the policeman. Following this
resolution is a homosocial exchange between "the cop" and Boots when the
policeman looks at Lutie and says, "'Don't know that I blame you for being
late, Mack'" (166). Lutie, who had resisted Boots's sexual advances in the car
only moments before, "couldn't see the denomination" of the bill, but she
understood the "difference" that money made, "even with cops . . . even if
you're colored." Money could even "keep Boots out of the army, because she
didn't believe that business about there being something wrong with one of
his ears. He had acted too strangely when he said it" (166).

The story of Boots's evasion of the draft is indeed "strange," even though
his rationale for not participating in the war is principled. The chapter that
represents Boots's consciousness reveals his dependence on his employer,
Junto, as much as his angry opposition to fighting for the United States in the
war. What's strangest, though, is the method Junto recommends for disquali-
fying Boots from military eligibility. When Boots receives his notice to report
to the draft board for his physical examination, he says to Junto, "'Fix this
thing'" (258). Junto then asks him why he does not want to fight, and Boots
expresses his disdain for the U.S. military clearly and directly: "'Because, no
matter how scared they are of Germans, they're still more scared of me. I'm
black, see? And they hate Germans, but they hate me worse. If that wasn't
so, they wouldn't have a separate army for black men'" (258–59). After Boots
persuades Junto with a litany of Jim Crow humiliations he had experienced,
especially as a Pullman porter and as a struggling young musician, Junto
agrees to help him. He "sent him to a doctor who performed a slight, delicate,
dangerous operation on his ear" (259). Given that he owes his living as a
pianist to Junto, Boots has little choice, even though he is momentarily wor-
ried. No more is said about this operation, however. To propose a "dangerous
operation on his ear" suggests not only Junto's power over his employee but
also the precariousness of Boots's professional existence as a jazz musician.
But neither Boots nor the novel dwells on the implications of this operation,

as Junto tells Boots moments later: "'That girl—Lutie Johnson. . . . You're to keep your hands off her. I've got other plans for her'" (262). Not only does Junto make it clear that he controls Boots professionally, but he also presumes similar control over his "girl." There is nothing "slight" or "delicate" about Junto's demands, although *this* "operation" proves to be more "dangerous" than either Junto or Boots expected.

Lutie's initial encounter with Boots is determined, if not overdetermined, by her desire to escape "the street." The more that she can imagine herself as a professional jazz singer, the more she can imagine leaving her apartment on 116th Street for a new home, a home "where there were trees and the streets were clean and the rooms would be full of sunlight" (151). Coinciding with this pastoral image, though, is the predatory image of the cat approaching its prey. Her experience of the drive north from Manhattan is fearful, at first because of the speed and ferocity of Boots's driving, but even more when he stops and holds her "so tightly and his mouth was so insistent, so brutal" (161). Her fear is figured in the very landscape through which they speed: "'I don't like mountains,' Lutie said. . . . 'I get the feeling they're closing in on me'" (159–60). This image evokes the "racial mountain" of Langston Hughes's famous manifesto, but with a gendered difference: it is the black man, Boots, who is here identified with the mountain "closing in" on her. He responds to her fear by saying, "'Probably why you sing so well. . . . You feel things stronger than other folks.'" His interpretation of her singing ability identifies her with sentimentality, although his praise of her "singing" is of course inseparable from his desire for her. When Boots asks her what songs she knows, the sequence of titles she names ironically evokes her predicament in this scene: "All the usual ones. Night and Day. Darlin'. Hurry Up, Sammy, and Let's Go Home.'" Boots's response to these titles of sentimental songs is abrupt: "'You'll have to learn some new ones'—he steered the car to the side of the road and parked it where there was an unobstructed view if the river" (160). Thus, there is a dramatic tension between the sentimental and the naturalistic, between the romantic song titles and Lutie's fear of Boots's sexual aggression. This tension is further complicated by Lutie's thoughts as she gazes at the river: "That was what had been wrong with her these last few weeks—she hadn't known where she was going. As a matter of fact, she had probably never known. But if she could sing—work hard at it, study, really get somewhere, it would give direction to her life—she would know where she was going" (160). The problem, of course, is that at this moment she is not driving the car, and she has no control over where she is going. As she does repeatedly, Lutie resorts to the individualist work ethic as her model for "getting somewhere." As optimistic as this momentary reverie is, it is escapist if not dangerously delusional. At this moment, Lutie underestimates the persistence of Boots and the power of Junto to enforce their ideas of what it means to "sing."

"Night and Day. Darlin'. Hurry Up, Sammy, and Let's Go Home": as disconnected as these titles seem—from each other and from the dramatic moment in which they are uttered—this sequence can also be read as a narrative montage of Lutie's anxieties while she is riding with Boots, even if the titles ironically allude to expressions of romantic desire. The sequence of titles signifies even more about Lutie's characterization: what is representative of her self-image as a singer and what is psychologically distinctive about her. As the song that attracted Boots's attention in the first place, "Darlin'" is especially notable, even though it is "typical of the countless sentimental torch songs popular in wartime America" in that it expresses an intense longing for an absent lover (Grandt 33).[14] Less typical but no less popular than "Darlin'" is the first song that Lutie names, "Night and Day," which Cole Porter wrote for the 1932 comic musical *Gay Divorce*. *Gay Divorce* became better known as *The Gay Divorcee* in the 1934 film version, which starred Fred Astaire and Ginger Rogers. The original title was changed for the film in accordance with the Hays Code, to avoid the impression that divorce could be considered "gay." The idea of either "gay divorce" or a "gay divorcee" is irrelevant for Lutie, not because the concept of "gay divorce" is incongruous, but because she simply cannot afford to divorce her husband, from whom she had separated. And the lyrics of "Night and Day" are likewise ironically suggestive. A song of almost obsessive passion, "Night and Day" begins with an extensive repetition of the opening note through the words, "Like the beat, beat, beat, of the tom-tom when the jungle shadows fall, / Like the tick, tick, tock of the stately clock as it stands against the wall," before it finally arrives with the release of the melody: "Night and day, you are the one, only you beneath the moon and under the sun" (C. Porter 108).[15] Lutie is indeed the object of Boots's relentless desire, but this desire is oppressive. At the same time, the opening image of this song evokes stereotypes of jazz as at once primitively African and modernly mechanical. As unusual a composition as "Night and Day" is, it became Porter's best-selling song. And it was recorded by numerous musicians, including two of the most influential female jazz musicians of the time: Mary Lou Williams, who recorded the song in 1944, and Billie Holiday, who recorded it in 1939, shortly after she recorded her most famous song of social protest, "Strange Fruit" (Schuller 544).

While Boots's disdain for the American pretense of democracy is clear, Lutie's characterization is more contradictory. Throughout the novel there is a dramatic tension between her understanding of herself as an African

American woman and her belief in self-reliance as the primary means for upward mobility. This tension is personified through the figures of her grandmother, who raised her after her mother's death when Lutie was seven, and Benjamin Franklin, whose autobiography inspired her when she was growing up.[16] At moments of crisis, Lutie recalls the ancestral figure of Granny, who represents oral folk knowledge, but she relies more often on what she sees as the more practical written advice of Franklin. When Lutie first recalls Granny in chapter 1, she dismisses her folk wisdom as a "whole lot of nonsense. . . . All those tales about things that people sensed before they actually happened. Tales that had been handed down and down and down until, if you tried to trace them back, you'd end up God knows where—probably Africa" (15–16). Lutie rejects "Africa" for the presumably more practical self-reliance she identifies with Franklin: if you try hard enough, work hard enough, and live frugally enough, you too can prosper, she tells herself, regardless of the Depression, regardless of her plight as a single black mother who is the sole provider for her child, regardless of her knowledge of the socioeconomic conditions that make her situation more typical than exceptional.[17] If Franklin inspires Lutie with a "feeling of self-confidence" that she too could "live on a little bit of money and could prosper" (64), the memory of Granny recurs when she feels most threatened, from the opening scene with the Super to the scene after her separation from her son, Bub. She acknowledges that Granny's presence had saved her from the insecurity and danger that Bub experienced: "Granny had always been there, her rocking chair part of the shadow, part of the darkness, making it known and familiar. She was always humming. It was a faint sound, part and parcel of the darkness. Going to sleep with that warm sound clinging to your ears made fear impossible" (404). Granny is invoked as a singer, as a protective figure, whose sustaining voice is contrasted with the noise of the radio in her apartment. As for Franklin, it is no coincidence that the owner of the clubs where Lutie sings is named "Junto," the name of Franklin's influential business, civic, and social "club of mutual improvement."[18]

Lutie sees jazz as a means for her "improvement," as it was for many musicians from working-class families. The two chapters that represent Lutie's brief "experience" as a jazz singer, though, reveal how this belief in upward mobility is so sadly misguided. Her performances at the Casino, the large dance hall that resembles the Savoy, reveal both the importance of jazz as a medium of democratic, interracial social interaction and the exploitative racial economics of the music industry. On the one hand, these chapters celebrate the collective joy and release from everyday pressures experienced by the dancers at the Casino. Remarkably, for a novel so concerned with race and racism, the Casino dance floor is vividly represented without any obvious signifiers of racial differentiation. As Lutie sings, the "dance floor spilled over with people—young girls, soldiers, sailors, middle-aged men and women" (223). These dancers are described by their appearance, but only the appearance of their clothing and movement:

> The soft rainbow-colored lights played over the dancers. There were women in evening gowns, girls in short tight skirts and sweaters that clung slickly to their young breasts. Boys in pants cut tight and close at the ankle went through violent dance routines with the young girls. Some of the dancing couples jitter-bugged, did the rhumba, invented intricate new steps of their own. The ever-moving, ever-changing lights picked faces and figures out of the crowd; added a sense of excitement and strangely the quality of laughter to the dancers. People in the boxes drank out of little paper cups, ate fried chicken and cake and thick ham sandwiches. (223)

This "rainbow-colored" scene of exhilarating pleasure, of sexual allure and creative improvisation, of a "sense of excitement" and a "quality of laughter" is quite different from the most familiar scenes of dance hall tension in New Negro Renaissance fiction. The dance floor is a democratic site of pleasure, of momentary release from the everyday tensions of whatever "street," whatever neighborhood, whatever city, state, or country the dancers come from. The tension that does exist at the Casino exists outside the dance floor, among the workers who depend on tips for their living. And it exists on stage among the musicians, who depend on one another but especially on the Casino's owner to make their living. And the economic tensions between the black musicians and their employer are inherently racialized, even though, according to Boots, Junto "treated the white men who worked for him exactly the way he treated the black ones" (263).

The tension between the black musicians and Lutie is more pronounced. "'Boys, meet Lutie Johnson,'" Boots says when she first rehearses with them at the Casino. "'She's singin' with us tonight'" (221). It's immediately evident to Lutie, though, that "the boys" in the orchestra assume she's there because she's "singing" with Boots—after hours:

> She avoided the eyes of the men in the orchestra because what they were think-ing was plain on their faces. The fat pianist grinned. One of the trumpet players winked at the drummer. The others nudged each other and nodded knowingly. One of the saxophonists was raising his instrument in mock salute to Boots. It was quite obvious that they were saying to themselves and to each other, Yeah, Boots has got himself a new chick and this singing business is the old come-on. (221)

She is suspect because she is a woman, and the phallic power of their gaze is suggested when she begins to sing "Darlin'": "As she held the mike, she felt as though her voice was draining away down through the slender metal rod, and the idea frightened her" (221).[19] While she proves her merit as a singer and earns their respect, and while the act of singing transports her far from "the street," the business of singing is indeed inseparable from "the business of being nice" to Boots. And whatever dreams Lutie has about a singing career are soon shot down by the more menacing figure of Junto. There's no contract, no salary, no compensation whatsoever, just "experience," Boots tells her later, until she agrees to "be nice" to the man who owns the Casino.

Lutie's initial reaction to this news is to blame herself, even as she "could feel a hard, tight knot of anger and hate forming within her." She seeks "some philosophy with which to rebuild her shattered hopes. The world hadn't collapsed about her. She hadn't been buried under brick and rubble, falling plaster and caved-in sidewalks. Yet that was how she had felt listening to Boots" (307). While this metaphor for her psychological state evokes the bombed-out cities of wartime Europe as much as the crumbling streets and tenements of Harlem, it repeats Lutie's earlier reflections on the suffocating effects of "the street." But she refuses to accept the naturalist logic of environmental determinism and instead acknowledges her own delusional dreams of success: "The trouble was with her. She had built up a fantastic structure made from the soft, nebulous, cloudy stuff of dreams. There hadn't been a solid, practical brick in it, not even a foundation. . . . It had never existed anywhere but in her own mind" (307–308). So what does Lutie do? She renews her commitment to "hard work and self-sacrifice," even as she partially recognizes the symbolic power of Junto, the "implacable figure of a white man blocking the way, so that it is impossible to escape" (315). Indeed, she does not give up her dream of a singing career, as she answers a "Negro newspaper" advertisement for a singing job through the "Crosse School for Singers" (318). But she is double-crossed: not only does the white man tell her she has to pay for "training" before she can be hired; he also suggests that "if you and me can get together a coupla nights a week in Harlem, those lessons won't cost you a cent" (321).

This is the end of Lutie's career as a jazz singer, but it is not the end of Lutie's story, nor is it the end of jazz in *The Street*. While scenes of jazz performance are few in *The Street*, the recorded sound of jazz also figures prominently in the novel's plot, from the radio in Lutie's apartment, where she learns to sing popular songs, to the jukebox at the Junto Bar and Grill, where she is first heard singing. Jazz is especially present in the soundscape of Lutie's building, constantly blaring from radios in other apartments as well as her own.

Most notably, when she returns home from the Casino, dejected about her short-lived "experience" as a singer, she returns to an oppressive cacophony of radio sounds: "'Buy Shirley Soap and Keep Beautiful' was blared out by an announcer's voice. The sounds were confusing. Someone had tuned in the station that played swing records all night, and she heard, 'Now we have the master of trumpet in Rock, Raleigh, Rock'" (312). This "medley of sound" only becomes more "confusing" as she ascends and hears "the sounds of a revival church which was broadcasting a service designed to redeem lost souls" (312), which mingles "with the high sweetness of the trumpet playing 'Rock, Raleigh, Rock' and the soap program joined in with the plunking of a steel guitar, 'If you want to be beautiful use Shirley Soap'" (313). While this confusion of sounds, this blurring of commerce, entertainment, and religion, can be read as an auditory objective correlative for Lutie's consciousness, it also reminds us of the importance of recorded sound throughout *The Street*. The radio in Lutie's apartment, for example, functions dramatically in a number of contradictory ways. It relieves Lutie's loneliness at times, and it intensifies her loneliness at others. She relies on the radio for companionship when she is alone, to obliterate the silence of her apartment, but she also hears "the silence under the sound of the radio," especially when she recollects her childhood with Granny (81). The radio is a stimulant for social interaction, specifically when the dance music she hears provokes her initial decision to visit the Junto (78). But the radio is also a poor substitute for social interaction: the Junto is appealing precisely because it offers an escape from the empty routine of "listening to radios or trying to read an evening paper" (145). One thing the radio is not in *The Street* is a source of meaningful information: the Junto is the place to "pick up the all the daily news," whether local or national, while the radio is more often white noise.[20]

Lutie's everyday experience of music is comparable to what Ralph Ellison describes in his essay "Living with Music," published a few years after *The Street*. This essay reflects on the difficulty of writing amid "the noise" surrounding Ellison's "tiny ground-floor-rear-apartment" (228). Like Lutie, Ellison is subjected to the "chaotic sounds" (233) of the street and the apartments surrounding him, including the noise of a restaurant jukebox next door and the louder noise "of a night-employed swing enthusiast who took his lullaby music so loud that every morning promptly at nine Basie's brasses started blasting my typewriter off its stand" (228). Unlike Lutie, however, Ellison figures out a solution to counter this noise: he invests in new audio equipment to play music loud enough that he can't hear anything else. As Alexander Weheliye has written, Ellison's essay dramatizes the "fluid sonic boundaries in the city," which complicate distinctions between public and

private space (123).²¹ Lutie, of course, cannot afford a sound system like Ellison's, but she does play the radio to control her domestic space, to counter
silence as well as noise. By the end of *The Street*, however, it also seems like
the radio plays Lutie. After her aspirations for a singing career have been
defeated, she returns home to find out that her son, Bub, has been appre-
hended by the "post-office investigators" and taken to the Children's Shelter.
She begins to cry:

> All through the house radios went on full blast in order to drown out this
> familiar, frightening, unbearable sound. But even under the radios they could
> hear it, for they had started crying with her when the sound first assailed their
> ears. And now it had become a perpetual weeping that flowed through them,
> carrying pain and a shrinking from pain, so that the music and the voices
> coming from the radios couldn't possibly shut it out, for it was inside them.
> The thin walls shivered and trembled with the music. Upstairs, downstairs,
> all through the house, there was music, any kind of music, tuned up full and
> loud—jazz, blues, swing, symphony, surged though the house. (390–91)

What begins as a series of individual defensive measures to drown out the
noise of Lutie's sobbing becomes a collective commiseration with her pain.
While each person turns on the radio to escape the sound of Lutie's desperate
sadness, the chaotic noise of the radio—"jazz, blues, swing, symphony"—instead intensifies the sound of her sorrow.

When Lutie subsequently calls Boots for a loan to pay a predatory lawyer
to defend her son, another metaphor of recorded sound comes into play: "He
didn't understand what she was saying and she had to begin all over again, going
slowly, so slowly that she thought she sounded like a record that had got stuck
on a victrola" (397). This metaphor is then repeated in the next paragraph: "And
thought again that she sounded like a victrola, but one that had got stuck, like
one that had run down, that needed winding" (397). As familiar as the metaphor
of a "broken record" would become, its repetition is especially appropriate at
this point in the novel. Because she is desperate, Lutie returns to Boots and,
as she later finds out, Junto in order to escape her sense of entrapment, only
to become entrapped in the same exploitative male plot she had found herself
in before. The metaphor of the broken record thus recalls the doubleness of
"Do you sing for a living?" And it functions psychologically for Lutie as what
Freud would characterize as a repetition compulsion, as a restaging of the past,
a return to a past conflict that she cannot escape. Indeed, in the conclusion of
the novel, she becomes quite literally "stuck" between Boots and Juno, without
any viable means of escape.

The repetition of the metaphor of the broken record is actually a repetition
with a difference, however. Initially, "she sounded like a record that had got

stuck on a victrola," while subsequently, "she sounded like a victrola, but one that had got stuck." This distinction between a broken record and a broken Victrola, between Lutie's contrasting identification with the record being played and with the Victrola playing the record, suggests uncertainty not only about her voice but also about her agency, her degree of control over her predicament. This reminds us of Lutie's persistent but tragic belief in self-reliance, her belief that she is ultimately responsible for all that has gone wrong in her life, despite the overwhelming evidence otherwise, evidence that she often recognizes but refuses to accept. Because she adamantly believes about her child that "it was her fault he'd got into this trouble" (407), it is a revelation to her that that her predicament is not unlike that of the other women at the Children's Shelter:

> Lutie sat down near the back of the room. It was filled with colored women, sitting in huddled-over positions. They sat quietly, not moving. Their patient silence filled the room, made her uneasy. Why were all of them colored? Was it because the mothers of white children had safe places for them to play in, because the mothers of white children didn't have to work? (408–409)

Lutie here recognizes the shared predicament of "colored" women, although even here she distances herself from "them." She is separate from these women as she has been throughout the novel, partly because she believes in her individual ability to escape such a predicament, and partly because she is always working so hard that she has little time to spend with other women. Remarkably, though, she soon realizes that she is mistaken in her judgment of these women: "She had been wrong. There were some white mothers, too . . . sitting in the same shrinking, huddled positions" (409). And at this moment she identifies herself with the other women in the Children's Shelter waiting room: "Perhaps, she thought, we're all here because we're all poor. Maybe it doesn't have anything to do with color" (409). This revelation is tentative, but it suggests a class consciousness, and specifically an identification with working-class women, that Lutie has been reluctant to accept throughout the novel. But at this moment, when she "felt as though she were bearing the uneasy burden of the sum total of all the troubles these women had brought with them" (409), it is too late. Alone and disconsolate, Lutie has already decided that her only hope for saving her son is to depend on the black man who had already deceived her, the black man who is himself dependent on the white owner of "the street."

If the "broken record" aptly characterizes the repetition of events, the return engagement with Boots and Junto, it also describes the formal repetition in the novel's concluding chapters. Repetition of specific sentences and phrases occurs throughout *The Street*. Such repetition dramatizes both Lutie's sense of confinement and her obsessive consciousness, but it also functions formally like jazz riffs, as narrative fragments that are comparable to the theme statements of popular swing compositions. The theme statements of *The Street*, which mostly concern the destructive effects of the street itself, are answered by repeated phrases about more specific features of Lutie's life. For example, when Lutie finds out that Bub has been arrested, "her thoughts were like a chorus chanting in her head," a chorus of familiar statements that begins: "The men stood around and the women worked. The men left the women and the women went on working and the kids were left alone. The kids burned lights all night because they were left alone in small, dark rooms and they were afraid. Alone. Always alone" (388). This recitation tells us nothing we do not know already, but the cumulative effect of this repetition is powerful, powerful because Lutie sees no escape from her predicament, but powerful also because the formal repetition objectifies such obsessive thoughts into a musical form that has collective implications beyond Lutie's feeling of aloneness. This formal repetition evokes both the specific compositional patterns associated with swing and the more general African diasporic musical principle of rhythmic circulation and equilibrium.[22]

Lutie's process of recognizing how Boots and Junto intend to "play" her in the concluding chapter likewise seems like a broken record. It begins with the familiar refrain of Mrs. Hedges as Lutie leaves for Boots's apartment: "'A friend of mine, a Mr. Junto—a very nice white gentleman, dearie—'" (417). The sound of "nice" resonates in Lutie's mind—"A nice white gentleman . . . a nice warm colored girl . . . All of it nice, nice gentleman, nice girl" (417)—until she is in the presence of Junto and Boots, who tells her to "'be nice to him . . . Just be nice to him . . . And bein' nice to Junto pays off better than anything else I know'" (421). And the voice of Boots reminds her of the Casino, of her scene of disappointment, her scene of humiliation, to what has become her scene of trauma, "straining to hear a thin thread of music that kept getting lost in the babble of voices, in the clink of glasses, in the bursts of laughter, in the bursts of laughter, so that she wasn't certain the music was real" (421). And, amazingly, she recalls the exact statements that Boots uttered to explain that her singing was "just experience," repeated verbatim from the earlier chapter. Her confirmation of what she had suspected but also had repressed, Junto's plot to "sleep with her," is too much for her to bear. She continues to hear "that floating drifting tune":

> It was inside her head and she couldn't get it out. Boots was staring at her, waiting for her answer. He and Junto thought they knew what she would say. If she hummed that fragment of melody aloud, she would get rid of it. It was

the only way to make it disappear; otherwise it would keep going round and round in her head. And she thought, I must be losing my mind, wanting to hum a tune and at the same time thinking about killing that man who is sitting, waiting, outside. (422)

Haunted by the "fragment of melody" but unable to sing it, Lutie's consciousness is figured as a broken record: the tune keeps "going round and round in her head." Her mind is stuck in this past moment of trauma as she is stuck in this present scene of entrapment. As absurd as it does seem, to hum the tune would be at once an act of claiming it and releasing it, an act that correlates with her desire to claim her son and release him from detention. To hum the tune would also make it hers, would give her agency, would counter the masculine authority of Boots and Junto, who "thought they knew what she had to say." But instead of singing, she becomes enraged, so enraged that she kills Boots, not Junto, so filled with "the hate, the frustration, the resentment she had toward the pattern her life had followed" (428) that she finds herself alone, separated from her son, with a one-way ticket to Chicago.

The "floating drifting tune" that Lutie recalls is the most notable moment of jazz improvisation in *The Street*. It takes place during intermission at the Casino, immediately preceding Lutie's conversation with Boots about her salary. A pianist and a trumpeter are "experimenting with a tune that had been playing in [the trumpeter's] head for days" (302). The trumpeter asks the pianist if he had ever heard the tune before and says, "'Sometimes tunes play tricks in your head and turn out to be somep'n you heard a long while ago and all the time you think it's one you made up'" (303). The "faint melody" of this song, a "slight, ghostly sound running through the room" (303), is so haunting because it occurs during the unregulated period of intermission, a moment of creative freedom from the pressures of big band "show business." As for Lutie, this happens to be the final moment of musical joy and hope before her fall to the exploitative reality of her position. While the musicians are "experimenting," she is sitting at a table with Boots and asking him, "'When will my salary start? And how much will it be?'" (303). As a moment of unfettered improvisation, this scene suggests the after-hours jam sessions that were creating the new sound of bebop. The fact that Lutie is outside this scene, as a woman who is expected to "sing" for months before she can "earn her living by singing" (304), reminds us of the exploitative economics of jazz. The contrast between the art of jazz and the business of jazz could not be starker.

The trumpeter's comment about jazz composition also speaks to Lutie's consciousness and to the structure of *The Street*. His comment especially describes Lutie's consciousness at the end of the novel, when she recalls but cannot sing this tune, and when she becomes so bitterly aware of the patterns of repetition that define her life. His comment also speaks more generally to her fatalistic confusion of what is with what has to be, a confusion that is only intensified by her determined belief in self-reliance. This is an ideological confusion that isolates her, that separates her not only from the ancestral "African" wisdom of her grandmother but also from a transformative collective identification with the women she joins at the Children's Shelter. The structure of *The Street* also "plays tricks in your head" with its repetition of sentences and phrases, its variations on the theme of "the street" and its many subplots. The effect of such tricks is not just a narrative approximation of jazz form, as brilliantly inventive as this is; it is also a process of disrupting narrative expectations of naturalism and accentuating the contradictions of an individualist ideology that is isolating, if not fatal. It's no wonder that Lutie recalls this scene of improvisation when she feels most imprisoned, because improvisation suggests the possibility of both creative expression within the tradition of jazz music as well as creative action. The fact that she tries to remember the song exactly but cannot suggests the limitations of her jazz "experience" and her internalized exclusion from this masculine world. However, the conclusion of *The Street* also suggests patterns of historical and intertextual repetition that relate Lutie's predicament to African American cultural and literary history more generally. As fatalistic as the conclusion seems, the design of circles that Lutie draws on the train window suggests patterns of improvisatory expression that defy the seemingly deterministic linear progression of her narrative. The figure of the circle itself suggests the power of literacy and the power of music as modes of African American resistance, a power expressed most famously by Frederick Douglass in his 1845 *Narrative*: "I did not, when a slave, understand the deep meaning of those rude and apparently incoherent songs. I was myself within the circle; so that I neither saw nor heard as those without must see" (qtd. in Grandt 119, note 6).[23] The novel, then, defies the dismissive words of Lutie's "grammar school" teacher—"I don't know why they have us bother to teach your people to write" (435)—even as Lutie herself reiterates her teacher's judgment.

The fact that Lutie envisions Chicago as her refuge from the law does not simply relegate her to the harshly naturalistic streets of *Native Son*, even as the concluding snowstorm of *The Street* recalls the frigid streets of Wright's novel.[24] Lutie's departure for Chicago also recalls earlier New Negro Renaissance novels such as Claude McKay's *Home to Harlem*, Nella Larsen's *Quicksand*, and especially Langston Hughes's *Not without Laughter*, all of which feature scenes of jazz and, in Hughes's novel, a female protagonist who overcomes adversity to become a successful jazz and blues singer. Post–World War I Chicago is both a migrant refuge and an alternative "black metropolis" to Harlem that resonates with jazz improvisation and the possibility for social transformation. But these novels also all represent the disruptive psychological and social effects of World War I on African Americans, and one of the few conversations about World War II in *The Street* compares its effects to the earlier experience of World War I. On the street outside Lutie's building, an African American veteran of World War I says to his friend, "'I been in a war. I know what I'm talking about. There'll be trouble when them colored boys come back. They ain't going to put up with all this stuff'—he waved toward the street" (338). Whether *The Street* suggests the inevitability of such change or agrees with the veteran's skeptical friend that it has "been like this all these years, ain't nothing a bunch of hungry soldiers can do about it'" (339) is debatable, but the sense of needed change, as well as the sense of historical repetition, is undeniable. In signifying on previous narrative journeys to Chicago, Lutie's departure suggests tunes that "play tricks in your head and turn out to be somep'n you heard a long while ago.'" If *The Street* similarly recalls narratives from a previous war and a previous generation of African American dreams deferred, its improvisation on such narratives underscores the urgency for recognizing and transforming the patterns of repetition that Lutie alone cannot overcome.

4 "Cultural Exchange"

Cold War Jazz and the Political Aesthetics of Langston Hughes's Long Poems

What—wonders the African—is really happening in the shadow of world events, past and present—and of world problems, old and new—to an America that seems to understand so little about its black citizens? Even so little about itself. Even so little.
—Langston Hughes, liner notes to *Ask Your Mama: 12 Moods for Jazz*

Langston Hughes is better known than any other African American poet for his inventive adaptations of African American vernacular forms, especially musical forms, from his blues poetry of the 1920s to his ambitious postwar jazz sequences, *Montage of a Dream Deferred* and *Ask Your Mama: 12 Moods for Jazz*. Hughes's poetry is distinctively African American in its language and social locations, but it is also modern in its engagement with "world events, past and present." Like Ann Petry, Hughes situates the African American "dream deferred" in 1940s Harlem in his best-known long poem, *Montage of a Dream Deferred* (1951). And as in *The Street*, the scenes of jazz performance in *Montage* enact a dramatic tension between utopian desire and frustration, between the "dream" and the recognition of the dream's deferral. It does so, however, more explicitly and more assertively, through the emergent 1940s jazz sound of bebop. In his introductory statement for *Montage*, Hughes suggests how bebop both intensifies and extends the vernacular forms of African American music that Hughes had adapted in his poetry since the 1920s:

> In terms of current Afro-American popular music and the sources from which it has progressed—jazz, ragtime, swing, blues, boogie-woogie, and be-bop—this poem on contemporary Harlem, like be-bop, is marked by conflicting changes, sudden nuances, sharp and impudent interjections, broken rhythms, and passages sometimes in the manner of the jam session, sometimes the popular song, punctuated by the riffs, runs, breaks, and disc-tortions of the music of a community in transition.[1]

The dramatic principle of montage, the dialogue of voices that occurs within poems as well as in longer sequences, informs Hughes's early jazz poetry as well as later book-length poems such as *Montage* and *Ask Your Mama*. The interplay of perspectives in early poems such as "The Cat and the Saxophone (2 a.m.)," "Harlem Night Club," and "Jazz Band in a Parisian Cabaret" evokes both the creative dynamic of jazz performance and the racial tension of jazz clubs, especially between musicians and their audiences. In introducing how *Montage* relates to the social world it represents, however, Hughes associates his poetry with the more aggressive sound of bebop. In the 1940s the improvisations of bebop musicians such as Charlie Parker and Dizzy Gillespie seemed to casual listeners more discordant, and thus rebellious, than the more popular swing music that is featured in *The Street*. The dramatic sequencing of poems in *Montage* evokes a Harlem "community in transition" precisely through its rendering of bebop's rapid rhythmic and harmonic changes. The sudden, sometimes disorienting shifts in voice, mood, and dramatic scene convey the anxiety and tension of a postwar urban black experience that is contemporaneous with *The Street* but that also anticipates the revolutionary movements, political and cultural, that Hughes underscores in his more challenging long poem a decade later, *Ask Your Mama*.[2]

Ask Your Mama is Hughes's most experimental blend of jazz and poetry, and recent approaches to the poem have underscored its performative qualities. New historicist readings of *Ask Your Mama* have likewise addressed the political implications of its Cold War and African diasporic contexts.[3] There has been less attention, however, to the political significance of jazz as a medium of protest and black transnationalist expression. This essay will show how the jazz form of *Ask Your Mama* enacts the challenge of developing a progressive black transnationalist public. I will look most closely at its opening section, "Cultural Exchange," where Hughes introduces the black transnationalist network of musical forms, proper names, and social locations that reverberate throughout the poem. Through its formal and specifically sonic patterns of defamiliarization, *Ask Your Mama* unsettles conceptualizations of "culture"—and cultural production—that assume hierarchical oppositions of white and black, European and African, American and African American, modernist and popular, and written and vernacular. In doing so, *Ask Your Mama* draws our attention to the contradictions of racialized aesthetic categories as it displays an encyclopedic knowledge of African diasporic expressive forms and history.

Ask Your Mama underscores the contradictory perceptions of jazz that emerged with the development of bebop during World War II. The notion that bebop was "revolutionary" had as much to do with the timing of its emergence as with its break from jazz tradition. Bebop's perception as a revolutionary movement also varied among different constituencies for jazz, from African Americans who were part of bebop's development in Harlem to young white jazz enthusiasts who identified with the rebelliousness of bebop after the war. As a movement of the early 1940s war years, bebop coincided with the African American "Double V" campaign, the dual commitment to victory over fascism overseas and Jim Crow racism in the United States. The growing sense of African American disappointment in the lack of racial progress during the war years, most memorably evoked by the 1943 Harlem Riot, informs the early African American reception of bebop.[4] Bebop's aggressive sound corresponded with the growing militancy and anger among young African Americans especially. It first developed after hours in Harlem nightclubs such as Minton's and Clarke Monroe's Uptown House as a distinctively African American form of jazz innovation. Because it did not reach a broader public until after the war, partly because of the 1942–1944 recording ban, it seemed to emerge as a fully formed "underground" movement. Because of its complexity and unfamiliarity, bebop was perceived by many as a defiant protest against popular swing music and commercialism more generally. As the idiom of primarily young African American musicians, it was also perceived as the rebellious expression of a black subculture. Unlike more popular, commercially successful forms of jazz that preceded it, bebop was thus both avant-garde, in assuming the modern artist's prerogative to disregard an audience's sensibilities, and revolutionary, in that its innovations seemed socially disruptive (DeVeaux 7–8). Such perceptions of bebop were more likely among young jazz fans, whether black or white, who were disaffected from mainstream postwar American culture. As Scott DeVeaux has emphasized in *The Birth of Bebop*, however, bebop musicians did not generally see themselves as revolutionaries; they saw themselves primarily as professionals in a music industry that offered opportunity, albeit limited, for African American social and economic advancement. However, because such opportunity was scarcer during the war years, bebop can be seen as a response to the economic restrictions of a profession that was itself structured by Jim Crow racial policies: "Bebop was a response to this impasse, an attempt to reconstitute jazz—or more precisely, the specialized idiom of the improvising virtuoso—in such a way to give its black creators the greatest professional autonomy *within* the marketplace" (27). If bebop was an "anti-assimilationist sound," as Amiri Baraka wrote in *Blues People* (181), the very signs of its rebelliousness as a black subculture, from its distinctive style and slang to the musician's refusal to play the role of entertainer, also defined bebop's appeal in the marketplace (DeVeaux 23–24).

Ask Your Mama extends the questions raised by bebop's reception to the post-bop development of jazz in the later 1950s. With the proliferation of jazz styles and subcultures, the potential for confusion and conflict intensified, especially with the arrival of the "new thing," free jazz, by the early 1960s. The occasion that inspired *Ask Your Mama* exemplifies the discordant cultural politics of jazz at this time. On July 4, 1960, Langston Hughes began composing *Ask Your Mama* in Newport, Rhode Island, in the aftermath of the Newport Jazz Festival. The festival had ended, prematurely, the day before, with a program that Hughes introduced, appropriately enough, on the history of the blues. The 1960 Newport Jazz Festival was so notorious that it was discontinued the following year. Most notably, it received international attention after a mob of mostly drunken young white men had rioted so violently that local police required the assistance of the National Guard to restore order. The weekend also became famous in the jazz world for the alternative "Newport Rebels" festival, organized by younger musicians to protest the increasingly commercialist ethos and exploitative pay scale of the Newport Jazz Festival. The Rebels festival featured performances by Charles Mingus and Max Roach, who were its primary organizers, along with Ornette Coleman, whose controversial engagement at the Five Spot Café in Manhattan that year had already generated intense debates about the future of jazz.[5]

Hughes, then, began *Ask Your Mama* during one of the most tumultuous years of jazz history, a year of intensifying debates about the economics, international politics, and aesthetics of jazz. Of course, 1960 was also one of the most tumultuous years of modern African history. It was the "year of Africa," declared the United Nations, as seventeen nations achieved their independence. But it was also the year of the Sharpeville massacre of apartheid protesters in South Africa and the civil war in the Congo, with the notorious assassination of Premier Patrice Lumumba in January 1961, which galvanized radical black activists in the United States.[6] Finally, 1960 was a tumultuous year for Hughes in that while there was increasing demand for his skills as a speaker, reader, and diplomat, he encountered renewed anticommunist threats, which left him wearier—and warier—than ever.[7] Given the urgency of "world problems, old and new," as Hughes wrote in his "liner notes" to *Ask Your Mama*, to represent the contradictions of "an America that seems to understand so little about its black citizens" was a challenge that defied existing rhetorical and formal strategies, including those that Hughes had pioneered himself. How, then, could the poem that Hughes began composing in Newport incorporate so many contradictory threads—musical and literary, personal and political, national and international—into the fabric of its design? More specifically, how could Hughes relate the history of jazz to a transnationalist consciousness of black liberation? *Ask Your Mama* is his most extensive, and most demanding, response to these questions, because it invokes traditional as well as more recent avant-garde permutations of jazz within a global geography of African diasporic movement.

Hughes's writing in the late 1950s and early 1960s was increasingly motivated by several intersecting historical developments: the rise of black liberation movements in Africa and the Caribbean; the accelerating movement for African American civil rights in the United States; and the growth of jazz as an increasingly international, and increasingly politicized, medium of expression. Hughes's role in promoting African writers became increasingly pronounced by the 1960s, when he edited two Pan-Africanist anthologies: *An African Treasury: Articles, Essays, Stories, Poems by Black Africans* (1960) and *Poems from Black Africa, Ethiopia, and Other Countries* (1963). This work coincided with his growing involvement with African diasporic cultural productions that combined music with the literary arts—from his participation in the 1959 Carnegie Hall Africa Freedom Day celebration and the 1961 American Society of African Culture festival in Lagos to his collaboration with Randy Weston on his groundbreaking recording, *Uhuru Afrika*. So it is not surprising that *Ask Your Mama* features the interaction of African cultures in the Americas and Africa, through its evocation of Afro-Caribbean as well as African American music and its movement between different sites of black revolutionary struggle. In this context, jazz plays an explicitly political role for expressing the revolutionary desire for black liberation in the United States, Africa, and the Caribbean, in contrast with U.S. Cold War propaganda that presented jazz as evidence of racial equality in the United States.

When *Ask Your Mama* was first published, readers struggled to comprehend its unfamiliar form and widely allusive content. Hughes's book-length poem was not commercially successful, and, as Arnold Rampersad has written, it did not attract scholarly attention: "No scholar, whether black or white, apparently was prepared to take the poem seriously. No one was challenged sufficiently by its allusions or references, or by its possible novelty as a fusion of jazz and literary language."[8] Given how unprecedented *Ask Your Mama* was, the challenges it posed to its early readers are understandable, but why has it taken so long to attract the sustained critical attention that it has begun to receive in the twenty-first century?[9] One explanation for the limited reception of *Ask Your Mama* is that preconceptions about Hughes's poetry have made his long poems seem anomalous. As Meta DuEwa Jones has written, Hughes's reputation as a representative black writer has been largely shaped by his "authentic" representation of African American vernacular forms of expression, not by his more technically experimental approach to jazz in his longer sequences, *Montage of a Dream Deferred* and *Ask Your Mama*. It is precisely the "abrupt tonal variation between individual poems and the use of varied vernacular expressions" in these sequences that distinguish Hughes's accomplishment as a modern jazz poet and contradict his reputation as a "folk poet" who wrote primarily for the masses (M. Jones, "Listening" 1148). The structure of *Ask Your Mama* is straightforward enough: twelve movements, or moods, that are based on the theme introduced by "Hesitation Blues": "How long must I wait? Can I get it now—or must I hesitate?" Within this structure, as Hughes writes in his introductory notes, *"there is room for spontaneous jazz improvisation, particularly between verses, where the voice pauses"* (CP 475). Each of the twelve moods follows the African American oral form of ritual insult known as "the dozens," and the twelve moods correspond with the twelve bars of "Hesitation Blues." As straightforward as this twelve-part structure is, and as rhetorically consistent as each mood is, there is considerable "room for spontaneous . . . improvisation," for readers as well as for musicians. *Ask Your Mama* follows a pattern of juxtaposition similar to the earlier *Montage of a Dream Deferred*, in which the gaps between voices, scenes, and sections are as important for the reader's interpretation of the poem as the more evident thematic continuities. This structure enhances the thematic significance of the poem's intercultural dialogue. The structural principle of juxtaposition engages the reader in an active process of constructing meaning, of improvising within the gaps, while simultaneously underscoring the potential for discord, for confusion, even for unintelligibility, which applies to the reception of jazz as well as to intercultural communication.[10] What differentiates *Ask Your Mama* from *Montage*, however, is its more challenging juxtaposition of different modalities. One reason that it has appealed more to twenty-first-century readers is that it resembles a DJ's mix of converging sounds rather than a more conventional jazz poem.[11]

Ask Your Mama also alludes to an international history of jazz that is only beginning to be fully appreciated. By the time that Hughes wrote his long poem, jazz was playing an increasing role in Cold War international diplomacy, as the U.S. State Department was sponsoring numerous jazz tours to counter the presumed threat of Soviet communism. As Penny Von Eschen and Ingrid Monson have documented, the promotion of jazz as the embodiment of the "free world" was full of ironic contradictions. U.S. policy makers viewed jazz as a Cold War weapon to counteract the perception of the country abroad, at a time when black liberation struggles were becoming central to domestic and international politics. The most obvious contradiction of the jazz tours was the promotion of black artists as symbols of American democracy when the United States was still largely a Jim Crow nation. As Von Eschen writes, a corresponding contradiction was the promotion of the "universal, race-transcending quality of jazz while depending on the blackness of musicians to legitimize America's global agendas" (*Satchmo* 4). Not surprisingly, the tours also had unintended effects, as African American musicians were able to witness more directly the freedom struggles taking place in Africa and elsewhere. Through this "cultural exchange," the idea of democracy that motivated the tours was transformed by many African American musicians, who saw their participation in the tours as a critical alternative to rather than an extension of Western cultural imperialism.[12] There was thus a fundamental paradox inherent in these tours: they were organized on behalf of the ascendancy of the United States as a global power, but they also enhanced transnational formations of Pan-African and Third World solidarity.[13]

Hughes consistently stressed the cross-cultural appeal of jazz in the 1950s and early 1960s. His claims, however, were based more on a diasporic consciousness of the music's evolution rather than nationalist promotions of jazz as the embodiment of American democracy. For Hughes, jazz encompassed the musical fluctuations of African diasporic expression: "Jazz is a great big sea. It washes up all kinds of fish and shells and spume and waves with a steady old beat, or off-beat" ("Jazz as Communication" 369). Jazz is recursive, then; while it reiterates the ancient beat of Africa, its permutations are unlimited. Such an inclusive understanding of jazz underscores Hughes's assertion that the blues, swing, bebop, and rock-and-roll are more closely related than most of his peers assumed. The figure of the sea was at once an identification of jazz with the beat of the human heart and the persistence of African rhythms as a life-affirming force, for black people throughout the diaspora and for everyone else who is moved by black music. As the expression of and defiant response to adversity, jazz is "a montage of a dream deferred," whether it be expressed through instrumental music or language, "a great big dream—yet to come—and always *yet*—to become ultimately and finally true" (370). Such debates about the international significance of jazz and black music more generally are integral to *Ask Your Mama*. The intersecting discourses of African American civil rights and African liberation movements are dramatized, often surprisingly, by the sonic mix of African diaspora music that Hughes develops in the first mood of his long poem, "CULTURAL EXCHANGE." Hughes also develops recurring thematic and sonic patterns through the figures of black celebrities, especially performing artists and activists, in the introductory sections of *Ask Your Mama*. The specific locations in which these figures recur transform jazz into a progressively activist form of "cultural exchange."

"CULTURAL EXCHANGE" begins by stressing what is culturally distinctive about racial formation in the United States. It does so, however, to satirize racial stereotypes and invert national—and international—racial hierarchies. First of all, the "cultural exchange" takes place in the United States, "IN THE QUARTER OF THE NEGROES" (*CP* 477), and the "ambassador" is

> AN AFRICAN IN MID-DECEMBER
> SENT BY THE STATE DEPARTMENT
> AMONG THE SHACKS TO MEET THE BLACKS. (478)

This reversal of the more familiar route of African American cultural ambassadors sent by the State Department to Africa not only disrupts the liberal worldview of the United States as the epicenter of "freedom," but it also recalls the misadventures of African diplomats who had previously toured the States, from Liberian president William Tubman in 1954, whose train was sabotaged by white Atlanta railroad workers in his tour of the South, to Guinean president Sekou Touré in 1959, whose unexpectedly circuitous Southern trip was also disrupted by racial hostility.[14] In reversing the more familiar route of "cultural exchange" between the United States and Africa, Hughes not only disrupts hierarchical perceptions of cultural difference, but he also underscores the challenges, as well as the possibilities, for Pan-Africanist alliances that are developed later in the first mood and throughout *Ask Your Mama*.

"CULTURAL EXCHANGE" accentuates the confusion that arises from the term "culture" as a term that evokes systems that define difference hierarchically, whether difference is based on social class, nationality, or race. Cultural "exchange" further complicates such conflicting notions of culture with the economic associations implicit in "exchange." "Exchange" suggests, most generally, an act of reciprocal giving and receiving or an act of substituting or trading one thing for another. "Cultural exchange," then, is presumably a substitution or trade of cultural representatives, but it is a substitution with a "price" (subsequently evoked in the figure of "LEONTYNE" Price). "Cultural exchange" also recalls the trade of black people as commodities, in slavery and the marketplace more generally, including the marketplace of cultural work. At the same time, "CULTURAL EXCHANGE" refers to the poem's own act of disrupting cultural expectations, an act that begins with the unstable "QUARTER" that is repeated in the first three lines:

> IN THE
> IN THE QUARTER
> IN THE QUARTER OF THE NEGROES
> WHERE THE DOORS ARE DOORS OF PAPER
> DUST OF DINGY ATOMS
> BLOWS A SCRATCHY SOUND. (477)

The "QUARTER" is introduced hesitatingly—"How long must I wait?"—but also repetitively, underscoring its associations with an economic order that depends on the perpetuation of a segregated social system to sustain racial and economic inequality. The insufficient living space and economic power of the "QUARTER" is the cost, in a sense, of a socioeconomic order that retains the physical space of separate but unequal slave "quarters." At the same time, however, "THE QUARTER OF THE NEGRO" is also a refuge, "AMORPHOUS" (477) to outsiders, but familiar to insiders, including the poem's speaker, in its resourceful capacity for improvisation. If "THE DOORS ARE DOORS OF PAPER," with the economic, legal, and textual suggestiveness of "PAPER," if the doors are insufficient to withstand the wind, they are also more open to possible change, "cultural" or otherwise.

The opening lines of "CULTURAL EXCHANGE" establish an intercultural dynamic of uncertainty, if not suspicion; as permeable as the "DOORS OF PAPER" appear, they mean something quite different to those within, whether flimsy protection or weak containment, than to those outside. This dynamic is produced formally through the "AMORPHOUS" nature of the poem's speaker but also through the permeability of the poem's lines. With minimal punctuation, and thus minimal subordination, the poem's enjambed lines create syntactic ambiguity. The line "WHERE THE DOORS ARE DOORS OF PAPER" functions, appropriately enough, as what Charles Bernstein has defined as a "hinge":[15] its syntactic uncertainty demands that it be read as a modifier of both "IN THE QUARTER OF THE NEGROES" and "DUST OF DINGY ATOMS." The syntactic doubleness of the hinge, here and elsewhere in *Ask Your Mama*, intensifies the poem's enactment of double consciousness, because it requires a double if not multiple reading of its resonance. It underscores the problem of cultural perspective, of the agency of and accountability for making meaning. The semantic ambiguity of these opening lines has a similar effect. What, for example, does "SCRATCHY SOUND" suggest, especially given the associations of "scratch" with writing and, specifically, barely legible or barely literate writing? And where *does* that "SCRATCHY SOUND" come from? Is it simply the impersonal power of the wind, or does this ATOM-ic power evoke the Manichean logic of the Cold War, which reduces meaning to the polar mentality of "us vs. them"? Or does the "SCRATCHY SOUND" blow from a "DUSTY" record on a phonograph, a sound that is at once modern in its transmission and as folksy as the *rhythmically rough scraping* of the Afro-Caribbean *"guira"* that appears in the musical directions in the corresponding right column of the page? Or could the "SCRATCHY SOUND" suggest a more discordant, and more rebellious, sound of the latest jazz horn blowing, black noise to adversarial or naive listeners, experimentation or innovation to those in the know? And might such a sound be as threatening, if not as profound, as the dreaded sound of atomic bombs? Later lines in "CULTURAL EXCHANGE" imply that these questions are hardly unrelated:

IN THE QUARTER OF THE NEGROES
ORNETTE AND CONSTERNATION
CLAIM ATTENTION FROM THE PAPERS
THAT HAVE NO NEWS THAT DAY OF MOSCOW. (479)

The association of black music, and jazz specifically, with racial anxiety, of "ORNETTE AND CONSTERNATION," is an underlying current throughout *Ask Your Mama*. Yet, the tendency to ascribe essentialist qualities to African diasporic cultural production, and especially music, is rendered as absurd as the association of "free jazz" with the threat of communism. Hughes accentuates the absurdities of setting cultural parameters for black music throughout *Ask Your Mama*, even as he celebrates pioneering performing artists who cross racialized cultural boundaries. The unlikelihood of the sonic mix that follows the opening scene of "CULTURAL EXCHANGE" brilliantly exemplifies this method. The initial musical directions take us from the scraping of the *guira*, to a "*lonely flute call*," to "*piano variations on German lieder*," to "*old-time traditional 12-bar blues*," to the "*throb*" of African drums (477–78). This "AMORPHOUS" sequence makes sense only with the arrival of the iconic, but, in this context, also absurd, figure of Leontyne Price:

BY THE RIVER AND THE RAILROAD
WITH FLUID FAR-OFF GOING
BOUNDARIES BIND UNBINDING
A WHIRL OF WHISTLES BLOWING
NO TRAINS OR STEAMBOATS GOING—
YET LEONTYNE'S UNPACKING. (477)

These lines evoke the mythic sounds of the blues, of train and steamboat whistles, yet they are unsettling as well, in their negation of hopeful departure ("NO TRAINS OR STEAMBOATS GOING") and their semantic uncertainty. Like the initial verse paragraph, these lines exemplify a blurring of possibility, "WITH FLUID FAR-OFF GOING / BOUNDARIES BIND UNBINDING." This blurring is again as descriptive of the poem's textuality, its material binding as a book that resembles a record album as well as its syntactic ambiguity, as it is of the poem's geography and temporality. No one could possibly evoke the paradox of "BOUNDARIES BIND UNBINDING" more complexly than Price, whose own life exemplified the contradictions and misperceptions of

black musical celebrities. Born in Laurel, Mississippi, where she began singing in her church, Price initially became famous for her portrayal of Bess in
George Gershwin's *Porgy and Bess.* Her performance in this 1952 revival of
Gershwin's opera was so successful that President Eisenhower orchestrated
a State Department tour of the opera through Europe, South America, and
the Middle East. Price, then, was among the first African American cultural
ambassadors and set the precedent for later jazz musicians' tours.[16] She soon
became a renowned opera star and in 1961 became the first African American
to sing a leading role (as Aida) at La Scala. Her debut recording, however,
which appeared the same year that *Ask Your Mama* was written and won
a 1961 Grammy award, was quite different from her performance of Bess:
A Program of Song was a recording of European art songs, and particularly
lieder, that she had performed at New York's Town Hall in 1959. Given the
complex significance of Price's celebrity status, as a figure identified with
the civil rights movement as well as with classical music, it is not surprising
that Hughes accentuates the ironies of her life, mixing the sound of collard
greens stewing, as well as the blues, with the sound of lieder. He does so as
a dramatic introduction to the multifarious reputations of black celebrities,
whether they are musicians, actors, or even writers: "LEONTYNE SAMMY
HARRY POITIER / LOVELY LENA MARIAN LOUIS PEARLIE MAE," and
"COME WHAT MAY LANGSTON HUGHES" himself (*CP* 478).

This segregated and, from the perspective of an African emissary, exotic
world that begins "CULTURAL EXCHANGE" is not limited to the South;
Hughes also exposes the violent backlash against black families moving to
the suburbs of New York City, from Mount Vernon, in lower Westchester
County, to St. Alban's, in eastern Queens. Significantly, he situates postwar
attempts to enforce racial segregation in these areas within an implied history
of West African contact with the "New World," from slavery to the liberation
movements of the 1950s:

COME WHAT MAY—THE SIGNS POINT:
   GHANA   GUINEA
AND THE TOLL BRIDGE FROM WESTCHESTER
IS A GANGPLANK ROCKING RISKY
BETWEEN THE DECK AND SHORE
OF A BOAT THAT NEVER QUITE
KNEW ITS DESTINATION. (479)

This passage acts as a bridge from the U.S. locales that are introduced in
"CULTURAL EXCHANGE" to the global struggles of Third World liberation
movements, signified by the names of "NKRUMAH," "NASSER," "AZIKIWE,"

"CASTRO," "TOURÉ," and "KENYATTA" (479). This bridge also suggests the Middle Passage, the historical memory of slavery that links these figures. It is surprising, perhaps, that "THE TOLL BRIDGE FROM WESTCHESTER" would bear so much weight in *Ask Your Mama*, but it exemplifies the interaction of local manifestations of racial oppression with the global liberation movements of the African diaspora that we see throughout the poem. It links the practice of housing segregation in Northern suburban communities like Mount Vernon with the more widely recognized practices of the Jim Crow South. At a time when the national perception of the civil rights struggle was focused on the South, the attempt to overturn the practice of housing covenants and other forms of segregation in the North was almost as obscure to casual observers of the civil rights movement as the nationalist liberation movements taking place in Africa. Finally, this passage also evokes the plight of the previously named African American celebrities, whose names recur with the African revolutionary leaders throughout *Ask Your Mama*. Success—and upward mobility—meant the opportunity to move into more integrated communities for many African Americans, yet this dream was often thwarted. This passage links the individual African American artist with American and African collective memory, the "*Hesitation Blues*" with "*distant African drums*" (478–79). It does so in the form of alternatives that are neither clearly opposed nor separable. But it does so to insist on the recognition of shared oppression that links people of African descent and the need for black transnationalist alliances to counteract this oppression. The satiric reversal of Jim Crow social roles that concludes this mood, the "cultural exchange" that places African Americans in positions of power with white servants, is as absurd in its parody of minstrelsy as it is prescient in its assertion of revolutionary desire.

The mix of African diasporic scenes and sounds that is initiated by "CULTURAL EXCHANGE" undergoes numerous permutations throughout *Ask Your Mama*. For example, the second mood, "RIDE, RED, RIDE," reiterates the book's title through Spanish permutations, in a sequence of Latin American, Caribbean, and African locations, referring specifically to Castro and Lumumba, and asking again, "*TELL ME HOW LONG—/ MUST I WAIT? / CAN I GET IT NOW?*" As indeterminate as "*IT*" is, with its reflexive reference to the text of *Ask Your Mama* and its leitmotif as well as to the object of desire implied by the question, "*IT*" signifies a desire and frustration that is crosscultural and multilingual in its demand for a revolutionary response. The response to this question, "ÇA IRA! ÇA IRA!" (483), adds another language to the diasporic mix, but this allusion to a French Revolutionary song appeals to black solidarity as it also accentuates linguistic division.[17] The soundtrack for this mood is likewise an African diasporic blend of maracas, calypso, and New Orleans jazz, reminding us of the creole roots of jazz in the United States. The title of this mood itself has revolutionary associations, from communism, to the freedom riders in the South, to Malcolm X ("Detroit Red"), while the recurring questions about "TU ABUELA" remind us of the shared roots of slavery that link those of African descent in Latin America and the Caribbean with African Americans, despite different histories of racial formation. In appealing to a black transnationalist commonality, even to those who would be considered black in the United States but not necessarily in the Caribbean or Latin America, "RIDE, RED, RIDE" does not dissociate itself from a Marxist revolutionary vision. The names of Castro and Lumumba are as symbolically potent for this vision as the equation of civil rights activism with communism is absurd in the United States:

> SANTA CLAUS, FORGIVE ME,
> BUT YOUR GIFT BOOKS ARE SUBVERSIVE,
> YOUR DOLLS ARE INTERRACIAL.
> YOU'LL BE CALLED BY EASTLAND.
> WHEN THEY ASK YOU IF YOU KNEW ME,
> DON'T TAKE THE FIFTH AMENDMENT. (484)

As ridiculous as it seems to implicate Santa Claus within an "interracial" communist plot, the costs of such red-baiting were too painfully clear, professionally and personally, for writers of gift books who knew what it might mean to take the Fifth Amendment.

The multicultural blend of African diasporic geographies and sounds that we encounter in "RIDE, RED, RIDE" reverberates throughout *Ask Your Mama*. If *Ask Your Mama* is "African American poetry's first Afro-Cuban jazz poem" (Kun 172), it looks back to earlier formations of black transnationalism, Marxist as well as Pan-Africanist, as much as to emergent formations propelled by African and Caribbean independence movements.[18] *Ask Your Mama* likewise recalls earlier modes of jazz, most notably early New Orleans jazz, as it formally resembles more unpredictable blends of traditional and new modes of jazz, not unlike the recordings of Charles Mingus that Hughes admired. "SHADES OF PIGMEAT," the third mood of *Ask Your Mama*, exemplifies this sonic movement across cultures and cultural histories. It also exemplifies the tonal range of the poem's sense of humor, as humor functions as a political weapon as well as collective release from pain and disappointment. "SHADES OF PIGMEAT" extends "THE QUARTER OF THE NEGROES" to the imperialist realms of King Leopold, Downing Street, and the Bourse as well as the segregationist quarters of Eastland and Malan. It celebrates their decline but also recognizes the shadows cast by their ghosts. The international journey of this mood takes us to the Brechtian musical stage of Lotte Lenye and Mack the Knife as well as to the political stage of international relations:

IN THE QUARTER OF THE NEGROES
ANSWER QUESTIONS ANSWER
AND ANSWERS WITH A QUESTION
AND THE TALMUD IS CORRECTED
BY A STUDENT IN A FEZ
WHO IS TO JESUIT
AS NORTH POLE IS TO SOUTH
OR ZIK TO ALABAMA
OR BIG MAYBELL TO
THE MET. (*CP* 487)

As is the case earlier in the book, to accept such "poles" is at best misleading. The textual juxtaposition of such logic with a sonic mix of "'*Eli Eli' merging into a wailing Afro-Arabic theme with flutes and steady drum beat changing into blues*" (486–87) challenges such preconceptions, disrupts received truths, suggests unforeseen possibilities. If North and South are more alike than not, whether the opposition designates hemispheres or regions in the United States, then there is certainly a need to imagine Nigerian president "Zik" Azikiwe, Hughes's classmate at Lincoln University and a formative theorist of Pan-Africanism, in Alabama. There is need also to imagine Big Maybelle, the popular rhythm and blues singer Mabel Louise Smith, performing at the Met. There is need to mix unfamiliar categories—philosophical, religious, cultural, or musical—in the spirit of "Pigmeat" Markham, the African American comedian, singer, dancer, and actor, in the spirit of black traveling music, burlesque, and vaudeville shows, which "SHADES OF PIGMEAT" and other sections of *Ask Your Mama* evoke. There is need, that is, to improvise, through whatever rhetorical means that are necessary, to convey the urgency of Hughes's claims in his liner note for "SHADES OF PIGMEAT": "Oppression by any other name is just about the same, casts a long shadow, adds a dash of bitters to each song, makes of almost every answer a question, and of men of every race or religion questioners" (528). By making "every answer a question," and by making its readers "questioners," *Ask Your Mama* compels us to imagine new cultural combinations—Africa/America, North/South, or high/low—and new political alliances: "ME / IN THE WHITE HOUSE / (AND AIN'T NEVER HAD A BLACK HOUSE)" (487). Imagine!

While "SHADES OF PIGMEAT" enacts a burlesque of colonial and Jim Crow practices of segregation, other moods of *Ask Your Mama* are more direct, and often more poignant, in their critique of racist logic. The binaries that "SHADES OF PIGMEAT" comically deconstructs are, of course, not innocuous; they have a direct impact on black movement and black expression, and the sense of entrapment evoked by "THE QUARTER OF THE NEGROES" requires more direct measures as well. Music plays an integral role in asserting more direct forms of action, often as an agent of action rather than as a mode of accompaniment. This is especially true where the subjects of the poem are themselves professional performing artists, struggling to make a living from their art, like Hughes himself, or struggling to exercise rights long denied to African Americans. Nowhere is this truer than in New York City itself, which was known worldwide as the commercial and artistic center of jazz in the 1950s, but which itself exemplified practices of segregation and discrimination more often identified with the Jim Crow South. The sixth mood of *Ask Your Mama*, "HORN OF PLENTY," most dramatically interrogates how the commodification—or "exchange value"—of black celebrities relates to their everyday lives. The opening sentence of this mood is a catalog of black celebrities, from "ODETTA" to "JACKIE WILLIE CAMPENELLA," and includes jazz musicians who had little else in common but their blackness ("DUKE AND DIZZY ERIC DOLPHY / MILES AND ELLA AND MISS NINA"), with each line punctuated by dollar signs (*CP* 498). However, this opening sentence of "HORN OF PLENTY" introduces a more sober exploration of housing segregation within New York City that reduces the individuality as well as the dollar value of these celebrities to the common denominator of race.

The commercial exploitation of African American performing artists, especially of jazz musicians, was widely known by the time Hughes wrote *Ask Your Mama*. The "Newport Rebels" counter-festival was only the latest, if most visible, example of jazz musicians uniting to protest their treatment by the music business. Less well known was the struggle of African American jazz musicians, like other black celebrities, to live in suburban neighborhoods. Nowhere was this more famously shown than the destination of the black celebrities Hughes cites in "HORN OF PLENTY":

> TO MOVE OUT TO ST ALBANS $$$$$$$$
> WHERE THE GRASS IS GREENER $$$$$$$
> SCHOOLS ARE BETTER FOR THEIR CHILDREN $
> AND OTHER KIDS LESS MEANER THAN   ¢¢¢¢
> IN THE QUARTER OF THE NEGROES   ¢¢¢¢ (*CP* 499)

St. Alban's, bordering Nassau County on the eastern edge of Queens, was famous for two reasons in the 1950s: (1) its black celebrity residents, especially jazz musicians, and (2) a concerted and often violent effort to limit the influx of black homeowners. St. Alban's was the "most exclusive Negro residential section in America," according to *Ebony* magazine in 1951 ("St. Alban's" 34). The neighborhood of St. Alban's known as Addisleigh Park offered musicians like Ella Fitzgerald, Illinois Jacquet, Count Basie, and Mercer Ellington "happy havens far removed from the grind of one-nighters or the fetid atmosphere of big-city night clubs" (36). Its bucolic calm also "disproved the theory that Negro ownership automatically depreciates property value" (35). Only a few years before the *Ebony* tribute to Addisleigh Park, it was more famous for the legal efforts of the local homeowners association to legally prohibit the sale of homes to blacks. While the Supreme Court ruled in 1948 that such restrictive covenants violated the 14th Amendment, St. Alban's remained a contested area throughout the 1950s. If it could be portrayed by *Ebony* as a suburban refuge from racial hostility in the early 1950s, the harassment and intimidation of black families, including a 1952 cross burning near the homes of Jackie Robinson and Fitzgerald, suggested otherwise.[19] The story of St. Alban's was not altogether different from Lorraine Hansberry's *A Raisin in the Sun*, which famously adapted its title from Hughes's "Harlem."

Hughes was also aware of the peculiar ironies of African American upward mobility in a community with so many celebrities as St. Alban's. Celebrity status might be achieved through extraordinary talent and hard work, or it might be granted the "HARD WAY":

> GOT THERE! YES, I MADE IT!
> NAME IN THE PAPERS EVERY DAY!
> FAMOUS—THE HARD WAY. (*CP* 499)

The costs of having "made it" are painfully evident in "HORN OF PLENTY," including the psychological costs. And while Hughes accentuates the dehumanizing logic of commerce encountered by black performing artists, whether in the recording studio or the suburban real estate office, he does not lose his comic edge in portraying white perception of black celebrities:

> THEY WONDERED WAS I SENSITIVE
> AND HAD A CHIP ON MY SHOULDER?
> DID I KNOW CHARLIE MINGUS? (500)

Or what about the most notorious literary figure of black anger?

> AND WHY DID RICHARD WRIGHT
> LIVE ALL THAT WHILE IN PARIS
> INSTEAD OF COMING HOME TO DECENT DIE?
> IN HARLEM OR THE SOUTH SIDE OF CHICAGO
> OR THE WOMB OF MISSISSIPPI? (500)

This question of "home," whether it be Harlem, the South Side of Chicago, Mississippi, or St. Alban's, is inevitably inflected with the national denial of racial inequality. And this denial is expressed through nationalist terms that conflate the struggle for equal rights with anti-Americanism: "AND ONE SHOULD LOVE ONE'S COUNTRY / FOR ONE'S COUNTRY IS YOUR MAMA" (500). In portraying the strange ordeal of African American suburbanization in such ironic, even surreal, terms, "HORN OF PLENTY" accentuates the dissonant impact of the Jeffersonian ideal on African American middle-class aspirations even as Hughes underscores the pain of this experience. The "HORN" of this mood's title is at once the cornucopian symbol of American capitalism and the brashly abundant notes of a Charlie Parker, singing its harsh contradictions through the "*gently yearning lieder*," through "*the old 'Hesitation Blues*,'" through "*the trills of birds*" (500–501)—"*BIRDS THAT REALLY SING*" (500).

The unlikely manifestations of "THE SHADOW OF THE NEGROES" that we see in "HORN OF PLENTY" are embedded within the global geography of racial oppression and resistance of *Ask Your Mama*, from the "TOWN NAMED AFTER STANLEY" (496) in the previous mood, "BLUES IN STEREO," to the multitude of African diasporic sites in the Americas in the following mood, "GOSPEL CHA-CHA." Accompanying these journeys to Africa, Cuba, Haiti, and Brazil are the creole blends of the blues and African drumbeats, cha-cha and mambo, gospel and maracas. The effect of such geographical and sonic blending is a defamiliarization of the "NEGRO," a proliferation of difference that defies fixed categories and renders ridiculous such naive questions as "IS IT TRUE THAT NEGROES—?" (509). The multilingual profusion of proper names, place-names, and names of contemporaneous, historical, and mythic figures has a similar effect: Hughes expands his readers' awareness of African diasporic history while challenging the reductive binaries that structure Jim Crow racism. The title mood of *Ask Your Mama* exemplifies these patterns of defamiliarization, with its ironic geography of "THE NOW KNOWN WORLD: / 5TH AND MOUND IN CINCI, 63RD IN CHI, / 23RD AND CENTRAL, 18TH STREET AND VINE" (511). "NOW KNOWN" to whom? To African American readers who recognize such black districts in U.S. cities? To other readers whose world has been expanded by the poem to recognize these street addresses? And how do these addresses relate to "FORT DE FRANCE, PLACE PIGALLE . . . BAHIA LAGOS DAKAR LENOX / KINGSTON TOO GOD WILLING" (512–13)? This black Atlantic geography suggests that black music, and especially jazz, is a shared language, even if the juxtaposition of "LUMUMBA LOUIS ARMSTRONG" (512) reiterates the urgency for

Pan-African solidarity as well as skepticism toward state claims for the "universal" appeal of jazz.

The correlation of black music with political activism, of jazz with Pan-Africanism, is especially pronounced in the moods that are identified most specifically with controversial jazz musicians, "BIRD IN ORBIT" and "JAZZ-TET MUTED." "BIRD IN ORBIT" identifies the poem's African diasporic geography with the figure of "CHARLIE YARDBIRD PARKER." While Parker was hardly a political revolutionary, his famously rebellious reputation out-lived his tragically abbreviated life. In Hughes's invocation to "BIRD IN ORBIT," Parker circulates among the most prominent proponents of négritude—"ALIOUNE AIMÉ SEDAR" (*CP* 517) (Alioune Diop, Aimé Cesairé, and Léopold Sédar Senghor)—as well as renowned civil rights activists in the United States, from Du Bois, to King, to the first-graders in New Orleans, "WHERE SIT-INS ARE CONDUCTED / BY THOSE YET UNINDUCTED" (516). As a figure of improvisation as much as rebellion, Parker can be identi-fied with the innovative form of *Ask Your Mama* as well as with the revolu-tionary "STARS" (518), past and present, religious and secular, who populate the pages of "BIRD IN ORBIT." Again, Hughes ponders the contradictory appeal of "STARS," especially when these stars are African political figures:

> TOURÉ DOWN IN GUINEA
> LUMUMBA IN THE CONGO
> JOMO IN KENYATTA. (518)

On the one hand, these revolutionary figures have an international celebrity status comparable to that of African American jazz musicians such as Parker, even if their significance is only vaguely understood by most Americans. In the context of U.S. foreign policy, however, their fame represents a more threatening reality, but a reality that is itself surreally distorted by the hysteri-cal lens of anticommunism, which conflates black liberation movements in Africa and the United States with communism:

> THOSE SIT-IN KIDS, HE SAID,
>   MUST BE RED!
> KENYATTA RED! CASTRO RED!
>   NKRUMAH RED! (518)

Such anticommunist fervor, which Hughes knew so well and which saw black cultural production as inherently suspect, does not negate the appeal of black music, however. The concluding figure of "BIRD IN ORBIT," "THAT GENTLEMAN IN EXPENSIVE SHOES / MADE FROM THE HIDES OF

BLACKS," is, after all, "SOAKING UP THE MUSIC," even when this music is a *very far-out boopish blues*" (519).

"THE MUSIC" of "BIRD IN ORBIT" is at once celebratory and foreboding. In "JAZZTET MUTED" the music is incendiary, *"very modern jazz burning the air eerie like a neon swamp-fire cooled by dry ice."* It is the fire lit "FROM THE WING TIP OF A MATCH TIP / ON THE BREATH OF ORNETTE COLEMAN" (521). The correlation of black liberation with jazz innovation no longer has to be cataloged—it is implicit, explosively implicit. And while Coleman takes center stage in "JAZZTET MUTED" as the avant-garde voice of this mood and the free jazz voice of black liberation, Parker is still the ancestral figure, the *"bop blues"* spirit of rebellion, invoked in the mood's concluding lines: *HELP ME, YARDBIRD! HELP ME!"* (522). The tone of this appeal is tricky to decipher. On the one hand, the firestorm of "JAZZTET MUTED" seems apocalyptic, inevitably so, given the rising "PRESSURE OF THE BLOOD" and the "SMOLDERING SHADOWS" of resentment that emerge from the "QUARTER" (522). On the other hand, this fire is an act of rebellion, an act of asserting an individual and black collective agency, as mischievous and destructive as it might be. The identification of such creative destruction with the improvised sounds of Coleman is certainly fitting, but the apocalyptic impact of his "BREATH" seems as outlandish as the paranoid association of Coleman with communism in the introductory mood of *Ask Your Mama*. The appeal to Parker for help, then, is more ironic than nostalgic; his *"bop blues,"* like Coleman's free jazz, seemed to represent the death of jazz, if not the world, when he appeared on the scene. What goes around comes around, the fire this time sparks the fire next time, and jazz, in the spirit of black liberation, will continue to improvise new modes of incendiary expression. Hughes asks in his liner notes for "JAZZTET MUTED": "Forcing cries of succor from its own unheard completion—not resolved by Charlie Parker—can we look to monk or Monk? Or let it rest with Eric Dolphy?" (531). The question is purposefully open-ended, but even more importantly, the question is at once intrinsic to and seemingly far removed from the mood that follows, where the "QUARTER" becomes twenty-five cents, where "CHANGE" becomes pocket money, where "ASK YOUR MAMA" becomes a child's appeal to his mama for "SHOW FARE," where *"bop blues"* and *"modern jazz"* give way to *"'The Hesitation Blues'* very loud, lively and raucously" (525). "Hesitation Blues" is as "haunting" as it sounds in the poem's first mood; however, the song is transformed, desperately, angrily, but also defiantly, by the dramatic insistence of its asking, "How long must I wait? Can I get it now—or must I hesitate?"

Hughes waited the rest of his life for a performance of *Ask Your Mama* that would precisely interpret the musical score, as well as the poetry, that he had so carefully composed. Almost fifty years after Hughes wrote *Ask Your Mama*, the most unlikely event of course did happen: a black man was elected president of the United States. And two months after President Obama's inauguration, *Ask Your Mama* was finally performed as Hughes might have hoped—in Carnegie Hall, with a full orchestra, with classical and jazz vocalists, with the unlikely combination of Jessye Norman and the Roots taking center stage. Laura Karpman's multimedia interpretation of what she called Hughes's "stylistic 'mashup' of American music" (30) was stunning, although more specifically "American" in its frame of reference than Hughes might have expected. Such current interest in *Ask Your Mama* is not surprising. With a president whose inspiring life story and family history are as complicated as the international geography of Hughes's poem, the "age of Obama" could also very well become the age of *Ask Your Mama*. The confused and often hostile public response in the United States to Obama's family history, especially to his "anticolonialist" Kenyan father, however, suggests that the words Hughes wrote for his liner notes of "CULTURAL EXCHANGE" are more timely than ever: "What—wonders the African—is really happening in the shadow of world events, past and present—and of world problems, old and new—to an America that seems to understand so little about its black citizens? Even so little about itself. Even so little" (*CP* 527).

5 "A Silent Beat in Between the Drums"

Bebop, Post-Bop, and the Black Beat Poetics of Bob Kaufman

Why are all blacklists white? Perhaps because all light lists are black,
the listing of all that is listed is done by who is brown, the colors of
an earthquake are black, brown & beige, on the Ellington scale, such
sweet thunder, there is a silent beat in between the drums.

—Bob Kaufman, letter to the *San Francisco Chronicle*, Oct. 5, 1963

Bob Kaufman's second book of poems, *Golden Sardine* (1967), concludes with an atypically documentary note, an October 5, 1963, letter to the editor of the *San Francisco Chronicle* (*Cranial Guitar* 96–97).[1] Immediately following the intensely sensual affirmation of jazz in his "O-JAZZ-O" poems, this letter is conspicuously formal with its full address and salutation to "Gentlemen." It is soon clear, however, that the letter is as much a manifesto as a statement of opinion. While not as outrageous as Kaufman's famous "Abomunist Manifesto," it is no less sharp in its social criticism as well as its rhetorical enactment of its claims. The letter begins: "Arriving back in San Francisco to be greeted by a blacklist and eviction, I am writing these lines to the responsible non-people. One thing is certain I am not white. Thank God for that. It makes everything else bearable." As direct an affirmation of blackness, or not-whiteness, as this is, the letter becomes increasingly cryptic: "Why are all blacklists white?" This meditation on the whiteness of blacklists and the blackness of light lists, not unlike the meditation on the "Blackness of Blackness" in Ralph Ellison's prologue to *Invisible Man*, seems more absurd than profound, although perhaps profoundly absurd, until it metamorphoses into a seemingly free association on "black, brown & beige." The rhetorical structure of this sentence, which begins as a logical "answer" to the blacklist question, dissolves into a seemingly improvised series of fragmentary reflections, with the concluding assertion that translates color into sound: "Perhaps because all light lists are black . . . there is a silent beat in between the drums" (96).

The date of Kaufman's "Letter to the *San Francisco Chronicle*" coincided with the latest report of a Buddhist monk setting himself on fire in South Vietnam to protest the Diem government's repressive policies against Buddhists. International news was dominated by reports of growing violence in Vietnam as well as U.S. consideration of a planned military overthrow of the Diem regime. There were also contrasting stories about the Soviet Union. On the front page of the *Chronicle* was a story titled "Russia's Crisis over Harvest." This was juxtaposed with a report on negotiations between the United States and the Soviet Union about atomic weapons in outer space. National news also included numerous accounts of battles in the United States between government forces and civilians, in Alabama, South Carolina, and Louisiana, where a suspected "Red Front" group was arrested (*San Francisco Chronicle* 9). The leading front page stories in the October 5 *Chronicle*, however, were titled "Ticket Chaos in Dodgerland," "A Plan to Save the View on San Francisco Waterfront," and "U.S. Report of Bodega—It's Unsafe," the story of an earthquake fault discovered at the site of the proposed Bodega Bay nuclear power plant. Amid this California news was a prominent photograph of Jacqueline Kennedy above a story titled "Jackie in the Sun," an account of her luxury cruise in the Greek islands, taken the month before the assassination of her husband, which Kaufman would commemorate by taking a Buddhist vow of silence that lasted until the end of the Vietnam War. Kaufman's letter to the *Chronicle* seems especially absurd in the context of the newspaper's cover stories for that day. His housing problems seemed as far removed from the view on the northern waterfront of San Francisco as they did from Jackie Kennedy's Greek cruise. At the same time, though, his reflection on the whiteness of blacklists certainly does intersect with the national and international news stories of the Cold War and the black freedom movement that were less prominently featured in the *Chronicle*.

Why, then, would Kaufman refer to *Black, Brown and Beige*, which was not only obscure but seemingly anachronistic by the early 1960s? Who would expect a writer best known for his celebration of Charlie Parker to identify with Duke Ellington's most extensive composition, a jazz symphony on the history of African America that was associated with the wartime Popular Front? The concerns of the Popular Front, after all, seemed like a lifetime before the more skeptical postwar period of the Beats and bebop. Kaufman is so commonly identified with the Beat obsession with bebop, and bebop is so commonly understood as a rebellious reaction to the popularity of swing, that the thought of serious engagement with *Black, Brown, and Beige*; with

the program music of a previous era of African American race consciousness; or for that matter, with a social aesthetic associated with the Popular
Front itself seems absurd. This chapter will address the question of Kaufman's
identity—or identities—as a jazz poet, beginning with the notion that jazz is
a form of social protest in his poetry. For Kaufman, jazz is a mode of social
protest that is inseparable from the surrealist Afro-modernism of his poetics.
Kaufman's poetry accentuates the African American and African dimensions of modernism, in the United States and internationally, and it does so
through the interplay of jazz performance with the multiple discourses and
social locations of his poems. His poetry also accentuates the continuities and
discontinuities of African diasporic history, including jazz history. Whether
alluding to the Popular Front "swing" of Ellington or the Cold War "bop"
of Parker, Kaufman's "post-bop" poetics enact the power of Afro-modernist
music as a both painful testimony and revolutionary inspiration.

Black, Brown, and Beige premiered at Carnegie Hall on January 23, 1943,
as a benefit for the Russian War Relief agency. Ellington's "tone parallel to
the history of the American Negro" (Ellington 181) was divided into three
historical periods of African American history and music. "Black" featured
the importance of work songs and spirituals prior to emancipation. "Brown"
introduced West Indian as well as African American music, including the
blues, to demonstrate the New World history of blacks in the Revolutionary
War, the Civil War, the Spanish-American War, and World War I. "Beige"
emphasized the jazz most popularly associated with Ellington's orchestra
while complicating the "common view of the people of Harlem, and the
little Harlems around the U.S.A., as just singing, dancing, and responding
to the tom-toms" (182). It concludes with a patriotic wartime affirmation of
African American commitment to the "Red, White, and Blue."[2] Although it
was enthusiastically applauded by the Carnegie Hall audience, *Black, Brown,
and Beige* received mixed reviews in the mainstream media. These reviews
revealed racial preconceptions about Ellington's music and about the relationship of jazz to concert music more generally. Among the critics of Ellington's
composition were advocates of jazz, most notably John Hammond, who
argued in "Is the Duke Deserting Jazz?" that *Black, Brown, and Beige* was too
complex and thus diminished the emotional power of black music.[3] Classical
music critics, who were also skeptical about the incorporation of African
American popular music into symphonic compositions, criticized the composition's lack of formal unity.[4] While the reception of *Black, Brown, and Beige*
was mixed enough that Ellington never again performed this composition in
its entirety, he was satisfied with the attention it received and especially with
the positive response in the black press. It was, after all, a composition that

was designed to raise the consciousness of its listeners at a time of increasing protest against racial segregation in the U.S. military. The fact that it was dismissed on formalist grounds by classical musical critics revealed their ignorance of African American history as well as their criteria for evaluating concert music based on African American vernacular forms of expression.[5] It was not, after all, the first extended piece about African American life that Ellington had composed, as it followed *Creole Rhapsody* (1931), the soundtrack for the short film *Symphony in Black* (1934), *Reminiscing in Tempo* (1935), as well as the musical revue *Jump for Joy* (1939), which also refuted minstrel stereotypes and contested Jim Crow social and economic conditions. *Black, Brown, and Beige* was also not the last extended composition Ellington would write: among the longer compositions he would write was a similarly ambitious historical account of African American history titled *My People*, which premiered at the Century of Negro Progress Exposition in Chicago only weeks before the date of Kaufman's letter to the *Chronicle*. *My People*, which includes some songs from *Black, Brown, and Beige*, begins with Africa and the Middle Passage and builds to one of Ellington's most overtly political songs, "King Fit the Battle of Alabama." Following this tribute to Martin Luther King's leadership in the black freedom movement, is the concluding song, "What Color Is Virtue?" with its insistent refrain, "What color is virtue? What color is love?"[6]

Kaufman's reference to *Black, Brown, and Beige* is not as unlikely as it might seem, then. If the reception of *Black, Brown, and Beige* revealed conflicting ideas about "the universality, the artistic genius, and Americanness of Ellington's music," as Kevin Gaines has written (598), it likewise brought up Popular Front questions about the mix of high art and indigenous music as well as the mix of art and protest. These were questions that recurred with renewed intensity by the early 1960s, with the jazz protests of racism and anticolonialism by musicians such as Charles Mingus, Max Roach, and Abby Lincoln.[7] They were questions that also applied to poetry, and especially jazz poetry, from Langston Hughes to Kaufman to the Black Arts movement. The "silent beat in between the drums" in Kaufman's letter to the *Chronicle* is not only the secret sound of African American rebellion, perceptible only to those in the know; it is also the sound that relates the most advanced jazz of the postwar years to the history of African American—and African—music. The "silent beat" is the secret rhythm of African drumming, from the years of slavery in the United States to the syncopated sounds of bebop and hard bop, the secret language of African American cultural continuity and resistance to white authority. At the same time, the "silent beat" is what Hughes called "the heartbeat of sorrow," the sound of sadness that accompanies the "rhythms of joy" in the history of African American music ("The Roots of Jazz" 370). The "beat," then, is not so much the mystical sound of beatitude as the beat that Hughes's Jesse B. Semple identifies with the blues roots of bebop:

> "Every time a cop hits a Negro with his billy club, that old club says 'BOP! BOP! . . . BE-BOP . . . MOP! . . . Bop! . . . That's where Be-Bop came from, beaten right out of some Negro's head . . .
>
> Bop comes out of them dark days. That is why real Bop is so mad, wild, frantic, crazy—and not to be dug unless you've seen dark days, too. Folks who ain't suffered much cannot play Bop, neither appreciate it. They think Bop is nonsense—like you. They think it's just *crazy* crazy. They do not know Bop is also MAD crazy, SAD crazy, FRANTIC WILD CRAZY—beat out of somebody's head!" (*Best of Simple* 118–19)

While Kaufman's poetry is full of such bebop "craziness," such pain is implied rather than stated in his letter of "blacklist and eviction." There is no doubt, though, that the silent beat between the beats, the beat that is inaudible to those who either do not know or deny the history that informs African American music, is the "sound" of "Bob Kaufman, Poet."

Bob Kaufman knew a thing or two about being beaten on the head, and the word "beat" is as likely to evoke a policeman's nightstick in his poetry as a jazz drumstick. Kaufman's understanding of the Beat movement differed from the "ragged beatific" vision that Jack Kerouac associated with beatitude. In a retrospective 1958 article in *Esquire*, Kerouac famously wrote:

> The Beat Generation, that was a vision that we had, John Clellon Holmes and I, and Allen Ginsberg in an even wilder way, in the late forties, of a generation of crazy illuminated hipsters suddenly rising and roaming America, serious, curious, bumming and hitchhiking everywhere, ragged beatific, beautiful in an ugly graceful new way—a vision gleaned from the way we had heard the word *beat* spoken on street corners in Times Square and in the Village, in other cities in the downtown-city-night of postwar America—*beat*, meaning down and out but full of intense conviction. ("Philosophy" 24)

Kerouac's prototypical Beat, while disenchanted with the values of a conformist, materialist American society, was individualistic—"characters of a special spirituality who didn't gang up but were solitary Bartlebies staring out the dead wall window of our civilization." His prototypical Beat was also most likely to be a white young man who deeply admired the music and style of "strange beatific Negro hepcat[s]" (24). Kaufman certainly identified with the Beat movement, and he recognized that even "white Negroes" (to use Norman Mailer's notorious designation) were subject to "Jazz cops with ivory nightsticks" who beat on "the heads of imitation Negroes" as well as actual "Negroes" ("San Francisco Beat," *Solitudes* 31). His vision of the Beat movement, however, was more aggressively subversive and more collectivist than Kerouac's vision. His "Abomunist Manifesto" most famously exemplifies his absurdly insistent, or insistently absurd, assertion of an alternative mass movement, but the early issues of *Beatitude* that he edited perhaps best exemplify his characteristic comic irreverence and revolutionary spirit. For example, *Beatitude* 7 (July 4, 1959), which included excerpts from the forthcoming *Abomunist Manifesto* broadside, includes a representative range of Beat poetry, including poems by Kerouac and Ginsberg. Its masthead, however, is full of the comic wordplay and surrealist irony associated with the "Manifesto." The title of the magazine is listed as "BEETITOOD," and Kaufman identifies himself as "B. Kofman," presumably not to be confused with the author of the "Abomunist Documents," "Bomkaf," or the "Bobby Kaufman" who is mentioned in the concluding statement of this issue. The "Bored of Directours" lists "A. Ginsboig, R. Wise, B. Uuraniame, J. Korewax, P. Ononoffkey, Ann Otherkats," and the founding date of the magazine includes an asterisked comment: "Some place. don't esk where." As playfully irreverent as this masthead is, the concluding statement about the Beat generation is more politically assertive. Contesting claims that the Beat movement is simply a continuation of earlier forms of bohemianism, this statement offers an alternative explanation:

> Why not a military one? A sort of guerilla warfare waged against the organized forces of befuddlement by the Knights of the human spirit. The brave commandos, Ginsberg Kerouac Rexroth & al versus the Hearse Press, the Loose Enterprises and so forth, who have all but succeeded in stifling the human spirit. With incredible courage they have parachuted down and established a beach-head. Now they are tired and wounded from the struggle, but young and eager reinforcements are coming from all over. You see the proof here in this magazine, and the material has been arranged with this in view. (*Beatitude* 7)

The poems this statement cites as evidence of this "guerilla warfare" include Ginsberg's "Afternoon Seattle," which is "full of nostalgia for the days of the Wobblies, and yet connecting those days with these." And among the "reinforcements" is "the new Voltaire of our day, Bobby Kaufman, dissolving the forces of Befuddlement with his corrosive jeering and mockery," evident in the "Abomunist Documents Discovered during Ceremonies at the Tomb of the Unknown Draft Dodger" and "Abomusual," included in this issue of *Beatitude*.

Kaufman also knew what it meant to be blacklisted. After joining the merchant marines as a young man, Kaufman became politically active in the

National Maritime Union and was "banned from shipping out" by the federal government during the early Cold War years because of his union affiliation (Damon, *Dark End* 33). Although the evidence of Kaufman's subsequent political affiliations is uncertain, he had additional experience as a radical activist before becoming involved with the Beat movement in the 1950s. He reputedly worked as a communist labor organizer in the South and served as an area director for Henry Wallace's 1948 Progressive Party presidential campaign before eventually moving to New York in the early 1950s.[8] However, this experience is not mentioned in the most famous portrayal of Kaufman: the brief biography on the New Directions back cover of *Solitudes Crowded with Loneliness*:

> Kaufman, one of fourteen children born in Louisiana to a German Jewish father and a Black Catholic mother, ran away to sea when he was thirteen, circling the globe nine times in the next twenty years. In the 1950s, while working as a waiter at the Los Angeles Hilton, he met another erstwhile member of the Merchant Marine, Jack Kerouac, and soon thereafter both moved north to found, along with Allen Ginsberg, Gregory Corso, and others, the San Francisco literary "renaissance" of the time.

This biography presents a romanticized version of Kaufman's trajectory toward the Beat movement even as it emphasizes the proletarian and cosmopolitan sources of his poetic vision. The mention of his work as a waiter at the Los Angeles Hilton, where he first met Kerouac, even recalls the mythic debut of another famous African American poet decades before: Langston Hughes, whose poetry was "discovered" by Vachel Lindsay at the hotel restaurant where Hughes was working as a busboy.[9] Like Hughes in the early 1920s, Kaufman's vision as a poet preceded his affiliation with white writers such as Kerouac, Ginsberg, and Corso. And this vision was informed by a radical commitment to social justice, especially racial justice, that was inseparable from his enthusiasm for jazz. He is surprisingly close in spirit, then, if not in his own practice as a poet, to the radical black internationalism associated with the Popular Front generation of artists, even as he embraced the avant-garde jazz of bebop and its subsequent hard bop transformations. In 1972 the influential African American literary critic Barbara Christian wrote one of the earliest, if not the earliest, academic essays on Kaufman, titled "Whatever Happened to Bob Kaufman?" Her essay begins by asking why Ginsberg, Kerouac, and even Ted Joans were still familiar while Kaufman was forgotten. Christian's premise for reconsidering Kaufman anticipates subsequent recoveries of his literary life and legacy: "Bob Kaufman . . . is one of the poets who helped shape the Beat movement in American poetry, and, as usual when somebody black makes something new in America, he's the one who's apt to be forgotten" (107). Her portrait of Kaufman belies the romantic individualist image of the poet so often identified with the Beats as she underscores his dual critique of racism and imperialism: "His poems always couple domestic racism with American criminal behavior abroad. He attacks the basic values of America, seeing the race problem in its midst and its behavior toward the rest of the world as reflections of the country's internal corrosion" (109). In short, Christian's Kaufman is a black radical, and jazz is a form of "protest music" (110) for countering the dehumanizing impact of racism. Christian's portrayal of the forgotten "revolutionary" poet informs more recent accounts of Kaufman's significance as an African American poet, whether looking forward to his impact on the "Black Aesthetic" or back to his engagement with radical modernist poetics. The late poet Lorenzo Thomas, for example, himself a member of the early 1960s Society of Umbra writing group that sometimes included Kaufman, has written that Kaufman's invocation of jazz is comparable to that of Black Arts writers such as Amiri Baraka, Larry Neal, and Henry Dumas: "For these writers, the jazz musician is not merely the custodian of an authentic folk culture or even the conscious avant-garde artist; he is the leader of rebellion against postwar conformity and the spiritual agent of the politically powerless" ("Communicating" 291).[10] Kathryne V. Lindberg, Aldon Lynn Nielsen, and James Smethurst have likewise emphasized the continuity of Kaufman's radical critique of racism and imperialism with the Black Arts movement while demonstrating how his poetry constructs an alternative vision of international modernism, a left surrealist modernism associated with the poetics of Federico García Lorca and Aimé Césaire.[11] Finally, the critic who has done the most to reconstruct Kaufman's life, Maria Damon, has emphasized how the mythic identities of Kaufman themselves suggest a revision of modernism, as his reputation as a Beat legend and forgotten African American poet make him both "paradigmatic" and "marginal" ("Unmeaning Jargon" 36). The myth of Kaufman's family history—"one of fourteen children born in Louisiana to a German Jewish father and a Black Catholic mother" (back cover, *Solitudes*)—has resonated more profoundly than any narrative about his experience as an activist. Despite Kaufman's own claims about his "German Orthodox Jewish father" and "Martiniquan Catholic voodoo mother," Kaufman grew up in a successful middle-class African American Catholic family (Damon, *Dark End* 33). His father was a Pullman porter with some Jewish ancestry, and his mother was a schoolteacher from an old New Orleans family. Kaufman's mythic genealogy enhanced his life story of diasporic roots (or routes), from his childhood in the jazz city of New Orleans to his later literary affiliations with Lorca and

Césaire as well as Hughes. His poetry, like his persona as a poet, can be seen as "a meeting place of cultural influences" (Damon, "Unmeaning Jargon" 36), a meeting place of Euro- and Afro-modernisms, musical and literary.[12]

Perhaps more than any other poet of his generation, Kaufman is associated with bebop, largely because of his poetry's engagement with the music, life, and legend of Charlie Parker. As Sascha Feinstein has written, more than any other poet of the 1950s, Kaufman resembled "the stereotypical jazz musician of the time" in his dedication to his art: "addicted to nightlife, to drugs, and to the avowedly non-academic, non self-promoting world of the arts." He was also the most successful poet in adapting Parker's sound, through "broken syntax, flurries of imagery, and conscious rejection of standard narrative" (Feinstein, *Jazz Poetry* 104). As incisive as Feinstein's assessment of Kaufman's adaptation of bebop is, I suggest that Kaufman's approach to Parker is more multivalent than the intense identification with Parker and his sound enacted in "Walking Parker Home." Kaufman admired Parker enough to name his son after him, and his commemorations of Parker—in "His Horn," for example, as well as "Walking Parker Home"—aspire to Parker's improvisatory virtuosity. Parker appears in a number of contexts in Kaufman's early poetry, however, as a mythic presence as well as a musician whose life is commemorated. More often than not, the mood of Parker's appearance in Kaufman's poetry is elegiac, as is the case in "A Remembered Beat" and "On," but he also appears more surreally, if not ironically, in poems such as "Fragment," which concludes, "Charlie Parker was a great electrician who went around wiring people" (*Solitudes* 12). Parker can also be found in Kaufman's more somber reflections on interracial social relations, as in "Bagel Shop Jazz," or, more mysteriously, as the "Bird" whose spiritual presence is more suggestive than definitive, as in "Tequila Jazz." Thus, Charlie Parker is more than a source of inspiration for Kaufman's poetry, as Kaufman is as concerned with his legacy, with his contested reputation, with the myth of Parker as well as his own memory of him. Kaufman's poetry suggests how Parker's reputation circulated, socially as well as musically, and his elegiac commemorations of Parker are as much inquiries into the racial politics of bebop's reception as they are tributes to Parker's influence as a musician.

No musician embodies the contradictory perceptions of bebop as famously as Charlie Parker.[13] He is now acknowledged as a transformative figure in jazz history, whose complex approach to harmony and unprecedented velocity of phrasing expanded the possibilities for improvisation. As revolutionary as his improvisations sounded, though, his music was very much based on the blues. His playing was distinguished by its "sudden and disorienting shifts of rhetoric," its combination of blues riffs with more discordant music, but at such a speed that made the process seem "abrupt and startling" (DeVeaux 380). His music was revolutionary, as DeVeaux has noted, precisely because he attempted to reconcile newer forms of music with the blues. However, Parker did not become the legendary "Bird" because of his impact on jazz history; his brilliance as a musician was not widely recognized in his lifetime. His mythic significance, especially among the Beats, instead resulted from what was enigmatic about his brief life as a musician. His emergence as a bebop musician seemed especially sudden; in contrast with the musicians who played after hours at Minton's, for example, his development into the quintessential bebopper was somewhat mysterious. He also did not live long enough to develop beyond bebop, which meant he not only would be eternally identified with bebop, but he also would seem "perpetually youthful, rebellious, and vital" (Panish 43). There was also minimal documentation of his life. Because he was not considered prominent enough to be covered extensively by the jazz media in his lifetime, and because the mainstream press either ignored him or misunderstood him, his public reputation was based mostly on the testimony of those who knew him. The Beats played an especially important role in elevating Parker into an iconic figure of rebellion, identifying with his alienation from mainstream American society as much as with his creativity as an artist. Ralph Ellison summarized this identification of the Beats with Parker succinctly:

> For the postwar jazznik, Parker was Bird, a suffering, psychically wounded, law-breaking, life-affirming hero. . . . He was an obsessed outsider—and Bird was thrice alienated: as Negro, as addict, as exponent of a new and disturbing development in jazz—whose tortured and in many ways criminal striving for personal and moral integrations invokes a sense of tragic fellowship in those who saw in his agony a ritualization of their own fears, rebellions and hunger for creativity. ("On Bird" 262)

As Ellison suggests, the Beat "jazznik" legend of Bird was as much a projection of the Beats' alienation as bohemian artists as it was a glorification of his accomplishments as a musician. This legend is less coherent, though, than casual readers of the Beats might assume, as African American writers who were associated with the Beat movement, such as Ted Joans and LeRoi Jones/Amiri Baraka, as well as Kaufman, portrayed his life and legacy quite differently from the more familiar figure of the rebellious outsider that Ellison describes. As Jon Panish has concluded, white writers' portrayals of Parker in the 1950s tended to stress the "bankruptcy of the dominant white culture and celebrate[d] the greater spontaneity and emotionality of black culture" (55–56), renewing the romantic primitivism so famously associated with the Harlem Renaissance. In portrayals of Parker in novels such as Kerouac's *The Subterraneans* (1958) or Ross Russell's *The Sound* (1961), he symbolizes individual freedom and nonconformity, a personal rebellion against authority rather than a political rebellion. In contrast with such images of romantic primitivism and personal rebellion, black writers tended to represent Parker's life and legacy in collective terms of African American group identity rather than in the universalizing terms of "victimization, the persecution and suffering peculiar to the plight of the artist" associated with white writers' representations of Parker (Panish 71). James Baldwin's "Sonny's Blues" and Jones/Baraka's *Dutchman* exemplify prominent African American portrayals of Parker as a problematic but representative figure of African American history and culture. While Baldwin's story is associated more with an integrationist social politics than *Dutchman*'s proto–black nationalist sensibility, both portray Parker as a racial symbol whose significance continued to be debated by African American writers.[14]

Before examining Kaufman's engagement with the legend as well as the life of Charlie Parker, it is instructive to contrast portrayals of Parker by two Beat poets whose identification with his music suggests how differently he was perceived by white and black listeners. Perhaps more than any other poets of their generation, Jack Kerouac and Ted Joans emulated Parker's creative rebelliousness as a musician, yet their interpretations of his social significance are remarkably divergent. While Kerouac and Joans have had lasting reputations as Beat poets, it was of course Kerouac who would become the iconic figure of the Beat movement in San Francisco. While best known for his novel *On the Road*, Kerouac was also celebrated as a jazz poet, especially because he performed and recorded his poetry with the accompaniment of jazz musicians. Kerouac idolized Parker, and Parker appears most extensively in Kerouac's melancholy novel of interracial love, *The Subterraneans*. His most emphatic and resonant portrayal of Parker occurs, however, in the concluding choruses of his *Mexico City Blues*. Comprised of 242 loosely related choruses, *Mexico City Blues* evokes Kerouac's desire to "be considered a jazz poet / blowing a long blues in an afternoon jam / session on Sunday," as he wrote in the book's introductory note. This "afternoon jam" concludes with three choruses on the life and legacy of the "Perfect Musician." Comparing Parker to Buddha, Kerouac writes that when he played,

> his expression on his face
> Was as calm, beautiful, and profound
> As the image of the Buddha
> Represented in the East, the lidded eyes,

The expression that says "All is Well"
—This was what Charley Parker
Said when he played, All is Well. (*Mexico City Blues* 241)

Paying tribute to the artistic genius of Parker, Kerouac portrays him as a holy figure, a figure who transcends his material life through his creative expression and transports his listeners to a spiritual bliss in the process. In contrast with this idealization of Parker are Joans's contemporaneous portrayals of Parker negotiating the cold streets of Lower Manhattan as well as the bandstands of Greenwich Village. In his 1958 commemoration of Parker, "Him the Bird," Joans concludes with the famous affirmation of Parker's lasting presence: "Bird Lives!" But before doing so, he also reminds us of the struggles Parker endured, struggles simply to survive as well as to succeed as profoundly as he did on the bandstand. Joans remembers specifically the time he spent living with Parker in utter poverty: "at a flophouse on Barrow Street and froze / With a Moslem and me during that winter of my time '53 / Eating canned beans sardines sipping wine and drinking tea." Joans historicizes Parker's life as a musician, even as he celebrates his legacy, resisting the exotic romanticization of Parker so common among the white Beats, even as he commemorates Parker's performance as a musician: "He blew for kicks and a few measly bills / Those solos he took on borrowed alto / Sax gave everybody their jazz-as-religious thrills" (*Teducation* 167). If "Him the Bird" only implicitly invokes the racialized reception of Parker, another poem included in *Teducation*, "Ice Freezes Red," recalls Joans's friendship with Parker in a more explicit scenario of racial hatred. Looking back on the same scene of coldness, poverty, and hunger as "Him the Bird," but a scene also of camaraderie and late-night conversation between "Joans, Basheer Ahmad the Moslem, / and him, the bird, Charlie Parker," when suddenly a car speeds by them in Sheridan Square and the passengers shout, "HEY NIGGERS!!!" (40). The poem then ends with the three united, "heated up, by hate" (41). This image of Charlie Parker as a black man, reduced to a racial epithet, but also fired up with anger, is also the Parker commemorated by Kaufman, even as he celebrates the transformative power of Parker's music as Kerouac does.

Like Kerouac, Kaufman portrays Parker in mythic terms, but he does not idolize Parker in the mystical language so familiar to San Francisco Beat poetry. His portrayal of Parker as a musician instead emphasizes the racial dimensions of his experience and inspiration as a musician. That is, he accentuates Parker's lived experience as a black man in the United States while also situating his innovations as a musician within the history of African American music. He also exceeds both Kerouac and Joans, as renowned as each is as a jazz poet, in approximating the sound of Parker's playing. This is especially true in his most intensive recollection of Parker's impact, "Walking Parker Home" (*Solitudes* 5). In this poem, as in other jazz poems in his first two books, Kaufman conveys the physical sensation of Parker's improvisations through processes of defamiliarization associated with surrealism—through synaesthesia and the juxtaposition of opposites, for example.[15] He also conveys the intensity and unpredictability of Parker's sound through the rhythmic complexity of his lines and his dramatic use of sonic devices such as alliteration and assonance. "Walking Parker Home" is comprised of twenty-seven enjambed lines that are broken into two sentences of almost equal length. The first sentence simultaneously narrates Parker's life and enacts the experience of his playing, while the second sentence reflects on the legacy of Parker's life and music. Like extended Parker improvisations, each sentence creates the effect of rapid dramatic movement and ultimate breathlessness. The form of the poem evokes at once the virtuoso performance of a Parker solo and the intensity of his short life. As continuous as the lines are, especially in the first half of the poem, "Walking Parker Home" does not read as a sequence of continuous run-on sentences, because the lines are broken internally with slash marks that indicate brief pauses. These slash marks accentuate the creative urgency of association but also the brokenness of these sentence fragments, replicating the sound of Parker's playing and the fragmentation of his life, from his earliest years in Kansas, to his migration to New York, to his ascent as a musician and his decline as a heroin addict.

"Walking Parker Home" begins by tracing Parker's roots, geographically and musically, locating his genius within African American history and jazz tradition. The poem's opening line is especially percussive with its strong alliteration as it introduces the paradoxical mix of beauty and violence, of assonance and dissonance, of creation and destruction that characterized Parker's playing and his life: "Sweet beats of jazz impaled on slivers of wind." Charlie Parker's genius as a musician begins with a "Kansas Black Morning," with "Historical sound pictures" that resonate on "New Bird wings." He does not suddenly arise as a "New Bird" in New York, though, as Kaufman underscores not only the "People shouts" of his youth but also the influence of his predecessors, "Lurking Hawkins / shadows of Lester." It is of course New York, though, where he begins his ascent to musical brilliance, which is also the beginning of his descent to dependence on narcotics. As Kaufman locates Parker's origins as a musician within the African American soundscape of his youth, he also suggests how his life in New York is not simply a story of individual creative success and self-destructiveness; it is also a story of the social and economic pressures of his professional life. His expressiveness as a musician is informed by his representative experience as a black man in the segregated city: "Bronze fingers—brain extensions seeking trapped sounds / Ghetto thoughts / bandstand courage / solo flight." But his anxiety is likewise fueled by the pressure to perform, night after night, set after set, and these "Nerve-wracked suspicions of newer songs and doubts" are the result of such pressure from "Culture gods / mob sounds / visions of spikes," which begins the descent to increasing dependence on heroin. Kaufman's Parker is heroic in his ability to perform so creatively despite his emotional and physical pain, and indeed to perform such pain so creatively, but he is also tragic, a casualty of "Money cancer / remembered pain / terror flights," a casualty of a socioeconomic and racial system that is more likely to destroy than nourish the creative genius of a black man.

"Walking Parker Home" concludes with a tribute to Parker that suggests that his legacy is ultimately inspirational:

> His legacy, our Jazz-tinted dawn
> Wailing his triumphs of oddly begotten dreams
> Inviting the nerveless to feel once more
> That fierce dying of humans consumed
> In raging fires of Love. (*Solitudes* 5)

In celebrating Parker's "triumphs," Kaufman underscores the stimulating impact of his playing, but he does not overlook his tragic suffering. He instead translates this suffering into a redemptive vision of "Love," a provocative and evocative vision that relies on the paradox of creative destruction to transform his readers' consciousness of the meaning of collective suffering. The pause at the end of "Inviting the nerveless to feel once more" suggests a double reading: Parker, through Kaufman's reenactment of his playing, wakens the senses of the "nerveless," inspiring "the nerveless to feel," but he also inspires them to feel more specifically "That fierce dying of humans," to bear testimony to collective suffering. While the "fierce dying of humans" seems to universalize this experience of suffering, this collective experience also resonates with the racialized experience of Parker's portrayal in the poem. The collective pronoun "our" also suggests a doubleness that is both universal and specifically "tinted" by the African American sources of Parker's jazz. Kaufman situates Parker's creativity, then, as well as his pain within the African American history of tragic suffering that recurs throughout Kaufman's poetry and especially in *Solitudes Crowded with Loneliness*.

The poems that frame "Walking Parker Home" at the beginning of *Solitudes* are suggestive for understanding its African American resonance as well as its elegiac tone. Kaufman was notoriously indifferent to the publication of his poems in books, but the sequential juxtaposition of "African Dream," "Walking Parker Home," and "Afterwards, They Shall Dance" exemplifies the jazz surrealism of Kaufman's poetry.[16] "African Dream" is at once mysterious, if not surreal, and deeply traditional, as it reflects on the question of African "heritage" that was so prevalent in the Harlem Renaissance, most famously in Countee Cullen's "Heritage." Kaufman's vision of Africa is an unconscious dream vision, however, a vision that is at once frightening and seductive. The explosive imagery and fragmentary lines of its opening are not unlike those of "Walking Parker Home":

> In black core of night, it explodes
> Silver thunder, rolling back my brain,
> Bursting copper screens, memory worlds
> Deep in star-fed beds of time,
> Seducing my soul to diamond fires of night. (*Solitudes* 4)

This sensual image of an unconscious ancestral "heritage" is then interrupted by a "Faint outline, a ship—momentary fright," a nightmare memory of the middle passage that provokes the sound of drums: "Drummed back through time / Hummed back through mind, / Drumming, cracking the night." Music, and specifically drumming, is a form of racial memory, a living racial memory that makes the "Strange forest songs, skin sounds / Crashing through—no longer strange." Music explicitly provides temporal and geographical continuity between Africa and African America in Kaufman's "African Dream," even though the dream image of Africa seems as threatening as it is seductive, whether because it is escapist or traumatic. As a preface to "Walking Parker Home," however, and a preface to the jazz poetry of *Solitudes*, "African Dream" suggests a vital continuity between African drumming and the most modern forms of African American musical expression.

The poem that follows "Walking Parker Home," "Afterwards, They Shall Dance," accentuates the elegiac tone of Kaufman's portrayal of Parker and bebop and earlier jazz more generally. It also suggests a dialogue between jazz and literature that becomes increasingly pronounced, more often than not surreally, in subsequent pages of *Solitudes*. The poem commemorates Maxwell Bodenheim (one of the earliest jazz poets as well as a legendary Greenwich Village bohemian), Dylan Thomas, Billie Holiday, and Edgar Allan Poe, an unlikely pantheon that posits a plurality of "underground" ancestors for Kaufman's poetics. Whereas Bodenheim, Thomas, and Poe are celebrated for their iconoclastic personalities, it is Holiday who is remembered most affectionately:

Billie Holiday got lost on the subway and stayed there forever,
Raised little peace-of-mind gardens in out of the way stations,
And will go on living in wrappers of jazz silence forever, loved. (*Solitudes* 6)

This vision of Holiday is hardly the glamorous but deeply troubled figure familiar to jazz poetry in the 1950s and afterward. As eternally "lost" as she is on the subway, her spirit is a sustaining presence in jazz memory. The interplay of these figures with the anxious reflections of the poem's speaker suggests a redemptive role for jazz as well as poetry. It also suggests that jazz and poetry, and indeed jazz poetry, can be most powerful when most provocative, most disorienting, as the speaker's response to the image of Holiday suggests: "My face feels like a living emotional relief map, forever wet. / My hair is curling in anticipation of my own wild gardening" (6). These bodily images are at once surreal and visceral responses to the emotional power of Holiday's voice—and her silence.

In juxtaposing his commemoration of Parker with a dream vision of ancestral Africa and a more fanciful vision of his literary ancestry, Kaufman suggests the range of moods and modes in play in *Solitudes*. The predominant mood, however, is elegiac, whether remembering the death of specific individuals, especially poets or musicians, or the collective death experienced in war or racial violence. As "Walking Parker Home" exemplifies, bebop is the musical mode that most powerfully responds to both the existential condition of individual mortality and collective forms of mass annihilation, past and present. As an African American movement that emerged in wartime, bebop stands for much more in the ears of its enthusiasts than an evolutionary moment of jazz history. In Kaufman's poetry it stands for the collective dreams and frustrations of African Americans and the socially marginalized more generally, even though its challenging sound appealed mostly to the jazz cognoscenti. Writing in the wake of World War II, in the wake of the early Cold War marginalization of the radical left, and in the wake of bebop's emergence as a "revolutionary" sound, Kaufman's poetry has the elegiac feel of being "post": postwar, post–Popular Front, and post-bop, although like "postmodern," the emphasis on war, on radicalism, on bebop, and on modernism acknowledges the lasting presence of what is presumably past. Parker's symbolic role in Kaufman's poetry can thus be seen as a tribute to the lasting impact of bebop and a retrospective renewal of its revolutionary energy. "Bird Lives"—"on yardbird corners" ("On," *Cranial Guitar* 92) and in the conversation of bohemians, black and white, "Talking of Bird and Diz and Miles" ("Bagel Shop Jazz," *Solitudes* 15). But Parker also appears as a "wounded bird," as a figure of melancholy alienation ("Tequila Jazz," *Cranial*

Guitar 61). Parker is the musician of thwarted desire, of perpetual outsider-hood, of beaten and Beat marginality, his "Swinging horn softly confirming / Anguished cries of eternal losers / Whose gifts outgrow their presence" ("His Horn," *Cranial Guitar* 63).

Parker's presence in "Bagel Shop Jazz" is only incidental, but the racial implications of his legacy are as pronounced as much here as anywhere in Kaufman's poetry. As Maria Damon has written, "Bagel Shop Jazz" (*Solitudes* 14–15) evokes the "triangulated desire" between the three groups represented in the Co-Existence Bagel Shop, where Kaufman regularly performed his poetry.[17] These three groups in the poem, the "Mulberry-eyed girls in black stockings"; the "Turtle-neck angel guys, black-haired dungaree guys"; and "Coffee-faced Ivy Leaguers, in Cambridge jackets," represent the uneasy "co-existence" of white ethnic ("Caesar-jawed, with synagogue eyes") and black men ("Whose personal Harvard was a Fillmore district step"). There is, of course, also an implied sexual tension between the groups of men and women, a tension that is heightened by the possibility of interracial sex. What unites these separate groups in the poem is the oppositional force of the "guilty police" who arrive in the poem's conclusion. They are presumably united as well by the "beat," but the poem stresses how this beat is interpreted quite differently by each group. For the women, the beat is overtly sexual, "As they fling their arrow legs / To the heavens, / Losing their doubts in the Beat." The white men, whose self-important bohemianism is portrayed somewhat satirically, are "Lost in a dream world, / Where time is told with a beat." While jazz is simply part of the conversational mix for these white Beats, it resonates more complexly for the black men:

> Weighted down with conga drums,
> The ancestral cross, the Othello-laid curse,
> Talking of Bird and Diz and Miles,
> The secret terrible hurts,
> Wrapped in cool hipster smiles,
> Telling themselves, under the talk
> This shot must be the end,
> Hoping the beat is really the truth. (*Solitudes* 15)

The "weight" of the conga drums, with their signification of Africanness, of the Pan-Africanist associations of Afro-Cuban jazz, but also of the "ancestral cross, the Othello-laid curse," is indeed heavy. In this interracial context, the black men wear the mask of "cool hipster smiles" while repressing the "secret terrible hurts," which are syntactically also the "secret terrible hurts" of "Bird and Diz and Miles." Their "Talking of Bird and Diz and Miles" is an implicit

identification with the musicians' double consciousness as performing artists, with the burden of concealing their "secret terrible hurts" with their cool
demeanor. As the consciousness of these black men is divided, their presence
in "Bagel Shop Jazz" is both part of and separate from the white groups of
women and men who project their romantic visions of blackness onto them.

"Bagel Shop Jazz," like so many poems in *Solitudes* and *Golden Sardine*, is
also a poem that is obsessed with time and memory, especially the time that
has elapsed since the war years of the 1940s. Its opening section reflects on
the presence of this past: "Shadow people, projected on coffee-shop walls. /
Memory formed echoes of a generation past / Beating into now" (*Solitudes*
14). The "shadow people" are presumably the images that are subsequently described more specifically, but the reference to "a generation past" cannot help
but evoke the traumatic violence of the war, of the Holocaust, of the atomic
bombing of Japan. It also cannot help but recall the music of a generation
past, given the sonic figuring of memory as "echoes" and the performance
location of the poem. The poem's concluding line—"Brief, beautiful shadows,
burned on walls of night" likewise suggests the violence "of a generation past"
(15), but with the difference that it follows the poem's reflection on African
American cultural memory. The reminiscence of "a generation past" reminds
us of the intensity, the sense of possibility as well as the sense of anxiety, that
informed bebop as well as African American social and political aspirations.
But this reminiscence also reminds us of the poem's historical distance from
this earlier moment, which makes Parker an ancestral figure as much as a
living jazz presence. The concluding line, which follows the intrusion of
the police, suggests both a return to the energy of a generation past and a
reminder of the continuity of violence against African Americans. It is also
an incendiary provocation—to remember, but also to recognize how the
"guilty police" extend the mass violence of the war.

Charlie Parker is remembered elegiacally throughout Kaufman's poetry,
as an archetypal blues figure as much as a bebop pioneer. But, as Kaufman
writes in the opening poem of *Solitudes*, his "traffic is not with addled keep-
ers of yesterday's disasters / Seekers of manifest disembowelment on shafts
of yesterday's pains" ("I Have Folded My Sorrows," *Solitudes* 6). As much
as Kaufman revisits the tragic brevity of Parker's life, Parker's legacy lives
in his music and in the music of those who extend his innovations. Parker
is the "remembered beat" among the pantheon of Beats whose intense but
tragic lives Kaufman commemorates, lives such as the young poet John Hoffman and the not so young Max Bodenheim a generation or two before ("A
Remembered Beat," *Solitudes* 44).[18] But even in the context of poetic Beats
where Parker's jazz so powerfully resonates, there is a noticeable dissonance,

a noticeable distance from mystical, if not mystifying, translations of his life story:

> When Parker, a poet in jazz,
> Gave one hundred seventy pounds to a one-ounce needle,
> His music, his life,
> Six hipsters from uptown
> Called it a religious sacrifice
> And wore turbans.
> Our poet wore lonely death,
> Leaving his breath in a beat. (44)

The distance between Kaufman's vision and that of the uptown hipsters is unmistakable: Kaufman remembers the pain that Parker experienced and the loneliness of his dying—that is, he remembers his humanity, not the martyrdom ascribed to his suffering. As a blues figure, Parker wanders throughout the surreal landscapes of Kaufman's poetry, unsettled and unsettling, not unlike the grandfather in "Grandfather Was Queer, Too." As often as Parker appears as a resilient trickster, however, he also resides in the depths of the poet's unconscious, as a "wounded bird / Hidden in the tall grass / That surrounds my heart" ("Tequila Jazz," *Cranial Guitar* 61). While Parker is a haunting "shadow person" in Kaufman's memory, a reminder of his own mortality, he is also a talismanic figure whose creative spirit sustains him in moments of desperate solitude. He appeals to this "wounded bird" in "Tequila Jazz"—"Unseen wings of jazz, / Flapping, flapping. Carry me off, carry me off"—at the very moment that "Thin melody ropes / Entwine" his neck. He is left "hanging," as the poem is left "hanging," with the tension between "hanging" loose or "hanging" from a noose, between being cool or being cooled. Like the poet, "Hanging, Man, / Hanging," the "bird" is a figure of temporary airborne equilibrium, but a figure precariously balanced between the threat of imminent danger and the traumatic memory of racial violence.

It is important to recognize that Kaufman's recurring invocation of Parker is not nostalgic, as distant as his revolutionary impact on jazz, and bebop's revolutionary impact on jazz more generally, had become by the late 1950s. Parker circulates among additional iconoclastic jazz musicians in Kaufman's poetry, such as Monk and Mingus, but also among musicians who moved fluidly between jazz and other modes of African American music, including gospel, blues, and rhythm and blues, such as Ray Charles ("Blues Note"). While Kaufman's jazz poetics are most often associated with bebop, his 1950s and early 1960s poetry coincides with the development of "hard bop" and its blending of bebop with more popular forms of African American music.

Kaufman's jazz poetry, with its formal hybridity and invocation of African American vernacular forms of expression, shares the Afro-modernist racial consciousness and assertive tone of hard bop. Kaufman recognizes and celebrates the transformative effect of bebop on jazz history, but he does not see jazz exclusively, or even primarily, as art music. He instead accentuates the interplay and continuity of bebop with other forms of African American music in the 1950s. By the mid-1950s bebop was no longer "revolutionary"; it had lost much of its initial appeal as a black subculture, and its musical innovations had become increasingly codified. The growing popularity of rhythm and blues, especially in urban black neighborhoods, also posed a challenge to the commercial viability of jazz, especially among African American listeners.

As David Rosenthal has documented, the emergence of hard bop can be attributed to the growing popularity of doo-wop, urban blues, and other forms of African American popular music associated with R&B. R&B appealed to younger musicians not only because of its popularity and expressiveness but also because so many jazz musicians were able to find work with R&B bands. R&B thus had an increasingly noticeable impact on jazz in the early 1950s, as the hard bop revisions of bebop that developed were more emotionally and formally expressive. Hard bop drew from gospel as well as secular African American dance music, and popular hard bop musicians such as Horace Silver and Art Blakey also integrated Latin American, Caribbean, and West African rhythms into their compositions. As Rosenthal concludes, by the mid-1950s hard bop had become increasingly identified with a mainstream jazz modernism, being distinguished from bebop by "heavier use of the minor mode and strong rhythmic patterning, along with slower tempos, blues- and gospel-influenced phrasing and compositions, and sometimes lusher melodies" (39). It was—and is—difficult to generalize about hard bop, however. Hard bop is often identified specifically with the popular "soul jazz" of musicians such as Silver, Cannonball Adderley, or Jimmy Smith, with the blending of jazz and popular black traditions such as gospel and the blues. But musicians such as John Coltrane and Sonny Rollins, who were subsequently open to free jazz and modally based improvisation in the 1960s, were also practitioners of hard bop in the mid-1950s. While hard bop has often been contrasted with more experimental forms of jazz as a more populist or commercial form of expression, innovative musicians such as Monk and Mingus exemplify how the most experimental forms of jazz innovation can also be deeply traditional.

Kaufman's portraits of Charles Mingus and Ray Charles in *Solitudes* demonstrate his "hard bop" mix of African American vernacular traditions and modernist experimentation. "Mingus" dramatizes the restless but assertive improvisations of the iconoclastic bassist and composer, while "Blues Note" celebrates the subversive power of Charles's soulful blend of sacred and secular African American music. Kaufman's brief portrait of Mingus evokes both the sensual intensity of hard bop performance and the ferocious audacity of his persona as a musician. "Mingus" (27) exemplifies Kaufman's dramatic use of synaesthesia to approximate the rapid call-and-response interplay of jazz musicians, both with one another and with their audiences. The poem begins by enacting the performance of Mingus with a densely alliterative blurring of the senses: "String-chewing bass players, / Plucking rolled balls of sound / From the jazz-scented night." The effect of such intensely sensual language is at once a defamiliarizing translation of jazz sound and an accentuation of the music's propulsive impact on its listeners, which is only momentarily relieved with the closure of "the jazz-scented night." The second section of the poem, comprised of present participle sentence fragments like the first, extends the initial focus on the musicians' performance to the music's impact on the audience of "hungry beat seekers." Again, the imagery is intensely physical and even more aggressively challenging: "Driving ivory nails / Into their greedy eyes." This portrait of Mingus conveys the power of his combative spirit as well as the improvisatory brilliance of his playing. It also conveys the plurality of styles and moods invoked by his music, as the initial plural "bass players" suggests. However, the power of Mingus's playing is attributed to the jazz traditions his music brings into play as much as to his iconoclasm as a composer and performer, to "Smoke crystals, from the nostrils / Of released jazz demons." The dramatic effect is not only disorienting but also enlightening, as the "smoke crystals . . . Crash from foggy yesterday / To the light / Of imaginary night."

In contrast with "Mingus," "Blues Note" (20) is more explicitly Afro-modernist in its interpretation of Charles's sound: "Ray Charles is the black wind of Kilimanjaro, / Screaming up-and-down blues, / Moaning happy on all the elevators of my time." The continuity between Africa and the blues, and between the blues and urban modernity, is no less explicit in the subsequent stanzas. The voice of Charles reveals "an African symphony hidden in his throat," and he "burst from Bessie's crushed black skull / One cold night outside of Nashville." For Charles, the blues both celebrate the Africanness of African American culture and mourn the loss of African Americans to Jim Crow violence and neglect.[19] And his blending of the blues with gospel, the "raw soul" of his singing, likewise affirms the strength of African American culture while asserting the utopian desire for social progress: "He separated the sea of polluted sounds / And led the blues to the Promised Land." "Blues

Note" states directly the social power of black music: "Ray Charles is a dangerous man." Kaufman's celebration of Charles, then, is written in language and syntax that approximates his more approachable, and more immediately affective, music, in contrast with the more abstractly synaesthetic lines of "Mingus." "Blues Note" is no less resonant, though, in suggesting the power of black music to enact an emphatically Afro-modernist ethos, as Kaufman's translation of Charles's affable persona into a "dangerous man" underscores the social urgency expressed by more popular as well as more experimental hard bop sounds.

If Kaufman's poetry can be compared with the hard bop modernizing of African American vernacular musical traditions, his hard bop poetics are also radically subversive in their challenge to U.S. Cold War—and Jim Crow—social norms. Scott Saul has argued cogently that "hard bop" is not simply an aesthetic term for the transformations of bebop that took place in the 1950s; the performance of hard bop also conveys a commitment to the civil rights movement and a "desire to make music that drew upon and publicized the black community's deep reserves of joy, defiance, and self-respect" (xii). Like the civil rights movement, Saul writes, hard bop "grounded new appeals for freedom in older idioms of black spirituality, challenging the nation's public account of itself and testifying to the black community's cultural power" (2). Hard bop was the musical expression of the freedom movement, especially as it extended the idea of direct action "into the realm of structurally improvised music," as Saul explains: "The hard bop group, with its loose, spontaneous interplay and its firm sense of a collective group, modeled a dynamic community that was democratic in ways that took exception to the supposed benign normalcy of 1950s America" (5–6). With its assertion of African American collective identity as well as individual creativity, hard bop challenged the fundamental premises of Cold War U.S. nationalism: that freedom was inseparable from the free market, and that this freedom was confirmed by a lack of organized dissent (12). These premises were fundamental to U.S. Cold War propaganda against Soviet communism, and jazz, with its reputation for improvisatory freedom, was enlisted in the "Goodwill Ambassador" tours and Voice of America programs to demonstrate the superiority of "free market" capitalism. As Saul notes, however, hard bop musicians, like the civil rights movement, challenged this correlation of jazz with individual freedom, situating freedom in "an arena of lively, unpredictable democratic participation" (15), while insisting that individual rights depended on collective empowerment. This idea of freedom was understood in spiritual terms: "The art of hard bop, like the street choreography of the civil rights movement, was a kind of spiritual dramaturgy—one that tested principles in the heat of instigated group conflict" (16).

Jazz plays an explicitly activist role, however outrageously, throughout Kaufman's poetry. Not only was Kaufman himself an activist for labor and civil rights as well as artistic freedom of expression, but his poetry frequently stages acts of symbolic defiance that correspond with the black freedom movement. The primary tactic of the movement was, of course, nonviolent direct action, in which activists would claim forbidden public locations as sites of protest. Such direct, collective action is figured as a jazz invasion in "Battle Report" (*Solitudes* 8), in which "One thousand saxophones infiltrate the city," followed soon after by a "fleet of trumpets," "Ten waves of trombones," "Five hundred bassmen," and "One hundred drummers." "Battle Report" is similar to the "Abomunist Manifesto" in its mockery of anticommunist anxiety. Its parody of military discourse is absurd, and its surreal espionage plot is likewise comical, yet its correlation of the "secret code" of jazz with a subversive infiltration of the city evokes the paranoid logic of anticommunism that informed federal government responses to civil rights activism. As music so deeply identified with African American culture, jazz is inherently suspicious: "Battle Report" evokes the recurring idea of jazz as contagious disease, from the post–World War I spread of jazz nationwide, through its unprecedented popularity during the swing era, through its underground resurgence as bebop during World War II. "Battle Report" suggests an amplified anxiety about the social impact of jazz, which from its earliest years was an anxiety about African American migration and urban interracial social relations, especially sexual relations. The mysterious emergence of bebop in the 1940s, with its subcultural style and lingo as well as its unfamiliar sound, intensified the anticommunist suspicion that jazz was "un-American." The primary practitioners of bebop, after all, were black, and not only was their music indecipherable but so was their spoken language. And not only were its audiences interracial, but they were also likely to be comprised largely of disaffected bohemians. In addition, bebop musicians and enthusiasts alike were notorious users of heroin and other illegal narcotics, further evidence of their "un-American" criminality. It is not surprising, then, that when the time comes for the jazz invaders to "attack" in "Battle Report," the "secret code" that is "flashed" to stage this attack is one of Charlie Parker's most memorable blues compositions: "Now is the time, now is the time." If this moment of "attack" culminates the surreal "plot" of "Battle Report," it can also be read allegorically as a drama of direct nonviolent action, not unlike the occupations of restricted public spaces by civil rights activists. Jazz is literally freedom music here, although more overtly "instrumental" than one might otherwise associate with jazz, and its "sound" attack on the city is overwhelming but nonviolent. The secrecy of this "attack," triggered by the resonant assertion that "Now is the time," evokes the creative success of the freedom movement to infiltrate public space that had long been the domain of Jim Crow legislative and police control.

If jazz is figured as a "secret" language of "guerilla war" in "Battle Report," as Amor Kohli has written (175), it is also a language explicitly opposed to war in Kaufman's "War Memoir" poems.[20] The first "War Memoir" appears in *Solitudes*, followed by the "O-JAZZ-O War Memoir" of *Golden Sardine* and the alternate version of this poem in *The Ancient Rain*, "War Memoir: Jazz, Don't Listen to It at Your Own Risk." The initial "War Memoir" (*Solitudes* 52–53) begins with an assertive statement about the power—and danger—of jazz: "Jazz—listen to it at your own risk." The tone of this opening warning, with the seemingly ominous seriousness of a public health pronouncement, resembles the mock-official tone of "Battle Report." "War Memoir" soon travels to another sonic realm, however, a realm in which the screams of childbirth converge with the wails of jazz. The poem locates jazz in the originary space of the womb, and the mother's act of childbearing is represented in the language of jazz and the blues. African American music is less an accompaniment to childbirth than its sonic manifestation, but the narrative sequence of birth is conveyed paradoxically, in a series of non sequiturs that defy narrative logic. The poem's "point of view" is a first-person-plural voice that at once experiences the process of being born and comments on the theological implications of this experience:

> Crying above the pain, we forgave ourselves;
> Original sin seemed a broken record.
> God played blues to kill time, all the time.
> Red-waved rivers floated us into life. (52)

These lines that follow the "trumpet laughter" of the mother's screams—"Not quite blues, but almost sinful"—figure her pain in the Judeo-Christian discourse of "original sin" and repentance. Yet, the solemnity of this language is undercut by the mechanical everyday simile of the "broken record." And God's power is itself portrayed in the secular terms of playing the blues to "kill time, all the time." The figuration of God as a bluesman is humanized in subsequent stanzas—"The heart is a sad musician, / Forever playing the blues"—but here the cliché of "killing time" attributed to God seems more like an existential absurdity than a recognition of divine power. The blues in "War Memoir" become the language of mortality, a language that correlates the experience of separation in childbirth with a consciousness of death. If the "blues blow life, as life blows fright," jazz is "Too soft for ears of men whose minds / Hear only the sound of death, of war" (52). The poem moves sonically from a raucous rendering of the blues, of the African American musical tradition most appropriate for negotiating the bodily experience of childbirth and metaphysical awareness of mortality, to the more subtle shades of jazz. Jazz is implicitly life-affirming, as the blues are explicitly life-affirming, in defiant contrast to the mass murder that is war, specifically the mass murder of "Japanese in atomic colorcinemascope" (53), the scene of genocidal annihilation that Kaufman returns to throughout his poetry. The concluding stanzas of "War Memoir" no longer express the paradox of life in musical terms, as there is nothing paradoxical about mass killing. The tone becomes one of outrage, and the images of death, cremation, and burial are themselves conveyed with "colorcinemascopic" vividness. Jazz is rendered mute by the "stereoscopic screaming" of the Japanese victims of atomic devastation.

Toward the conclusion of "War Memoir," following the "flagwrapped cremation" of soldiers and the "cries of children dying on deserted corners," a brief parenthetical statement interrupts the poet's diatribe against the thoughtless violence of warfare: "(Jazz is an African traitor)." Jazz is figured here not only as African but also as a "traitor" to the national cause of war. Jazz is thus figured as a defiant rejection of at least the most notorious manifestations of nationalism, if not of nationalism itself. Specifically, jazz is figured as a distinctively African alternative to an American militarist mentality that could rationalize the mass destruction of civilian populations, specifically Asian civilian populations. The Africanness of jazz and the blues is associated with the earlier experience of childbirth, with regeneration, in contrast to the methodical nihilism of mass destruction.

Kaufman's figuration of jazz as a form of protest against war is reiterated in "O-JAZZ-O" (*Cranial Guitar* 93), although in terms that more problematically blend the language of war with the more tragic dimensions of African American—and jazz—history. Jazz is initially figured retrospectively in "O-JAZZ-O" as "Where the string . . . Was some umbilical jazz," recalling the originary source of the blues in "War Memoir." The subsequent figuration of jazz in "O-JAZZ-O," however, as "A long lost bloody cross, / Buried in some steel calvary" is more overtly Christian in its suggestion of African American suffering as a source of jazz. This cultural "memory" resonates powerfully in "O-JAZZ-O," as the poem figures this suffering in terms that suggest both creative expression and destructive violence. The poem questions the alternative visions of temporality that it initially posits:

In what time
For whom do we bleed,
Lost notes, from some jazzman's
Broken needle.
Musical tears from lost
Eyes.
Broken drumsticks, why? (93)

The first-person-plural subject of this question suggests both the universality of the life cycle and the collective experience of African American cultural memory, questioning how jazz evokes not only the individual human consciousness of mortality, but also a collective fear of annihilation. The "jazzman's / Broken needle" figures death as a lack of sound rather than the repeated sound of the "broken record." More importantly, however, the "broken needle" suggests the destructiveness of heroin addiction, a destructiveness that is at once individual ("some jazzman") and collective, not only because of the communal loss of the musician's creative expression but also because of the disproportionate impact of heroin on urban black communities at the time. Such tragic suffering evoked by both the "bloody cross" and the "broken needle," accentuated by the fragmentary syntax of these lines, evokes the fragmentation of both African American communities and the African diaspora more generally.[21] But such tragic suffering is also integral to jazz, and especially bebop. When the concluding first-person subject of "O-JAZZ-O" figures jazz as "Pitter patter, boom dropping / Bombs in the middle / Of my emotions," he celebrates the explosive offbeat accents of bebop and hard bop drummers. Not coincidentally, he also alludes to the potentially devastating effects of narcotics. Finally, at the same time, he reminds us of the militaristic language that saturates jazz as well as the destructive mentality that jazz counteracts, evoking the assertiveness of bop and hard bop drumming through his own syncopated and alliterative lines. This celebration of jazz is ultimately not simply a celebration of individual creativity, however; by identifying these "bombs" with "My father's sound, / My mother's sound," he also celebrates the African ancestral power of his family and of jazz to offer "love" as a lasting antidote to destructive fragmentation.

"O-JAZZ-O War Memoir: Jazz, Don't Listen to It at Your Own Risk," which follows "O-JAZZ-O" in *Golden Sardine*, rewrites and expands the earlier "War Memoir." Inverting the opening pronouncement of "War Memoir" in its title, and starting instead with the seemingly biblical "In the beginning," "O-JAZZ-O War Memoir" proceeds from the same originary "warm dark place" as its predecessor. The vernacular language is initially more casual, however, and the existential angst and theological language of "War Memoir" is diminished. Most noticeably, the blues are displaced by jazz in "O-JAZZ-O War Memoir," and jazz performs as a trickster figure in the prewar narrative of the poem. Significantly, jazz is characterized as "secret" in "O-JAZZ-O War Memoir," as a language that is audible only to those who are receptive to its disruptive sound. As the baby emerges from the womb in childbirth, "Some secret jazz / Shouted, *wait, don't go.*" And as the child becomes more aware of the categorical absurdity of the adult world, "where laughter seems out of place," jazz is an emotionally expressive, life-affirming counterforce. The poem turns, however, as "War Memoir" turns, with the busy-ness of war: "Suddenly they were too busy to hear a simple sound / They were busy shoving mud in men's mouths, / Who were busy dying on the living ground" (*Cranial Guitar* 94). The most unsettling transformation of "O-JAZZ-O War Memoir" is the gradual conflation of "they" with "we," a conflation that becomes more explicit in the subsequent published version of this poem in *The Ancient Rain*, "War Memoir: Jazz, Don't Listen to It at Your Own Risk."[22] The demarcation of "we" who can hear jazz, of "we" who oppose warfare, from "they" who are deafened by the machinery of death in the initial "War Memoir" is not so clear-cut in "O-JAZZ-O War Memoir." At the moment when the "murderers must rest" in the conclusion of "O-JAZZ-O War Memoir,"

> they sat down in our blood soaked garments
> and listened to jazz
>   lost, steeped in all our death dreams
> They were shocked at the sound of life, long gone from our own
> (*Cranial Guitar* 95)

"Our death dreams" suggests at once the universality of "death dreams" and the hegemonic power of militaristic propaganda to occupy the consciousness of even those most resistant to its logic. Yet jazz proves to be transformative in a way that it was not in "War Memoir." The "sound of life" that is jazz, with its "whistling, thinking, singing, beating, swinging," allows the "murderers" to "feel" again. Jazz provides solace in "those terrible moments when the dark memories come / The secret moments to which we admit to no one," a solace to soldiers who have experienced the trauma of war as well as to those, such as the first-person-plural subject of the poem, who oppose the destructiveness of war but are not afraid to "admit" their own "dark memories" and "secret moments" to themselves. Jazz proves to be a different sort of "secret" weapon here than it is in "Battle Report," a benediction for those who "listen, / And feel" too late, and "die" (95).

The question that Barbara Christian asked in 1972—"Whatever happened to Bob Kaufman?"—seems dated now, as much a symptom of Kaufman's

Vietnam-era vow of silence as a recognition of his marginalization as a "black Beat." No poet is more identified with the transformative energy of bebop that Kaufman so memorably enacts in his "Battle Report" poems. And no poet is more profoundly associated with the life and legacy of Charlie Parker, as Ted Joans reiterates in the title of a commemorative poem, "Bird Lives and Bob Still GIVES."[23] And no writer except for Hughes has a greater impact on subsequent jazz poetry than Kaufman. Christian's provocative question is worth revisiting, however, because she not only underscores his marginal position within the Beat movement, as multicultural and transnational as this movement has become, but she also insists on his understanding and adaptation of jazz as "protest music," as music that is both utopian and pragmatic in its challenge to the white supremacist bases of racial inequality in the United States and U.S. hegemony abroad. Because Kaufman is identified primarily with the Beat movement, it is easy to forget his early affiliation with the Popular Front, which is manifested in his left internationalist historical consciousness and in his hybrid poetic forms, which allude to popular culture as much as European modernism. Kaufman has been the subject of important academic reconsideration in the late-twentieth and early twenty-first centuries, most notably in the special issues of *Discourse* and *Callaloo* dedicated to his writing.[24] His reputation in academia remains unstable, however, perhaps because he resisted the kinds of categorization that ensure long-term recognition. There is no question about his legacy among black poets, though. His writing informs the development of the Black Aesthetic in New York, where he participated in the early 1960s Society of Umbra writing group, founded by Tom Dent, Calvin Hernton, and David Henderson, and including poets such as Amiri Baraka, Clarence Major, Ishmael Reed, and Lorenzo Thomas. His poetry has been especially important for contemporaneous poets who combined jazz and surrealism with a black internationalist consciousness, including Baraka, Joans, and Jayne Cortez. And he has had a continuing impact on subsequent generations of African American writers, especially the writers associated with the 1990s Dark Room Collective, as Kevin Young recollects and celebrates in *The Grey Album*.[25] At the same time, the narrative of "whatever happened to Bob Kaufman" is still somewhat mysterious: it is a fragmentary, disjunctive, but urgent narrative, a post-bop narrative in which the silences resonate as profoundly as the sound of the beats.

Conclusion
"A New Kind of Music"

Paule Marshall, The Fisher King,
and the Dissonance of Diaspora

> After all, my life, as I saw it, was a thing divided in three: There
> was Brooklyn, U.S.A., and specifically the tight, little, ingrown
> immigrant world of Bajan Brooklyn that I had fled. Then, once I
> started writing, the Caribbean and its conga line of islands had
> been home off and on for any number of years. While all the
> time, lying in wait across the Atlantic, in a direct line with tiny
> wallflower Barbados, had been the Gulf of Guinea and the colossus
> of ancestral Africa, the greater portion of my tripartite self that I
> had yet to discover, yet to know.
> —Paule Marshall, *Triangular Road: A Memoir*

> Improvisation, commonly (and wrongly) thought of as a form of
> musical difference in which spontaneity is a dominant value (an
> art of the present), is . . . crucial to signifying how the space of the
> present can invoke spontaneity in the name of remembrance, in
> the name of lost practices and social formations that feed into the
> creative surge of energies that make the improvisational present.
> —Daniel Fischlin and Ajay Heble, introduction to *The Other Side
> of Nowhere: Jazz, Improvisation, and Communities in Dialogue*

Of the writers who are featured in *Jazz Internationalism*, Paule Marshall is
most often identified with the black Atlantic geography previously associated
with Claude McKay. From her first novel, *Brown Girl, Brownstones* (1959), to
her recent memoir, *Triangular Road* (2009), her writing has addressed the
conflicts that divide African diasporic communities and suggested resolutions
to these conflicts through movement toward sites that are more manifestly
African in their cultural practices.[1] This trajectory is explicit in the black
Atlantic geographical structure of *Triangular Road*, which begins with Mar-

shall's affectionate "homage" to Langston Hughes, the "travelin' man" who inspired her to become a "travelin' woman" (29). Following this reminiscence of her 1965 cultural tour of Europe with Hughes on behalf of the U.S. State Department, the subsequent chapters take us to the James River in Virginia, to the Caribbean, and ultimately to West Africa, where Marshall recalls her transformative experience at the 1977 Second World Black and African Festival of Arts and Culture (more popularly known as Festac '77) in Ibadan, Nigeria. As identifiable with black internationalism as Marshall's fiction is, she is less likely to be identified with either the politics or music of the "indignant generation."[2] Even though she was a radical activist and published writer in the 1950s, she is most often associated with the black feminist generation of the 1970s.[3] As she acknowledges in "Homage to Mr. Hughes," however, she already had a substantial "dossier" of radical civil rights activism when she was briefed by the State Department for her 1965 trip to Europe. Marshall is also infrequently identified as a novelist who features music as a mode of affirming or restoring a consciousness of African heritage, even though black music figures prominently as a mode of communal expression in two of her best-known novels, *Brown Girl, Brownstones* and *Praisesong for the Widow* (1982).[4] And like the fiction of Ann Petry, Marshall's fiction is rarely cited in studies of jazz fiction, despite the significance of jazz in her early fiction and especially her later 2000 jazz novel, *The Fisher King*. As I will suggest in this concluding chapter, *The Fisher King* is as much a "remembrance" of the "jazz internationalism" of writers like McKay, Hughes, and Petry as it is a compelling improvisational jazz narrative for the twenty-first century.

The Fisher King revisits a familiar site for readers of Marshall's fiction: the Brooklyn neighborhood of Bedford-Stuyvesant, familiarly known as "Bed-Stuy." The primary events of *The Fisher King* take place in this historic African diasporic neighborhood during the spring of 1984; however, the retrospective plot that underlies these events encompasses an extensive black Atlantic geography of migration, from the U.S. South and the Caribbean to New York in the early twentieth century, and from New York to Paris in the postwar years. What connects the characters who make these journeys is also what divides them: the life story of a jazz musician, the Barbadian American pianist Sonny-Rett Payne, whose rise and fall evokes legendary narratives of mid-century African American jazz musicians. Beginning in Bed-Stuy, developing his skills in Kansas City during the war, returning to establish his reputation in Brooklyn and then the Manhattan clubs where bebop came into being, Sonny-Rett eventually emigrates to Paris, where his career continues to ascend, only to come crashing down during the 1960s. In its narrative structure as well as the historical framework of its plot, *The*

Fisher King is at once an homage to and inventive revision of earlier African American narratives that feature jazz musicians as protagonists. Narrated through the dialogic interplay of the novel's multiple voices and memories, Sonny-Rett's life story evokes the tension between individual and collective expression associated with jazz performance. His trajectory as a musician recalls previous African American jazz narratives, especially those inspired by Charlie Parker, from James Baldwin's "Sonny's Blues" to John Williams's *Night Song* and William Melvin Kelley's *A Drop of Patience*. Like these narratives and other renowned African American jazz novels, from James Weldon Johnson's *Autobiography of an Ex-Colored Man* to Toni Morrison's *Jazz*, *The Fisher King* also dramatizes the historical impact of jazz through its narrative adaptation of specific jazz performance practices, including, most notably, practices of improvisation. *The Fisher King* features dramatic scenes of jazz improvisation, and like the process in which Sonny-Rett transforms popular songs through his improvisatory interpretations, the novel's narrative structure adapts and transforms Western myths of the Fisher King.[5]

What distinguishes *The Fisher King* from previous African American jazz novels is its dual emphasis on the intercultural significance of jazz and the social implications of improvisation. Marshall's novel dramatizes the link between improvisatory music and improvisatory social practice, between the group improvisation associated with jazz and new social formations. Jazz improvisation informs both the narrative structure of *The Fisher King* and the most unlikely improvisatory social relationships in the novel—sexual, familial, professional, and intercultural. Marshall's novel exemplifies how improvisation functions, as Daniel Fischlin and Ajay Heble have written, as a creative process of remembrance.[6] At the same time, however, the novel's focus on the narrative "rememory" of a black female character, Hattie, whose authority to represent Sonny-Rett's legacy is contested throughout the novel, complicates claims for jazz as a medium of democratic expression.[7] The dissonance of her life story accentuates how the novel's transgressive social alliances are subject to patriarchal, capitalist, and nationalist structures that inhibit the utopian potential of jazz improvisation.

Jazz is both the occasion for the retrospective plot of *The Fisher King* and an ongoing source of conflict between African American and West Indian families and between generations. Jazz is also the source for the novel's most unusual and most unified family, the "Inseparable Three" (184) of jazz pianist Everett "Sonny-Rett" Payne; his wife, Cherisse; and her closest friend, Hattie, who is also a singer and becomes Sonny's manager. From their teenage years in Brooklyn through their adult years in Paris, their "triangular" relationship represents an improvised queer alternative to the less supportive families in which they were raised, from the West Indian and African American families of Sonny-Rett and Cherisse to the foster families who raise Hattie. With the narrative focus on the ultimately tragic figure of Hattie, *The Fisher King* also accentuates the importance of the blues—and blues women—in jazz history. The character Hattie, an African American orphan who has endured abuse and hardship throughout her life, recalls the pain of numerous blues singers, most notably Billie Holiday, whose life story Hattie's most closely resembles. As a novel that narrates a jazz history partly through the testimony of a female character whose role might otherwise be considered marginal, *The Fisher King* enacts a revisionary process that Cheryl Wall has characterized as "worrying the line." *The Fisher King* exemplifies how black women writers "lay claim to Western tradition" but "rewrite canonical texts in order to give voice to stories those texts did not imagine" (Wall 13). Marshall's novel alludes most directly to Western myths of the Fisher King, but it also signifies on previous narrative representations of jazz. It not only "worries the line" of archetypal Western narratives, but it also imagines alternative narratives of jazz history through its African diasporic geography and its revisionist rendering of the profession and business of jazz.

As Farah Jasmine Griffin has written, studies of jazz literature have largely overlooked narrative fiction by women. While Morrison's *Jazz* is a notable exception, the narratives that have received the most attention in studies of jazz literature are those whose protagonists are male musicians. In addressing narratives by Shirley Anne Williams, Toni Cade Bambara, and Ntozake Shange, narratives that feature "the women who attend performances, the women in the booth or at the tables in the club, and women who share domestic space with the musicians," Griffin expands our understanding of jazz fiction ("It Takes Two" 348–49). Like Sherrie Tucker, the author of "'Where the Blues and the Truth Lay Hiding': Rememory of Jazz in Black Women's Fiction" (1992) as well as her better-known *Swing Shift: All Girl Bands of the 1940s*, Griffin underscores how black women's writing presents an "alternative historiography" to the more recognized modes of jazz critics and historians ("It Takes Two" 350).[8] Surprisingly, though, Griffin identifies *The Fisher King* with more canonical jazz narratives, such as James Baldwin's "Sonny's Blues" and Ann Petry's "Solo on the Drums," that emphasize "the virtuosic performance of an individual musician" (356).

As important as the scenes of Sonny-Rett's performance are to *The Fisher King*, Marshall's novel also enacts an "alternative historiography" through its narrative structure. Sonny-Rett's legacy is represented through multiple narrative memories of his music, and, most importantly, his most notable performances are conveyed through the consciousness of a woman whose relationship to him is both domestic *and* professional. The competing accounts of Sonny-Rett's life as a musician include those of his Barbadian immigrant mother, who disapproved of his "Sodom and Gomorrah music" (*Fisher King* 20), and his African American mother-in-law, who was equally as dismissive of his jazz and did not want her daughter to marry a West Indian. We learn more about Sonny-Rett from his brother Edgar and from Hattie, whose competing investments in Sonny-Rett's legacy, and specifically in his young grandson Sonny, form the novel's central dramatic conflict. As the novel begins, Edgar, who directs "The Three R's Housing Group of Central Brooklyn," has planned a commemorative concert fifteen years after his brother's death. This concert also celebrates the revival of the Putnam Royal, the Brooklyn nightclub that Sonny-Rett had made famous and that Edgar's company had subsequently restored and transformed into a concert hall. Edgar's vision of family reconciliation and urban renewal is contested, however, by Hattie, who has been invited to participate in this commemorative event. Most importantly, we have access to Hattie's private memory of her life with Sonny-Rett, an intimate counter-narrative to the public narrative that she performs for the family, friends, and musicians who gather to celebrate his life. If *The Fisher King* turns on the Brooklyn jazz performance that earned Sonny-Rett his name, it also underscores the crucial role that Hattie plays in sustaining his career and defining his legacy. Her interior counter-narrative, which is unspeakable in the public domain of the commemorative concert and is especially threatening to Edgar's authority, represents an alternative to jazz narratives that diminish the agency of women.

The Fisher King was inspired, Marshall has said, by a photograph of her cousin, Sonny Clement, whom she never met and who died mysteriously after he was drafted into the army in World War II. His commitment to jazz as a young man left a lasting impression on her, because, in Marshall's words, it was "a phenomenally brave thing to do in my part of the world. . . . It was an upwardly mobile community and they had no patience for children who wanted to be artists" (Stander). Yet, Bedford-Stuyvesant was also a remarkably important center for jazz when Marshall was growing up. "It is a well-kept secret, but my little corner of Brooklyn was a mecca for jazz during the forties and fifties," says Marshall. "I've wanted to write about it for a long time, to pay homage to the guys and a few women who braved family and community disapproval and became dedicated jazz musicians. Some made it big: Max Roach, Cecil Payne, Ernie Henry, Randy Weston" (qtd. in Doyle 73). According to Weston and Roach, who would become known for their inventive collaborations with African and Caribbean musicians in the early 1960s, the vitality of the jazz scene in Bedford-Stuyvesant had everything to do with the cultural mix of West Indian and African American families who had settled there. Weston's family exemplified the musical cosmopolitanism he associates with Brooklyn: "My dad's people came from Jamaica, Panama, and Costa Rica, and my mother's family is from Virginia. So I grew up in Brooklyn, New York. I was the first generation of New Yorkers, and I had the opportunity to savor and enjoy my mother's cooking and my father's cooking—different types of music. [There were] differences of accent, but I kept seeing the relationship between the two. And they were truly African people, just from different parts of the planet" (qtd. in Monson 142).

Weston's autobiography, *African Rhythms*, begins with an informative reflection on the cultural significance of the neighborhood where both he and Marshall grew up. As he recalls, his family's combination of West Indian and African American parents was not unusual in Bed-Stuy when he was growing up: it was "a really vibrant community . . . with a wonderful mix of black people from the South, from the Caribbean, and even a few from Africa" (11). For Weston, this African diasporic "mix" fostered both an appreciation of cultural difference and pride in a shared African heritage. Like Marshall, Weston's Pan-Africanist sensibility was shaped by his childhood exposure to Marcus Garvey's vision of black empowerment and self-determination.[9] Weston's father insisted that he "was an African in America" (Weston 18) and that "black people should strive to own their own businesses, work for themselves, be independent of the white man" (8).[10] The cultural importance of early jazz musicians such as Duke Ellington, Ella Fitzgerald, and Count Basie "was not just about their music, but the fact that their music was something for which we could claim ownership; it was definitely black music" (21). Weston celebrates the variety of black musical traditions that he experienced growing up in Brooklyn: "I was blessed with a combination of the black church, the blues, and calypso from our Caribbean side; plus hanging out at the Palladium and hearing music from our Afro-Caribbean side" (21). At the same time, he also emphasizes the openness to different musical forms that distinguished his parents' generation, and his childhood, from subsequent generations: "it wasn't so much about *styles* of music, they just loved *good* music; could be Cuban, could be calypso, jazz, blues, opera. . . . We grew up very healthy that way, with a lotta music in the house" (22). Unlike the elders in *The Fisher King*, then, the same generation of black immigrants and migrants to New York that Weston commemorates valued music of all kinds, whether Caribbean or African American, African or European, popular or classical.

As jazz historians Robin Kelley and Ingrid Monson have written, if the history of jazz in Central Brooklyn can be defined by any one characteristic, it is the creative blend of African diasporic musical traditions exemplified by the careers of Weston and Roach. This is most evident in their respective 1960 suites, *Uhuru Afrika* and *We Insist: Freedom Now Suite*, which combine African American, Caribbean, and African music (and musicians) in their affirmation of black liberation in Africa and the New World. *Uhuru Afrika*, although written specifically to celebrate the African independence movements of the late 1950s, remains one of Weston's most renowned compositions. Written in collaboration with composer and arranger Melba Liston and featuring lyrics and program notes by Langston Hughes, *Uhuru Afrika* "was not just another jazz record," Kelley writes. "It was a manifesto, a declaration of independence for Africa and mutual interdependence between the continent and its descendants. The entire project, from the music to the program notes, celebrates the bonds between Africans and the African diaspora—past, present, and future" (*Africa Speaks* 61). It was also a culmination of what the musician, educator, and writer Bilal Abdurahman has called the "Bedford-Stuyvesant Renaissance."[11] In jazz history Bedford-Stuyvesant has become identified with the experimental mixing of African, Caribbean, and African American musical forms that distinguish the compositions of Weston and Roach, partly because it became an important center for African music education as well as jazz in the 1950s (*Africa Speaks* 49–50). Its thriving jazz scene was especially eclectic in its postwar heyday, however. From ballrooms that featured big bands to neighborhood joints that hosted local musicians, there was ample opportunity and musical variety for jazz fans. And there was likewise opportunity for younger musicians and fans to hear the most prominent musicians of bebop and its post-bop permutations in Brooklyn, especially from the 1940s through the 1960s. Musicians such as Miles Davis, John Coltrane, and Thelonious Monk frequented the most prominent jazz clubs in Central Brooklyn. One of these clubs was the Putnam Central, which was known for weekly jam sessions that attracted both local and internationally known jazz musicians. It is, of course, no coincidence that the Putnam Central shares the name of the club featured most centrally in *The Fisher King*, the Putnam Royal.

The character who most clearly embodies such an African diasporic cultural mix in *The Fisher King* is Sonny, the eight-year-old grandson of Sonny-Rett. As the naive but sensitive consciousness through which much of the novel is narrated, young Sonny plays the role of the knight figure who seeks to restore the reputation of his Fisher King grandfather and heal the wounds that divide his family. The epigraph of the novel suggests that his role has a broader cultural importance as well, as it quotes his great-grandmother, who says, "'You got some of all of us in you, dontcha? What you gonna do with all that Colored from all over creation you got in you? Better be somethin' good'" (9). What is at stake throughout the novel is not only Sonny's future but the meaning of family more generally. Sonny is the biological son of an eighteen-year-old undocumented worker from Cameroon, who is deported from France shortly after his son's birth, and the fourteen-year-old African American Caribbean French girl, JoJo, who leaves him with her family and runs away when he is a baby. JoJo's family consists of her biological parents, Sonny-Rett and Cherisse, and their close friend Hattie, who plays the role of "materfamilias," especially when Cherisse becomes ill. Hattie's role in their family becomes increasingly crucial after JoJo's birth: she is Sonny-Rett's business manager, Cherisse's nurse when she is dying from breast cancer, their daughter JoJo's mother, and, eventually, their grandson Sonny's "fathermothersisterbrother and all the 'kin' he'd ever known" (16). Hattie's own childhood past, as the daughter of a mother who was institutionalized in a psychiatric hospital and as the subsequent victim of abuse from a series of foster parents, makes her love for her improvised family, and especially for Sonny, that much more intense. It's no wonder that her claim, "'There's all kinds of family and blood's got nothing to do with it'" (16), becomes such an important refrain in the novel.

As the novel begins, Sonny is visiting Brooklyn for the first time, having grown up in Paris with his "fathermothersisterbrother and all the kin he'd ever known" (16), Hattie. His method of coping with "this strange place called Brooklyn" (15) is no different from what he does in the more familiar working-class Paris district where he lives with Hattie: he takes out his drawing *bloc* and draws castles or fortresses, with his own signature image as the knight in each picture. His art is clearly a form of escape from painful situations, but it is also a creative form of adaptation, of translating the imagery of Arthurian legend into "castles and fortresses of his own invention" (74). It is not until late in the novel that we find out that Sonny's drawings are dedicated to the memory of his grandfather, who had fallen on the steps of the Paris Metro and died while running from the police. As Sonny tells his cousins, he had placed his grandfather in the castles for "'safekeeping. And not only was he safe, he was healed as well, all the bloody head wounds he had suffered in the Métro completely healed, his head, his face restored to that of his image above the entrance to the Club Belle Epoque'" (154–55). Sonny's imaginative act is at once a tribute to his grandfather's legendary reputation and an adaptation of his improvisatory practice as a musician. As the jazz musician transforms a popular song into an inventive and distinctive form of expression, Sonny translates the elements of Arthurian legend into a new image of restoration.[12]

Sonny's method of improvisation exemplifies the narrative structure of *The Fisher King* more generally, from its fabulist adaptation of the Holy Grail legend to its feminist revision of jazz narratives. As a novel that encompasses a century of African diasporic history, it likewise revisits narrative patterns of migration and urban settlement, including the very patterns that inform Marshall's earlier fiction, most notably *Brown Girl, Brownstones*.[13] If *The Fisher King* enacts and extends the improvisatory power of jazz through its intertextual allusion to Marshall's first novel, it also encompasses an extensive history of jazz, from the pre–World War II swing era through the postwar development of bebop and its subsequent transformations. By dramatizing the legacy of jazz, beyond the decades of its greatest popularity and prominence, Marshall underscores the ongoing vitality of jazz as a provocative and potentially regenerative mode of African diasporic expression. Thus, it is especially significant that the jazz life of Sonny-Rett Payne is initially refracted through his grandson Sonny's paradoxical perspective as an outsider in the extended family he has never met. Through Sonny's consciousness, his jazz musician grandfather is legendary, a living presence in the child's imagination but otherwise a larger-than-life figure from the distant past. This legendary presence is fractured, however, by the conflicting interpretations of his life story within the extended family. Before we have access to Hattie's consciousness, and before we hear the testimony of musicians who commemorate Sonny-Rett, we hear the accounts of relatives whose attitudes about jazz modify the legendary portrait that Sonny has constructed from the stories Hattie has told him. These dismissive accounts of Sonny-Rett's music that Sonny hears from his West Indian and African American great-grandmothers early in the novel evoke the controversial history of jazz, from the earliest years of its emergence through the postwar decades of Sonny-Rett's ascendance as a renowned pianist.

In the narratives of the great-grandmothers, Sonny-Rett's jazz career is figured as a rejection of both high cultural and commercial aspirations, the classical concert hall and the Broadway stage. It is clear from these opening chapters that Sonny-Rett's commitment to jazz was by necessity rebellious, even as he sought freedom from the restrictions of a parental generation that had itself struggled to make a new life in Brooklyn. Skepticism about Sonny-Rett's jazz life was not limited to this older generation, however. As we also find out early in the novel, his brother Edgar also did not appreciate his music during Sonny-Rett's lifetime. Between the first and third chapters, which introduce Sonny's great-grandmothers, is a brief chapter that consists entirely of a letter addressed to Hattie from Edgar DeC. Payne, director of "The Three R's Housing Group of Central Brooklyn: Reclamation. Restoration. Rebirth" (25). This letter of invitation to the memorial concert for Sonny-Rett both explains why Hattie and Sonny are visiting Brooklyn and foreshadows the later conflict about Sonny's future. Edgar's stated purpose for this memorial concert is the "restoration" of Sonny-Rett to his family and "home ground" of Brooklyn, after his vow never to return to the United States. Equally important to Edgar, though, is the introduction of young Sonny to his family, a "reclamation" project that becomes the primary dramatic conflict of the novel. The concert is planned to take place at the Putnam Royal, the club where Sonny-Rett had "first made his name," which, Edgar proudly proclaims, "'is no longer the run-down barn of a place'" that Hattie would remember. "'You'll be pleased at the transformation,'" Edgar writes. "'The concert will not only memorialize my brother, it will inaugurate a restored, reborn Putnam Royal'" (26). Edgar's motives for restoring family relationships are not altogether different from his housing and development work; they are based simultaneously on self-interest, whether emotional or economic, and commitment to developing a stronger community. Of course, there is inevitable collateral damage from this capitalist model of community development, whether it be the potential displacement of Hattie as Sonny's guardian or the dislodgment of poor tenants from their apartment buildings. Edgar's motives for restoring his brother's memory are more complex, however, and his changed understanding of jazz suggests a "transformation" of the jazz public as well as his own appreciation of his brother's music.

Edgar's stature as "the man" is perceived mostly through Sonny's consciousness, and his bonding with Sonny reveals a more sensitive character than his public image as a wealthy developer—the "Shylock of Central Brooklyn" (49)—initially suggests. For example, he appreciates Sonny's "castles and fortresses of his own invention" (74) enough that he is able to engage him in conversations about this otherwise private world of his imagination. And he pays attention to Sonny when other adults are "talking talking talking" (73), most notably at first at the planning meeting for the memorial concert, when Edgar and the musicians who had played with Sonny-Rett ask Hattie to participate in the event. Here, Edgar's role as a jazz enthusiast is muted, but his role as a developer is instrumental not only for this event but also for the resurrection of jazz in Bed-Stuy or, as he insists, "Central Brooklyn," more generally. The renovation of the Putnam Royal exemplifies the power and pride of black business ownership and community development that his company represents. Yet, as important a role as jazz has played in the history of Bed-Stuy and its renewal as "Central Brooklyn," Edgar's investment in jazz is more personal than public, and thus more suspect to Hattie. When she asks him directly about his motives, he narrates a long process of jazz education and increasing respect for Sonny-Rett's music, a process of extending himself to the challenges of Sonny's musicianship, but a process that eventually results in the domestication of what is otherwise defiant about his playing. When Hattie asks Edgar whether the "'concert is about making it up to him,'" his response is revealing: "'I suppose you could look at it that way. . . . But it's also about bringing him home in a manner of speaking and ending his anger with us and this place'" (86–87). This process of "reclamation," of "restoring" Sonny-Rett's music to its "home," a process that coincides with the "rebirth" of the Putnam Royal, necessarily mutes the anger expressed through Sonny's music. It is a process that, although admittedly personal here, has been an effective business model for reclaiming bebop and its subsequent transformations from their initially rebellious avant-garde associations. This process of reclamation, like the real estate name change from "Bed-Stuy" to "Central Brooklyn," changes the confrontational Afro-modernism of bebop into a musical product more marketable for middle-class consumption.

As important as Sonny's childhood perspective is to the novel's emotional impact, it is Hattie's perspective that challenges Edgar Payne's motives for reconciliation and represents a more knowledgeable, as well as more passionate, account of Sonny-Rett's significance as a musician. Her characterization initially underscores her maternal role. In the first few chapters we know her mostly through Sonny's love for her. But we are also gradually exposed to the economic precariousness of her bohemian life in Paris. The narrative of Hattie Carmichael certainly can be read as a sentimental tale of love and loss, of maternal attachment to and eventual separation from a child who is her primary connection to the past as well as her hope for the future, a child who never knew his biological parents and depends entirely on Hattie—until the intervention of his great-uncle Edgar Payne. Hattie's narrative also evokes the harsher sense of loss associated with African American blues narratives, beginning with her separation from her mother and concluding with the impending separation from the child she has raised. Hattie's life as a "kid around the block" (25) on Macon Street began as a "City child" (66) who lived with a series of foster parents after her mother had been institutionalized with mental illness. She endured sexual abuse and poverty as a child, but she eventually became close friends with Cherisse, whose mother would not allow "some foster care child" (70) into their home or even their yard. Hattie also became an accomplished doo-wop singer in a girl group that featured Cherisse (despite Cherisse's limited singing ability). This group, the Maconettes, appeared for the first time at the Putnam Royal that same day when Sonny-Rett debuted there, which was also the day when Sonny-Rett and Cherisse first "hooked up" (130). The debut of the Maconettes was a success, even if they never received a contract or payment from the owner of the Putnam Royal, but they were overshadowed by the performance that night by Sonny-Rett. Hattie's role in the novel is not eclipsed by Sonny-Rett, however, as each narrative account of his Putnam Royal performance is prefaced by the story of the Maconettes. Hattie not only sang in the group, but she was also the manager, as she was Sonny-Rett's manager after they moved to Europe. The novel accentuates both the continuum of black music, from doo-wop to bop, and the unheralded but crucial role that Hattie plays as a manager. When she imagines her future role at the moment when Sonny-Rett and Cherisse fall in love, she imagines her indispensable professional role as well as her intimate role in their lives: "She told herself it might not be as bad as it felt at the moment; that in fact, it might be the way things were meant to be, the three of them like the connected sides of the triangles she used to draw in geometry in high school, with her as the base, joining them to herself" (140–41). She concludes decisively, although somewhat desperately: "It might be the way—the only way—to have them both" (141).

If Hattie becomes the "base" in this triangular relationship, the foundational support for both Sonny-Rett and Cherisse, she is not always acknowledged as such. And she pays a heavy price for her involvement in their lives and in the music business more generally. The most visible sign of the price Hattie pays as a black woman in the music business is actually invisible throughout most of the novel, as she wears a turban to cover the fact that she has lost most of her hair, the result of too much Congolene as a young woman to transform "her thick, unruly bush into a sleek flapper 'do' reminiscent of the twenties" (133). While the physical cost of fulfilling 1940s expectations of beauty is evident in the damage to Hattie's hair, the more subtle, psychological scars result from the uncertainty and anonymity of her position as Sonny's manager. While Cherisse is the beautiful wife who accompanies Sonny-Rett in public, Hattie works behind the scenes, scheduling performances and negotiating contracts as she orchestrates Sonny-Rett's professional life, accompanying him on the road as well as taking care of business at home. The triangular relationship between Hattie, Sonny-Rett, and Cherisse becomes increasingly harmonious, however. Hattie becomes Sonny-Rett's lover, his primary source of emotional support, until he dies a violent death in a Paris subway station, pursued by "*les flics*" (201). She becomes Cherisse's lover, too, and her nurse when she suffers and dies from breast cancer, refusing to allow a doctor to "cut on" her (203). And she becomes the "materfamilias" to their daughter, JoJo, who runs away from home shortly before her mother's death. Then she becomes the mother of JoJo's baby, whom she names "Sonny," after JoJo returns home only to drop off the baby and disappear again, the baby whose face "reflected them all: Sonny-Rett, Cherisse, JoJo," the baby who "would be hers for the rest of her lifetime. She would do whatever it took to see to that" (208). After Cherisse had accepted Hattie's intimate relationship with Sonny-Rett, Hattie recalled an earlier moment when Cherisse whispered in her ear: "'*Partager*. It's the verb "to share"'" (192). *Partager* also means to divide, to separate, and Hattie recalls her experience of repeated love and loss as she shares the stage at the Putnam Royal with the musicians who accompanied Sonny-Rett. As she tells the story of Sonny-Rett on this stage, she also remembers the more intimate details of her life with him, and her public performance of his jazz life is accompanied by her private blues narrative. In her interior version of the story, Sonny-Rett shares his life with Hattie, and his success as a musician is inseparable from her accompanying role. However, the public separation of their life stories is as telling as the novel's positioning of Hattie—and her life story—center stage in a narrative about jazz history.

Hattie is both a participant and observer in the life story of Sonny-Rett that is the premise for *The Fisher King*. For Hattie, the Putnam Royal stage is not only a place of public commemoration; it is also a "place of silence," as Eugenia C. DeLamotte has written about the experience of previous female protagonists in Marshall's fiction. The process of narrative "double exposure" (DeLamotte 5), of superimposing Hattie's unspoken private narrative upon her public testimony, transforms this silence into a mode of recognition, of rememory, of claiming a narrative voice that can express a collective consciousness of oppression. Specifically, the structural separation of her private narrative from the public narrative of Sonny-Rett's life accentuates the marginalization of women as well as the repression of homosexuality in jazz history. Hattie is not unlike Billie Holiday in that her public persona is informed by perceptions of her tragic persona and compensatory excesses more than her professional integrity. Her characterization invokes perceptions of Holiday as "the tragic, ever-suffering black woman singer" who is defined by her emotions rather than her craft, as Farah Griffin discusses in her book *In Search of Billie Holiday* (31).[14] This perception of her by characters who want to separate her life story from that of Sonny-Rett, most notably Edgar, is contradicted by the interior narrative of their lives together. Although it is not evident in the story Hattie tells at the Putnam Royal, it is her blues life that is the "base" for the jazz narrative that is the story of Sonny-Rett, Cherisse, and jazz in postwar Paris.

Hattie's authority as a narrator—and interpreter—of Sonny-Rett's jazz life is apparent in each scene that includes the jazz musicians who have played with him. Her role is initially prominent during the recollection of the breakthrough performance in which "Everett Payne" became known as "Sonny-Rett Payne." Like Sonny-Rett's performance of his signature tune, "Sonny Boy Blue," Hattie's narrative recollections of this event dramatically reinvent this moment each time it recurs in the novel. As she recalls, he first "played the song straight through as written" (*Fisher King* 136). After "paying his respects to the tune as written," however:

> He hunched closer to the piano, angled his head sharply to the left, completely turned the curtain of his gaze, and with his hands commanding the length and breadth of the keyboard he unleashed a dazzling pyrotechnic of chords (you could almost see their colors), polyrhythms, seemingly unrelated harmonies, and ideas—fresh, brash, outrageous ideas. It was an outpouring of ideas and feelings informed by his own brand of lyricism and lit from time to time by flashes of the recognizable melody. He continued to acknowledge the little simpleminded tune, while at the same time furiously recasting and reinventing it in an image all his own. (136–37)

This synaesthetic reenactment of Sonny-Rett's performance underscores both his respect for the song as it was written and his dramatic defamiliarization of its "simpleminded" structure. He begins with what is familiar, with "that hokey-doke tune" (136), and transforms it into a version that would ever be identified with "Sonny-Rett."

This virtuoso performance is not simply improvisatory; it is a "reinvention" of a tune that becomes as defiant as it is brilliant. The descriptive language for this process emphasizes the musician's individual genius, his "ideas" as much as his "feelings," but it also accentuates the dialogue between the song "as written" and the transformative performance, which is very much of the moment but has a lasting impact on not only the audience but on jazz history as well. What is new and original about this performance, however, is based on Sonny-Rett's deep engagement with seemingly incompatible musical traditions. The playing of his right hand evoked a "new kind of music: splintered, atonal, profane, and possessing a wonderful dissonance," but a new kind of music attuned to "the Upper Room among the stars Mahalia sang about." At the same time, his left hand "remained earthbound, trained on the bedrock that for him was Bach and the blues" (137). Through this "joyous, terrifying roller coaster of a ride" that reminds Hattie of the "Cyclone and the Hurricane at Coney Island" (138), Marshall enacts not only the dramatic intensity of jazz performance but also the improvisatory dynamic that makes this intensity possible. And it is of course this moment that also represents Hattie's most imaginative improvisation: the realization that she did not have to be separated from either Sonny-Rett or Cherisse, that she could indeed play "the base" in their triangular relationship, "joining them to herself" (141).

This is not the story Hattie can tell when she takes the stage of the Putnam Royal to tell the story of Sonny-Rett's life in Paris, though. This commemorative event, the culmination of the novel's plot of healing and renewal, begins and ends with Sonny-Rett's signature tune. Within this musical "celebration of the man and his art" (209), Hattie narrates his ascent to musical glory and ultimate descent to his death in Paris. The public narrative that Hattie performs recalls the rapid growth of his reputation after "that Sunday in '47," from "little hole-in-the-wall, bucket-o'-blood joints in Bed-Stuy" (182) to such renowned Manhattan clubs as "Monroe's and Minton's and Connie's uptown and the Royal Roost and the Spotlight downtown" (185). After cutting three albums in 1948, "Europe came calling" and Sonny-Rett never looked back. The story of Sonny-Rett's career in Europe that Hattie presents is triumphant, a story of "two decades of steady work" (189), of exhilarating travel, and of gratifying appreciation of his music by audiences across the continent. It is, however, eventually a story of disappointment and decline, a story that ends with his deadly descent into the Châtelet station of the Métro. It is a story as well of French nationalism and hostility toward foreigners, especially foreigners of African descent, a story not familiarly associated with narratives of African American artists who sought refuge in postwar Paris.

The narrative trajectory of Sonny-Rett's ascent and decline as a jazz musician represents a broader transformation of Paris from its postwar reputation as a refuge for African American exiles. As Tyler Stovall, Michel Fabre, and other cultural historians of African American Paris have written, black artists from the United States moved to Paris after World War II to escape if not protest the continuation of racist policy in the States.[15] Sonny-Rett's motives for emigrating are explicit: he sought "a place, a country, a continent where he could breathe and create without a lot of hassle" (185). The primary hassle he flees is his mother's disapproval of his music, but he also seeks a country free of everyday racial discrimination. If Paris became an African diasporic literary capital in the 1950s and a communal site of exile, particularly for African American writers, it also became an important alternative for jazz musicians who sought acceptance as artists as well as opportunity as professional entertainers. Jazz became more popular than ever in France after World War II, partly because it had become a "cultural symbol of antifascism" during the occupation (Stovall 134). African American exiles also became politically appealing to French intellectuals, as their resistance to U.S. racism corresponded with growing skepticism on the French left toward U.S. Cold War foreign policy. Jazz symbolized what was most despicable about the United States as well as what was most appealing, since blacks were viewed as both "victims of American brutality and heralds of the New World's choicest offerings" (136). This paradoxical position of U.S. blacks, especially black jazz musicians, is suggested by the narrative chronology of Sonny-Rett Payne, who arrives in France as Dizzy Gillespie and Charlie Parker make their first concert appearances in Paris.[16] By the mid-1960s there were fewer opportunities for black jazz musicians throughout Europe and particularly in France, partly because of state policy that mandated preferential treatment of French musicians, and partly because of the rise of other forms of popular music (such as rock-and-roll) that displaced jazz among younger listeners. This was not a new story, as Hattie quotes Langston Hughes to her Putnam Royal audience: "'You done taken my blues and gone'" (200). But the degree of hostility to presumed black foreigners was new, she suggests, as it was fueled by racist resentment of anticolonial revolts in Algeria and elsewhere in Africa and the ensuing migration of refugees to France. After several "down-spiraling" years of increasing despair (200), Sonny-Rett becomes a direct casualty of this police hostility toward suspected "illegals" when he falls down the Métro stairs after an altercation with police who ask him for his *Carte de résident*.

Hattie does not present the details of Sonny-Rett's death in the celebratory scene of commemoration at the Putnam Royal. She does not summarize the police report that she has read, which claims that when the police asked Sonny-Rett to present his *Carte de résident*, "he told them they could find it hanging above the entrance to a certain nightclub on rue Monge" (201). His "fall" is less circumstantial in her public presentation than it is the result of an artistic trajectory from triumphant success to tragic decline that nonetheless does not diminish the vitality of his musical creativity. We find out most of the details of Sonny-Rett's life in Paris not through Hattie's public performance, but through "a counterpoint of other memories that were not for the public's ear as she spoke" (183). This "counterpoint" of public and private narratives that comprises the two chapters of the commemorative concert underscores the discretion of Hattie's testimony, her desire to protect her memory of a past that might hurt her or compromise the memories of her lovers. But this counterpoint also accentuates the limitations of what she can say from her indefinable position in the private and public life of Sonny-Rett, as a lover outside of his marriage and as a woman outside the recognized realms of jazz testimony. Her intimate relationship with Cherisse is, of course, even more unmentionable and even more unrecognizable. As with the scene of sexual intimacy between Hattie and Sonny-Rett, Hattie's memory of loving Cherisse "as when they were girls practicing their kissing and touching upstairs at Mis'

Dawson's" (206) is presented directly but briefly. And the novel's suggestion that JoJo's sudden departure from home is precipitated by her discovery of Hattie's sexual intimacy with Cherisse suggests how transgressive this relationship is, although this causation is only suggested rather than definitively asserted, through a series of questions that Hattie asks herself (206).[17]

What is unspeakable about the private lives of the "threesome ménage"— Hattie, Sonny-Rett, and Cherisse—is also presented as peculiarly French, as untranslatable. For example, when Hattie describes Cherisse's acceptance of Sonny-Rett's sexual relationship with Hattie, she says, "'As for Cherisse, who's become more français than the Français, it's all in the family to her'" (192). Cherisse's acceptance of French "family" arrangements exemplifies her embrace of Paris as a site of freedom from restrictive social and cultural conventions, even as she dedicates herself to learning and following French conventions. When Cherisse has her baby in Paris, she celebrates her expatriate French home by naming her after "the two Josephines, La Baker and Napoleon's empress" (193), or "JoJo." And Cherisse becomes so immersed in the French language that she stops speaking English: "She would not be satisfied, she said, until her French was such she could pass for some well-educated Parisian-born second- or third-generation Francophone African, or an Antillaise from Martinique or Guadaloupe" (195). The terrible irony, of course, is that Sonny-Rett dies because "*les flics*" do not distinguish him from a Francophone African or an Antillaise and ask him for his *Carte de resident*. An even more terrible irony is that shortly after her mother's death, JoJo runs off with a Francophone African, a young "*sans papier*" from Cameroon, who is deported soon after JoJo gives birth to his baby, leaves the baby with Hattie, and flees, presumably to Marseilles or Toulon. That baby, of course, is Sonny, soon to be displaced from the city his "fathermothersisterbrother" Hattie called home, even if her "scrambled, make-do French" was "terrible" (16).

With the narrative—and musical—framework of the commemoration of Sonny-Rett Payne, Hattie narrates a complexly intersecting set of African diasporic narratives. The interplay of public performance and private reflection reinforces the dramatic tension between the middle-class respectability, indeed the upwardly mobile success story, represented by Edgar, and the bohemian rebelliousness of his brother, Cherisse, and Hattie. It also dramatizes the struggle for Sonny's custody between Hattie and Edgar, who, as we find out in the final chapter, knows more about Hattie's life than she had thought and is willing to fight her in court for the custody of Sonny. Hattie's life story is a tragic tale of downward mobility, of almost desperate poverty as she raises Sonny, but also of perseverance and fierce love for her boy and the legacy that he embodies. Like her narration of Sonny-Rett's practice as a musician, her life story, indeed her character, is one of improvisation and creative adaptation, of continuous reinvention of self, family, and community from the most challenging situations. It is also a story that hinges on the French word that itself evokes both a communal ideal and its dissolution: "*partager*"—"to share," as Cherisse says to Hattie in Paris, but also to "divide." As the novel concludes, Sonny's future, and indeed the African diasporic future that he represents, is left suspended between irreconcilable interpretations of what "*partager*" signifies.

Narrating the ascent and decline of a black jazz musician, who leaves New York to find temporary fulfillment in Paris, *The Fisher King* complexly rewrites previous narratives of African American and West Indian migration as it rewrites the mythic tale of regeneration that structures the book. The story of African American expatriates in Paris has long challenged the American myth of immigrant upward mobility in that it represents the experience of those who *left* the country, crossing the ocean to Europe to find freedom and opportunity. However, as the precipitous fall of Sonny-Rett dramatizes, the idea of an expatriate refuge from racist "hassle" (185) changes with the French war with Algeria in the 1960s: Paris was no longer a refuge from racism, not only because of growing awareness of French colonial policy but also because of French hostility toward immigrant workers. In subtly interweaving narratives of African American and Caribbean migration with mythic narratives of African American expatriation and jazz history, and in locating her novel in late twentieth-century Brooklyn, a contested site of economic development *and* displacement, Marshall, like the pianist Sonny-Rett, creates "a new kind of music: splintered, atonal, profane, and possessing a wonderful dissonance," a music of utopian desire that is, at the same time, "earthbound," in its expression of the "hard, pure lyricism of the blues" (137).

The Fisher King accentuates what is implicit in the Afro-modernist jazz writing I have discussed throughout *Jazz Internationalism*: the correlation of jazz improvisation with improvisatory social practices. Marshall's fiction enacts what current critical improvisation theory asserts: the association of musical improvisation with "transgressive, critical, radical, and aesthetic practices in relation to the communities it engages" (Fischlin and Heble 12–13). This association of jazz improvisation with new social and cultural formations has a long history, from the group improvisation of New Orleans jazz to that of free jazz. And there is an equally long history of misconceptions about jazz improvisation, whether improvisation is idealized or dismissed as an African American musical practice, "Bolshevik" or otherwise. Ingrid Monson has written that improvisation is not "inherently moral, ethical, progressive, rebellious, or visionary" (*Freedom Sounds* 317), despite the activism of jazz musicians within the African American civil rights movement and black liberation movements worldwide. As theorists of jazz improvisation such as Monson have noted, improvisation is too often equated with freedom and spontaneity, even though the process of improvising has always involved an active engagement with traditional musical and cultural practices. The musician and musicologist George Lewis, for example, differentiates "Afrological" from "Eurological" understandings of improvisation, underscoring how Afrological improvisers assume that freedom can be achieved only through "discipline, defined as technical knowledge of music theory and of one's instrument as well as through attention to the background, history, and culture of one's music" ("Improvised Music" 153).

For the bebop musicians whose jazz innovations became most identified with Afro-modernism, improvisation was a means for asserting their self-determination as black musical artists. At the same time, bebop and subsequent jazz improvisation also became a means for "code-switching across traditions and genres," for enacting "exchanges across borders of language and musical culture" (Lewis, "Afterword" 165). Such improvisatory movement among musical traditions and cultures is also implicit in Graham Lock's temporal figuration of improvisation in *Blutopia*. He writes that African American improvisatory music is characterized by two impulses: "a utopian impulse, evident in the creation of imagined places (Promised Lands), and the impulse to remember, to bear witness" (2). As antithetical as these impulses seem—the utopian is associated with "space, the future, the sacred, and the spirituals," while memory is associated with "time, the past, the secular, and the blues"—Lock's account of improvisation also suggests how "visions of the future and revisions of the past become part of the same process" (2) in Afro-modernist jazz literature as well as music. While the concept of improvisation is notoriously difficult to apply to the more static medium of literature, the cultural and temporal implications of critical improvisation theory are similarly relevant. Recent jazz novels such as *The Fisher King* invoke earlier Afro-modernist novels such as *Banjo* and *The Street*, whether formally or thematically, implicitly or explicitly, as much as they allude to the performance practices of jazz. And because the formal conventions of jazz poetry are more codified than those of jazz fiction, intertextual allusions to earlier poetry by writers such as Hughes, Davis, or Kaufman are even more evident in recent jazz poetry. Like the history of jazz, the history of African American jazz writing is extensive and familiar enough that literary enactments of jazz performance recall this textual past as they project their visions of the future.

While *Jazz Internationalism* suggests a literary history of radical Afro-modernist jazz writing that coincides with the long civil rights movement, I am reluctant to generalize about the cultural politics of jazz suggested by these writings. As much as they assert a radical black internationalist understanding of jazz history, the cultural and political circumstances that inform the texts that I have emphasized are too specific, with their musical references as well as the cultural differences that they negotiate, to support comprehensive conclusions. Jazz historian Scott DeVeaux has made similar claims about "the jazz tradition," arguing that generalizations about the "tradition" are inherently reductive and therefore problematic:

> The narratives we have inherited to describe the history of jazz retain the patterns of outmoded thought, especially the assumption that the progress of jazz as art necessitates increased distance from the popular. . . . But the time has come for an approach that is less invested in the ideology of jazz as aesthetic object and more responsive to issues of historical particularity. Only in this way can the study of jazz break free from its self-imposed isolation, and participate with other disciplines in the exploration of meaning in American culture. ("Constructing" 553)

The twentieth-century narratives of jazz history that DeVeaux critiques have varied in their emphasis on the constitutive characteristics of "the jazz tradition," identifying jazz socially with African American cultural practices, economically with its presumed anti-commercialist ethos, or politically as an oppositional discourse. What constructs of "the jazz tradition" have shared, however, is an organic conceptualization of jazz that stresses its "universality and autonomy," a conceptualization that encompasses otherwise varied musical styles and practices within a transhistorical continuum (530). Since the 1991 publication of DeVeaux's "Constructing the Jazz Tradition," the new jazz studies have succeeded in complicating what jazz is and has been, through interdisciplinary practices that have been increasingly "responsive to historical particularity," including DeVeaux's exemplary social and musical history of bebop, *The Birth of Bebop* (1997). Perhaps most notable among these interdisciplinary practices of jazz studies has been an increasing emphasis on transnational and diasporic approaches to jazz, which have enhanced our understanding of the history and cultural politics of jazz. The jazz literary "tradition" has likewise been expanded and challenged by interdisciplinary approaches to the cultural and intercultural politics of jazz in recent years, including the black internationalist approaches that I have emphasized in this book.

From the New Negro Renaissance beyond Harlem to the Bedford-Stuyvesant Renaissance, this book has explored the internationalist dynamic of African diasporic cultural practices that have informed jazz as well as Afro-modernist jazz literature, which would also include more recent writers such as Amiri Baraka, Jayne Cortez, and Nathanael Mackey. In addressing the cultural politics of jazz that have informed Afro-modernist literature, I too have emphasized "issues of historical particularity" as much as the broader importance of "jazz internationalism" for the long civil rights movement. At the same time, the question that Langston Hughes asked in his essay "The Roots of Jazz" is no less relevant than it was over a half a century ago:

> The lacy gaiety of ragtime, the rolling rumble of boogie woogie, the happy dignity of Dixieland bands playing for funerals, parades, dances, picnics, to the swing of swing, the satire of bebop, the heavy beat of rock-and-roll, and the cool sounds of a Charlie Mingus, there is in all this music something of the question, "How long, how long before men and women, races and nations, will learn to live together happily?" (371)[18]

Adapting the lyrics of the classic blues song "How Long Has That Evening Train Been Gone?" to an international stage, Hughes underscores both the pleasure of jazz and its reminder of the experience of collective trauma, its "spontaneous improvisations, its syncopations, its infectious rhythms," and its roots in "men and drums stolen from Africa, songs and drums held in the harshness of a new world, rhythms tangled in the tall cane" (371). This mix of joy and sadness that Hughes attributes to jazz testifies to the African American experience of "sorrow and suffering" as well as to the power of African diasporic music to resist white supremacist nihilism.

The utopian impulse that Hughes attributes to jazz, its ability to foster a hopeful response to the question he asks about "men and women, races and nations," is inseparable from the blues echoed in that question, the memory of an African and African diasporic past that also emerges through jazz. It is no coincidence that Hughes names Mingus as the contemporary figure who represents the history of jazz. Not only was he a provocative collaborator with Hughes in their jazz poetry performances, but he was also a jazz musician whose compositions and improvisations exemplified the continuity and dialogue of African diasporic musical forms that Hughes notes, including, of course, the blues. He was also a jazz musician whose songs would become overtly identified with the black liberation struggle, historically and contemporaneously, from "Haitian Fight Song" to "Fables of Faustus." While seeming to invoke "the jazz tradition" as an organic continuum, Hughes underscores the "issues of historical particularity" that have informed African diasporic music through his reference to Mingus. It is not surprising that the most famous "travelin' man" of jazz writing would emphasize the routes as well as the roots of African diasporic music. Less well known, however, are the international routes of jazz that inform the Afro-modernist writing of McKay, Davis, Petry, Kaufman, and Marshall. If the question of "how long before men and women, races and nations, will learn to live together happily" remains urgent in the twenty-first century, the translations of jazz by these black internationalist writers remain important for imagining new ways "to live together" while reminding us of the African diasporic sites of struggle that they so powerfully commemorate.

Notes

Introduction

1. Europe's affection for Russian music also suggests what Kate Baldwin defines as the "historical affiliation between the Russian peasant and the American black as involuntarily indentured servants who were emancipated from servitude at roughly contemporaneous moments" (1). Europe's most popular adaptation of Russian music, however—his syncopated version of Sergei Rachmaninoff's "Prelude in C Minor," "The Russian Rag"—proved that modern Russian music also could be transformed into jazz.

2. See Welburn on Europe's importance for early jazz criticism.

3. See McCann 23–38 for a detailed reading of the cultural politics of jazz in "The Jazz Baby." For representative early 1920s moralist and musicological critiques of jazz, see, respectively, Faulkner and "The Jazz Problem." See Ogren for a more comprehensive account of the reception of jazz in the United States during the 1920s.

4. Bolshevism was a popular cultural obsession in the United States in the wake of the 1919 "Red Scare," and because jazz became a mass cultural phenomenon concurrently with the formation of the Soviet Union, it is not surprising that jazz would be associated with communism by its critics. Holder discusses the preoccupation with Bolshevism in late 1910s and early 1920s U.S. popular culture, particularly in ragtime.

5. I use the term "New Negro Renaissance" to describe the New Negro movement in more inclusive geographical, chronological, and political terms than "Harlem Renaissance" usually indicates. I will refer to the "Harlem Renaissance," however, when referring to "Harlem Renaissance" scholarship or other specific references to the New Negro movement in Harlem.

6. In addition to the scholarship that I discuss specifically in this chapter, my approach to jazz and Afro-modernist literature has been influenced especially by research on African American poetry by Meta DuEwa Jones, Nielsen, Sanders,

Smethurst, and Thomas. These studies stand out for their combination of precise formal analysis and historically informed cultural studies. While there are fewer comparative studies of Afro-modernist jazz narratives, the books by Grandt and Werner are notable for their lucid attention to the formal enactment of jazz in African American fiction.

7. Jackson adapts the term "indignant" from Ralph Ellison's characterization of the "indignant consciousness" of Bigger Thomas, the protagonist of Richard Wright's *Native Son* (Jackson 3). Jackson's periodization of "the indignant generation," 1934–1960, is less capacious than the "long civil rights movement," but it likewise underscores the sustained impact of radical black internationalism that informs *Jazz Internationalism*, from McKay to Marshall.

8. See, for example, the outstanding studies of black feminist internationalism by Higashida and McDuffie.

9. See especially the interdisciplinary collections that emerged through the Jazz Study Group at Columbia University: O'Meally, *Jazz Cadence* and O'Meally et al, *Uptown Conversation*. Other collections of new jazz scholarship that have approached jazz through cultural studies include the earlier volumes edited by Krin Gabbard, *Jazz among the Discourses* and *Representing Jazz*; the important collection of gender studies and jazz edited by Rustin and Tucker; and the two volumes on jazz and the African American arts edited by Lock and Murray.

10. My working definition of "jazz literature" includes any literary text that is informed by jazz music, formally or thematically. There has been substantial critical attention to jazz poetry, as the formal elements of poetry are more adaptable for enacting jazz performance. See Feinstein, *Jazz Poetry* for the most thorough history of Anglophone jazz poetry. There is less of a consensus about the generic expectations for "jazz fiction," although there is considerable scholarship on the representation of jazz in American and specifically African American fiction. For informative comparative studies of African American jazz narratives see Cataliotti, Jimoh, Gayl Jones, and Omry. For bibliographic accounts of the wide range of fictional narratives about jazz, see Albert and Rife.

11. As an Afro-modern mode of expression, jazz combines elements of Western and African music and performance. As a music that invokes the musical practices from which it evolved, practices that developed during slavery in the New World, jazz can also be considered a mode of historical recovery, as can the historiography and literature of jazz. More specifically, jazz enacts through its performance what Hanchard calls "time appropriation." As a response to the inequalities of temporality that constitute "racial time," such as the experience of waiting for basic services as well as civil rights, time appropriation is a form of "seizing another's time and making it one's own" (266). Jazz can be figured as symbolic time appropriation, as a musical mode of asserting a new temporality, "wherein new values, freedoms, and forms of expression are operative" (266). In jazz discourse, such time appropriation can be associated with the feature most often cited to distinguish it from Western classical music practice: improvisation, the performative practice of composing in

the moment. Whether perceived intrinsically by jazz musicians or extrinsically by jazz critics, the perception of jazz as Afro-modern music has often focused on the correlation of its improvised temporality with its assertion of social and political change for people of African descent. See Barnhart 6–7 on the implications of "time appropriation" for early jazz.

12. Baker's *Modernism and the Harlem Renaissance* (1987) initiated questions about modernism and African American literature that continue to reverberate. His provocative study addressed what were then dominant academic assumptions about the Harlem Renaissance: (1) that its literature was insufficiently modern and was thus peripheral to modernism, and (2) that it also failed as an African American cultural movement with its disintegration in the 1930s. In reconsidering the modernism of the Renaissance, Baker underscores "*modern Afro-American* sound as a function of a specifically Afro-American discursive practice" (xiv). Baker's argument for the lasting discursive practices that he identifies with the New Negro Renaissance—"the mastery of form" and "the deformation of mastery"—has remained important for several reasons: he extends the historical scope of the New Negro Renaissance to underscore its continuity with the late nineteenth century and the 1930s and later twentieth century; he does so through attention to the modernity of African American sounding, especially vernacular sounding; and he suggests an intertextual dynamic to African American literary history that is explicitly comparable to the history of African American music, what Amiri Baraka called "the changing same" (Baker 15). Scholarship following Baker's inquiry that discusses the literary and cultural significance of jazz in the Harlem Renaissance includes Paul Allen Anderson; Evans; Floyd, *Black Music*; and Ogren.

13. For a brief but thorough introduction to the international dimensions of "the New Negro," see Davarian L. Baldwin, "Introduction: New Negroes Forging a New World."

14. See Gates, "Trope of a New Negro," on the "New Negro" before the New Negro Renaissance.

15. Gilroy adapts his idea of a "counterculture of modernity" from Zygmunt Bauman's discussion of the Western left in "The Left as the Counterculture of Modernity."

16. See especially Maxwell's comprehensive account of communism (and suspected communism) and African American writing in *F. B. Eyes*.

17. For astute African Americanist literary and cultural studies of Marxist black internationalism in the early twentieth century, see Foley; Kelley, *Freedom Dreams* and *Race Rebels*; Maxwell, *New Negro*; Robinson; and Smethurst, *New Red Negro*. Important historical scholarship on communism and African Americans during this period includes Kelley, *Hammer and Hoe*; Naison; and Solomon. For the impact of Marxism on early twentieth-century Caribbean formulations of black internationalism, see James, *Holding Aloft*, and Stephens, *Black Empire*. Directly addressing Gilroy's black Atlantic paradigm, Stephens foregrounds the impact of Marxist formulations of black internationalism on Caribbean male intellectuals' attempt "to imagine a transnational form of black nationality that could both transcend nationalism and

reimagine the state itself" (4). As she examines the examples of Marcus Garvey, Claude McKay, and C.L.R. James especially, she emphasizes how the "colonial mentality" of Caribbeans limited national identifications and how the experience of living in Harlem informed their "internationalist black imaginary" and, more specifically, the idea of "the race as a multinational diaspora *within* the nation" (49).

18. For a compelling collection of approaches to the "New Negro Renaissance beyond Harlem," see Baldwin and Makalani.

19. See Ellison, *Collected Essays*; Murray, *Stomping the Blues*; Baraka, *Blues People*; Floyd, *Power of Black Music*; and Small, *Music of the Common Tongue*.

20. See Porter 35–39 for an incisive synopsis of Ellington's musical status in the 1920s.

21. See, for example, the accounts of 1930s swing in Denning, Erenberg, and Stowe.

22. A good example of how bebop has been conceptualized as a militant subculture is Lott, "Double V, Double Time." Jazz historians who have elucidated the culture and cultural implications of bebop at greater length include DeVeaux, Gendron, Ramsey, and Stowe.

23. For more extensive historical inquiry into the civil rights movement and U.S. Cold War foreign policy, see Borstelman, Dudziak, Meriwether, and Plummer.

Chapter 1. "Harlem Jazzing"

1. Among *Home to Harlem*'s initial reviews, there is the occasional mention of "Raymond, a Haytian chap who worked on the same dining car with Jake" (Bennett 6), or even of "the interesting Haytian, Raymond" (Brickell 151), but most reviews relegate his character to a minor status, if they mention him at all. Even a review titled "The Negro in King Christophe's Haiti, in Sir M. Garvey's Harlem, in Sunday School and at Large" (by Robert Cortes Holliday), which reviews *Home to Harlem* (mistitled "Back to Harlem") with John W. Vandercook's biography of the Haitian King Christophe, responds only to McKay's depiction of Harlem, ignoring Ray's narrative altogether. While Du Bois questioned the political impact of a novel that seemed to reinforce racist social prejudice, other readers, particularly younger African American artists, praised McKay's vivid depiction of the working-class "semi-underworld" of Harlem, agreeing with Langston Hughes that McKay's novel would become "the flower of the Negro Renaissance, even if it is no lovely lily" (Hughes, March 1, 1928, letter to Alain Locke, qtd. in Tillery 88). The most sympathetic reviewers of *Home to Harlem* praised its realist depiction of working-class Harlem, including Harlem nightlife. And while there was minimal attention to jazz performance in the book's initial reception, notable reviews characterized the novel's episodic structure in musical terms. Bennett, for example, calls *Home to Harlem* a "symphonic tone poem of dark brown workers" (6). Brickell argues that McKay's representation of Harlem is "a satire on civilization as we imagine it should be, a modern symphony scored for saxophones and snare-drums which were once tom-toms" (151). Both Cooper (84–87) and Tillery (87–106) discuss the significance of *Home to Harlem*'s polarized reception. For an annotated bibliography of reviews of *Home to Harlem*, see Bassett 90–95.

2. Critics who have examined *Home to Harlem* in relation to McKay's subsequent fiction have been more likely to foreground Ray's intellectual development, especially given the correspondence of his ideas about writing with McKay's. See, for example, Cooper, Giles, and Tillery, each of whom traces McKay's development as a fiction writer. None of these critics pays much attention to the political significance of Ray's Haitian national origins, however. Most recent studies of McKay's fiction with black internationalist or transnationalist studies have noted the implications of Ray's nationality. See especially Edwards, *Practice of Diaspora*; Holcomb; and Stephens, *Black Empire*.

3. Brennan argues for an understanding of New World African music as a critique of modernity and especially of U.S. "imperial ambition and a salvational sense of religious mission" (2). Emphasizing how early jazz developed through the interaction of New World African musical practices, he also notes that U.S. imperialist ventures in Cuba, Puerto Rico, and Haiti contributed to the musical hybridity of jazz. In addition to McKay, he cites Du Bois and Hughes as important figures who understood the interrelatedness of Caribbean, Latin American, and African American music (224).

4. Even studies of the Harlem Renaissance that accentuate McKay's Jamaican origins tend to situate *Home to Harlem* within a specifically African American national framework. David Levering Lewis's *When Harlem Was in Vogue* is a good example. In introducing McKay, he writes that "the racial burden afflicting McKay was of the cruelest duality—of being in but not of two cultures" (51). His discussion of *Home to Harlem*, however, concentrates not on the novel's cross-cultural dimensions but on its controversial resemblance to *Nigger Heaven* (224–28). An interesting exception to this pattern of reception comes from De Jongh, who examines how McKay's novel relates Harlem to other mythic "Afro-New World landscapes," particularly Haiti (26–32). For critics more interested in how Caribbean migration complicates African American nationalist paradigms, McKay's writing resonates more cross-culturally. See, especially, Hathaway, who emphasizes the African Caribbean (im)migration experience of "cultural dislocation" in McKay's writing. Both Edwards and Stephens address how identification of the New Negro Renaissance with the United States, and Harlem specifically, has limited the historical significance of interwar black internationalism. See Edwards's prologue to *The Practice of Diaspora* and Stephens's introduction to *Black Empire*.

5. De Barros explains how McKay's representation of jazz invokes the ideologies of Africanism, Freudianism, and Marxism. Lutz lucidly relates jazz and primitivism to the cosmopolitanism of McKay's fiction. Edwards also articulates the significance of jazz for imagining a "black transnational community" in *Banjo* (*Practice of Diaspora* 217–25). McKay's staging of jazz performance in *Home to Harlem* has also figured prominently in queer studies of Harlem cabaret culture; see, e.g., Holcomb 91–138 and Vogel 132–66.

6. See Baldwin, *Beyond the Color Line*; Edwards, *Practice of Diaspora*; Holcomb, *Claude McKay*; Maxwell, *New Negro* and "Claude McKay"; and Stephens, *Black Em-*

pire. Scholars who have emphasized McKay's early writing, in Jamaica as well as the United States, have likewise transformed his literary reputation. See especially James, *Fierce Hatred*, and Gosciak, *Shadowed Country*. For an excellent critical review of recent scholarship on McKay and black radicalism, see Smethurst, "The Red Is East."

7. Perhaps the most acclaimed book on music and the Harlem Renaissance, Paul Allen Anderson's *Deep River*, is a good example of such neglect. Ogren recognizes the importance of jazz performance in *Home to Harlem* in her important study of 1920s jazz, *Jazz Revolution* (126–28).

8. See Cooper 98–99 and Tillery 85–86.

9. For discussion of McKay's impact on Francophone black writers, see Cooper 214–16; 258–59; Fabre 92–113; and Kesteloot 56–74.

10. The intellectuals whom Gilroy studies most intensively are W.E.B. Du Bois and Richard Wright. While he mentions McKay only briefly, his formulation of the black Atlantic as a "counterculture of modernity" suggests how the reception of a writer like McKay is limited, if not distorted, by nationalist conceptual fields.

11. See Hutchinson, *Harlem Renaissance*; Douglas, *Terrible Honesty*; North, *Dialect of Modernism*; and Denning, *Cultural Front*.

12. The best-known argument of this period for a transnational model of cultural pluralism is Bourne's 1916 essay, "Trans-National America." Stephens relates Bourne's argument to early twentieth-century Caribbean black transnationalism as well as to current formulations of transnationalism in "Black Transnationalism."

13. See Hutchinson 387–433 for a lucid overview of the production and reception of *The New Negro*. The limits of the anthology's openness to radical social criticism are perhaps best exemplified by Locke's decision to change the title of McKay's poem "The White House" to the politically safer "White Houses." For McKay's angry response to this decision and his criticism of the anthology more generally, see his autobiography, *A Long Way from Home* (313–14, 321–22).

14. Johnson's mother was from Nassau, the Bahamas, while his father was an African American from Virginia. They spent the first eight years of their marriage in Nassau. For an overview of important African American cultural and political figures with Caribbean roots, see James, *Holding Aloft* 292–93, note 3.

15. Domingo's essay in Locke's *New Negro*, "Gift of the Black Tropics," makes the most specific case for the impact of Caribbean immigrants on Harlem society. Like New York City more generally, Harlem differed from other American cities with large black populations precisely because of its percentage of immigrants; about 25 percent of Harlem was foreign-born in the 1920s (Osofsky 131). Of course, as Domingo points out, Caribbean immigrants represented a plurality of cultures themselves, even though "to the average American Negro, all English-speaking black foreigners are West Indians, and by that is usually meant British subjects" (343). In contrast with such assumptions, Domingo stresses the cultural plurality of these "colored people of Spanish, French, Dutch, Arabian, Danish, Portuguese, British and native African ancestry," who "for the first time in their lives . . . meet and move together" (341). While American ignorance of cultural differences among Caribbean immigrants

intensified their identifications with their islands of origin, their common experience of migration was crucial for the development of a Pan-African consciousness among Harlem intellectuals. See James, *Holding Aloft*, for a lucid explanation of Caribbean leadership roles in radical international political organizations (such as the Universal Negro Improvement Association, the African Blood Brotherhood, and the Communist and Socialist parties). On early twentieth-century Caribbean migration to Harlem, see also Kasinitz 41–52; McKay, *Harlem* 132–35; Osofsky 131–35; and Reid.

16. Vogel's identification of McKay with the "Cabaret School" of Harlem Renaissance writers is important for considering how subjectivities are improvised to the syncopated sounds of jazz in *Home to Harlem*. Explaining how Cabaret School writers such as Hughes, Van Vechten, Hurston, Fisher, and Thurman rejected notions of racial uplift and sexual respectability associated with the Harlem Renaissance literary establishment, Vogel articulates how the "queer possibilities of Harlem's nightlife" were "not rooted in the regenerative essentialism of primitivism but in the productive force of performance and the creation of public intimacy" (16). As he writes, the cabaret in *Home to Harlem* is a site for cultivating "nonnormative intimacies" as well as the potential for "interclass solidarity" between "the working class and a criminal and sexually deviant underclass" (135). Vogel suggestively accentuates the "utopian potential" of the cabaret in *Home to Harlem*, but the cabaret is also a site of sexual conflict and of alienated labor in McKay's writing. See Marsh 169–74 for a cogent critique of Vogel's argument.

17. In her incisive study of representations of urban black migrant women in the 1920s, Carby notes that Felice becomes the object of Jake's narrative quest precisely because she returns his money for sex. Through this narrative "sleight-of-hand" Felice is transformed from a prostitute into the less-threatening "figure of wholesome sexuality" in Jake's representative journey of "black masculinity in formation" (749).

18. Ray's outsider status is accentuated further by his (understanding of) sexuality. When Jake meets him, he is reading a story by Alphonse Daudet about a woman named "Sapho." Their subsequent comic exchange about lesbians—"bulldykers," according to Jake (129)—reveals how their class differences affect their understanding of gender differences. Ray's character is feminized by his Pullman peers because he is both an intellectual and a French-speaking Haitian. While the homoeroticism of his friendship with Jake has received little attention in studies of McKay's fiction, the link between nationality and sexuality becomes more dramatically evident when they are reunited in *Banjo*. Upon seeing each other unexpectedly in France, they immediately embrace and kiss each other. Jake says, "'The fust time I evah French-kiss a he, chappie, but Ise so tearing mad and glad and crazy to meet you thisaway again.'" Ray responds, "'That's all right, Jakie, he-men and all. Stay long enough in any country and you'll get on to the ways and find them natural'" (292). Cooper discusses McKay's homosexuality in *Claude McKay* (esp. 29–32, 75, 149–51). On the significance of gay male subcultures in the Harlem Renaissance, see Chauncey 244–67 and Schwarz.

19. For a concise critical review of African American responses to the occupation, see Dash 45–60; Plummer, "Afro-American Response"; and Renda 261–300.

20. The best-known proletarian novels that treat Haiti's revolutionary past would be Arna Bontemps's *Drums at Dusk* (1939) and Guy Endore's *Babouk* (1934). Citing a wide range of African American texts on Haiti's revolutionary history, Denning relates this renewed interest to Popular Front cultural politics in *The Cultural Front* (396–97). See, also, Renda's overview of 1930s cultural work on Haiti (276–81). Her introduction to *Taking Haiti* is a cogent synopsis of U.S. attitudes toward Haiti during the occupation.

21. On the military conflict in Haiti and its political aftermath in the United States, see Schmidt 82–107. While the exact number of Haitians killed was not known, according to Gen. George Barnett, commandant of the Marine Corps from 1914 to 1920, only "14 or 16" marines died (Schmidt 103).

22. The most dramatic example of Du Bois's criticism of American policy in Haiti is his April 1920 editorial in *The Crisis*, in which he writes that the "greatest single question before the parties at the next election is the Freedom of Haiti" (297–98).

23. Dash assesses McKay's characterization of Ray only briefly but critically. According to Dash, McKay's Haiti conforms to the prevalent stereotype of an "aboriginal and pre-industrial paradise." He writes, "Perhaps the most famous Haitian protagonist in black American literature is McKay's Ray, portrayed as that whining, repressed Haitian mulatto who is a misfit because he does not have the courage to 'go and lose (himself) in some savage culture in the jungles of Africa.' Ray's heritage is an atavistic longing for the perverse and the carnal which his Westernization never permits him to fulfill" (55).

24. For a concise but cogent analysis of Ray's inability to represent Jake's speech in writing, see North 116–22.

25. As Smethurst notes in *African American Roots*, the travels of Banjo and Ray each represent "a diasporic arc that is global in reach and not simply transatlantic" (208). Smethurst discusses the significance of these trajectories, which disrupt expectations of the more familiar transatlantic geography of African American and Caribbean literature, in *African American Roots* 206–209.

26. As Maxwell has documented, McKay's journey to Europe was itself "something of a compulsory black Atlanticism" ("Banjo Meets the Dark Princess" 174), as he was officially denied return to the United States and the British colonies after his stay in the Soviet Union. On McKay's exile from the United States in the 1920s, see Maxwell, "Banjo"; "Claude McKay"; "F. B. Eyes"; and *F. B. Eyes*. See, also, Gosciak, "Most Wanted."

Chapter 2. "Black Man's Verse"

1. Cataliotti cogently explains the significance of jazz during the Black Chicago Renaissance in "African American Music." The writers he cites who represent jazz performance include Margaret Walker, Gwendolyn Brooks, and Frank London Brown, as well as Davis. On the historical development of early jazz in Chicago, see Kenney.

2. Hine, Introduction xxvi. In addition to this collection of essays, recent considerations of the literary Black Chicago Renaissance include Bone and Courage; Miller,

On the Ruins of Modernity; Mullen, *Popular Fronts*; and Tracy, *Writers of the Black Chicago Renaissance*. Additional important historical studies of Chicago's emergence as a modern black cultural center include Davarian L. Baldwin, *Chicago's New Negroes*; Green; Knupfer; and Schlabach.

3. Most discussions of Davis within the context of the Black Chicago Renaissance emphasize the social realism of his poetry. See, for example, Bone and Courage 208–11; Lawrence Jackson 101–2; and James D. Young 188–93. Morgan (184–205) makes an especially compelling case for the political significance of Davis's realist poetics. The most detailed considerations of the full range of Davis's poetry, including his jazz poetry, can be found in Smethurst, *New Red Negro*, especially 135–41; Takara, *Frank Marshall Davis: The Fire and the Phoenix* and "Frank Marshall Davis: A Forgotten Voice in the Chicago Black Renaissance"; and Tidwell, "'I Was a Weaver of Jagged Words'" and Introduction to Davis, *Black Moods*.

4. Feinstein mentions Davis as one of several poets who wrote jazz poems in the 1930s and '40s (62). He also suggests, somewhat apologetically, that Davis deserves greater recognition than he has received: "Although his influence cannot be compared to the careers of Langston Hughes and Sterling Brown, he may very well deserve more attention than I have offered in this book" (81, note 2). Davis's poetry is also not included in the first volume of *The Jazz Poetry Anthology*, edited by Feinstein and Yusef Komunyakaa, but "Jazz Band" is included in *The Second Set*.

5. Davis underscores the impact of *Others: A Magazine of the New Verse* on his early development as a poet in his 1985 interview with Tidwell. When asked about his first experience writing poetry, Davis notes that he was "influenced by a magazine called *Others* which featured the new revolutionary style called free verse." He goes on to say that this magazine "walloped me almost as hard as hearing my first jazz and blues some years earlier. I felt immediate kinship with this new poetry and felt I could write something in a similar vein" (105). Davis here reiterates the correlation of modernist free verse with early jazz that he attributes to his own poetry in the 1930s and afterward. It is interesting, though, that he would identify so intensely with a New York little magazine that featured modernist writers such as Mina Loy, William Carlos Williams, and Marianne Moore, whose experimentation was influenced more by European avant-garde movements in the visual arts than by jazz or the blues. The only African American poet published in *Others* was Fenton Johnson. The influence of *Others* on subsequent African American poetry such as Davis's suggests an area of modernist studies that has not been sufficiently explored. For interesting considerations of Johnson and his involvement with *Others*, see Thomas, *Extraordinary Measures* 11–44 and Smethurst, *African American Roots* 134–46. See Churchill for the most comprehensive account of *Others* and its importance for modern poetry.

6. For an incisive account of how Davis's self-fashioning in his autobiographical narratives represents alternatives to Black Arts autobiographies of the 1960s and '70s, see Tidwell, "Alternative Constructions."

7. As much as Davis insists on the retention of African cultural practices in African America, he does not romanticize his African roots. In one scene of *Livin' the Blues*,

he comically underscores the irony of identifying African Americans with Africa. He recollects that when Decca Records collaborated with Black Patti Records to "organize a group of native Africans to record sounds of the bush," Davis was asked to participate as one of the "'native Africans'" (118). After extensive rehearsals, Black Patti Records went bankrupt, thus canceling the opportunity to record. As Davis notes with his characteristic humor, "Thus was America deprived of a chance to hear rare and authentic music of the Dark Continent from the throats of assorted Chicagoans" (119).

8. See Gennari, *Blowin' Hot and Cool* (94–99), and "'A Weapon'" on the cultural politics of the United Hot Clubs, which were comprised primarily of white male jazz enthusiasts. According to Gennari, Davis was the only black member of the Hot Club of Chicago ("'A Weapon'" 24). Davis discusses his role with the Hot Club in *Livin' the Blues* (285–86), noting his disappointment that the Hot Club concerts generated little enthusiasm among black South Siders.

9. Locke actually relates Davis's poetry to that of "Willard Wright" in this review essay (10), but he explained in a later issue of *Opportunity* that he meant "Richard Wright" (Tidwell, Introduction to *Black Moods* lix, note 1).

10. The most notorious example of Locke's editorial decision to exclude potentially controversial poetry from *The Survey Graphic* special Harlem edition and later *The New Negro* was the change he made to the title of Claude McKay's "The White House." Without asking for McKay's approval, he published the poem as "White Houses."

11. Tidwell asserts that "the actual reason for his departure for Hawaii is rooted in his capitulation to the government pressure of McCarthyism" (Introduction to *Black Moods* xxx). As Davis notes, however, he was encouraged by his friend Paul Robeson's experience in Hawaii not only to move there but also to become politically active with the labor movement in Honolulu (*Livin' the Blues* 311). Hawaii also offered a degree of tolerance of his interracial marriage that was impossible in the mainland United States. The most thorough account of Davis's life in Hawaii, aside from his memoirs, can be found in Takara, *The Fire*. See especially 136–65.

12. See *Livin' the Blues* 327–33. Most of the manuscript of Davis's memoirs of "the Jungle," titled "That Incredible Waikiki Jungle," no longer exists. Tidwell includes a brief excerpt from an extant chapter of the manuscript as an appendix to *Livin' the Blues*.

13. These poems were subsequently combined with jazz poems that Davis wrote in the 1930s—"Jazz Band," "Cabaret," and "Dancing Gal"—and published in a 1977 chapbook titled *Jazz Interludes*.

14. *Negro Digest* was founded by John H. Johnson as a general interest magazine for African American readers in 1942. Like *Reader's Digest*, it was comprised of condensed articles from a variety of publications. As Davis notes in *Livin' the Blues* (274–75), *Negro Digest* was extraordinarily popular when it was first published, although subsequent competition with *Ebony*, also published by Johnson Publications, decreased its sales. It went out of business in 1951. The 1961 revival of *Negro Digest*, under the editorship of Hoyt Fuller, transformed the magazine into a more politically oriented journal of U.S. and international black issues.

15. For an insightful inquiry into the significance of Holiday's multiple reputations, see Griffin, *If You Can't Be Free,* and O'Meally, *Lady Day.*

16. See Stephen Henderson; Randall, Interview; and Redmond.

17. See Corsi, *Obama Nation*; D'Souza, *The Roots of Obama's Rage*; Klein and Elliott, *The Manchurian President*; and Kurtz, *Radical-in-Chief.*

18. Under the pseudonym of Bob Greene, Davis wrote a 1968 erotic novel titled *Sex Rebel, Black: Memoirs of a Gourmet Gash.* Because this novel is presumably based on Davis's own sexual experiences in Hawaii, it is not surprising that Obama's critics have identified Davis as the protagonist of this novel. See Tidwell, "Alternative Constructions," for a judicious consideration of this novel in the context of Davis's other autobiographical narratives.

During the 2012 presidential campaign, conspiracy theories citing Davis as Obama's illegitimacy as president became even more outrageous, alleging that Davis was not only Obama's mentor but also his biological father. See, for example, the widely circulated film, *Dreams from My Real Father: A Story of Reds and Deception,* directed by Joel Gilbert (Highway 61 Entertainment, 2012).

Chapter 3. *"Do You Sing for a Living?"*

1. Sherrie Tucker's introduction to *Swing Shift* (1–32) is an especially perceptive critical analysis of the gender politics of jazz during World War II. See also Erenberg (181–210) and Stowe (141–79) on the impact of World War II on female jazz musicians.

2. There were numerous popular novels about jazz musicians published in the late 1930s and 1940s. *The Street* stands out as the only notable jazz novel of this period written by an African American woman. The most commercially successful jazz novel of the swing era was Dorothy Baker's *Young Man with a Horn* (1938), which was loosely based on the life of Bix Beiderbecke. *The Street* was published in the same series as *Young Man with a Horn* by Houghton Mifflin. For bibliographic information about early jazz fiction, see Albert and Rife.

3. Petry writes about jazz in several stories, beginning with her first published story, "Marie of the Cabin Club," which appeared in the *Afro-American* under the name of Arnold Petri in 1939. This suspenseful love story takes place in a jazz club and features two employees of the club as protagonists, the cigarette girl Marie and the jazz trumpeter George. Petry's best known and widely anthologized jazz story is "Solo on the Drums" (147), which enacts the jazz performance of a drummer, Kid Jones, who laments the loss of his wife, who has left him for the piano player in his band. Another significant story that foregrounds African diasporic music is "Olaf and His Girl Friend" (1945). This love story features two Barbadian protagonists, the dockworker Olaf and his "girl friend" Belle Rose, whose parents prohibit her from marrying the lower-class laborer and send her to Harlem, where she becomes a successful calypso singer and dancer. This story is especially interesting for its evocation of *Home to Harlem.* Olaf's transatlantic pursuit of Belle Rose resembles the geography of McKay's novel, and the name of "Belle Rose" and of the club where she works, "The Conga," recall the character "Congo Rose" from *Home to*

Harlem. See Garvey and Rubin and Smethurst on the cultural politics of Petry's short fiction.

4. It is not surprising that early reviews of *The Street* compared it to *Native Son*, which was published only six years before Petry's novel. See, for example, the reviews collected in Ervin, *The Critical Response* (1–19). Christian presents an incisive feminist critique of the premises for reading *The Street* as a "foil" to *Native Son*. She emphasizes that "by constructing a proletarian protest novel from the point of view of a black woman, Petry both criticized and developed that genre" ("Checkered Career" 14). Wald also compares Petry's literary strategy in *The Street* to that of *Native Son*, noting that both underscore the ideological rather than "naturalist" forces that limit their working-class characters. More specifically, Petry's method "to avoid the pitfalls of reductive characterization and the interpolation of idealized solutions" is "one of subtraction" (127)—that is, subtraction of the social solutions to Lutie's predicament as a working mother whom Petry knew through her work as a reporter and activist in Harlem.

5. Drake, Garvey, and Jimoh (116–30) make interesting cases for reading Lutie as a blues figure, among other blues figures in the novel such as Mrs. Hedges, Min, and Boots Smith. See also Cataliotti (*Music* 138–44), who suggestively compares Lutie's life story to that of Billie Holiday.

6. Because of the growing commercialization of jazz during the swing era, leftist jazz critics disagreed especially about the relationship of commercially successful big bands, such as the orchestras of Count Basie and Benny Goodman, to earlier New Orleans jazz and contemporaneous African American "folk music" in the rural South. For an informative account of the cultural politics of the early 1940s "jazz wars," see Gendron. Denning (323–48), Erenberg (120–49), Eric Porter (40–52), and Stowe (50–93) explain specifically how swing was interpreted politically on the Popular Front left.

7. DeVeaux, *Birth of Bebop*; Erenberg; Lott; Eric Porter; and Stowe discuss the impact of World War II racial inequality on the development of bebop.

8. Petry writes knowledgeably about jazz in her journalism and fiction, but she has not written extensively about jazz otherwise. When asked about jazz in an interview with Hazel Arnett Ervin, though, she confirmed her lifelong interest in jazz: "I've been a jazz buff, or a fan, ever since I was a teenager—many a long year ago" (102).

9. Wald (108–122) and Rubin and Smethurst discuss the importance of *People's Voice* and Petry's experience as an activist in Harlem for the social vision of *The Street*.

10. A good example of Petry's feminist wit can be found in her account of a reception for the publication of Sterling Brown's anthology *The Negro Caravan* in the Feb. 21, 1942, issue. After listing the literary figures who were at the reception, she writes: "Incidentally the book is filled with superb writing—most of it by males. Why aren't there more Negro women writers? Are the girls too busy playing bridge or what?" ("Lighter Side" 16).

11. The initial entertainment pages of *People's Voice* also included the first serial selection of Richard Wright's *Native Son*. The opening pages of *Native Son* were ac-

companied by an illustration of Bigger chasing the rat with a frying pan. According to Roi Ottley, the serialization of *Native Son* was intended to raise circulation, but it was discontinued after four issues because of reader protests (275–76).

12. Gold presents a detailed account of the closing of the Savoy. The temporary closing of the Savoy is also commonly cited as one of many acts of racial and economic injustice that led to the 1943 Harlem Riot. See, for example, Capeci 134–47.

13. See, for example, the Nov. 4, 1944, case made by *People's Voice* for supporting Roosevelt. Under "Roosevelt's Deeds for the Negro: Things That Never Happened Before," the two primary categories are "Housing" and "Jobs."

14. Grandt (32–35) explains the historical and musical significance of this popular ballad by Lucky Millinder and Frances Kraft Reckling. Reckling was a close friend of Petry. In addition to her work as an arranger of songs for big bands and a writer of popular and gospel songs, she was the owner of Reckling's Music Store, which was on the same floor as the offices of *People's Voice* (Griffin, *Harlem Nocturne* 86–87).

15. The origins of "Night and Day" seem as unlikely as its extraordinary success; Porter claimed that the song was inspired by "a Mohammedan priest summoning the religious to prayers" in Morocco (McBrien 148). The song became so identified with Porter that it was also the title of a 1946 biographical film about him, starring Cary Grant.

16. See Garvey and especially Griffin, *"Who Set You Flowin'?"* (114–18) on the importance of Granny as an ancestral figure. Several critics have discussed how Franklin's vision of "the American dream" influences Lutie. See, for example, Bell, Clark, Lattin, and Pryse.

17. Although Lutie recognizes that her situation is not unique, her isolation is extraordinary. As Nellie McKay notes, she does not have a "supportive community (which is most unusual for black women in America)" and thus tragically relies on her own individual resourcefulness to overcome poverty (158). Wald emphasizes that there are moments in the novel when Lutie identifies collectively with African Americans, such as the momentary sense of coming "home" to Harlem when she arises from the subway in the second chapter, and with women, especially when she identifies with the poor women in the Children's Shelter waiting room after her son, Bub, is arrested. In each of these cases, however, Lutie is unable to sustain a sense of collective identification or to act on this recognition, largely because of the ideology of self-reliance she has internalized.

18. Franklin's philosophy has an indirect but especially destructive impact on Bub. Because he is aware of his mother's limited finances, he follows Franklin's industrious example and becomes a shoeshine boy. Lutie walks right past him on the street as she is thinking about Franklin and his loaf of bread (63–66). Bub's decision to steal mail for the Super is likewise what he sees as an ingenuous response to his mother's complaints about "being poor" (325). He does not know, of course, that the Super is using him to enact revenge on Lutie, who had earlier resisted his attempt to rape her.

19. As Grandt writes, the microphone "separates her body, the object of male sexual desire, from her voice, the instrument of individual human self-expression"

(28). This scene exemplifies how "the figurative territory of jazz is as dangerous as the literal territory of the unforgiving street" for Lutie (29), but it also shows her ability to improvise on a tune as ordinary as "Darlin."

20. Although Lutie mostly listens to music on the radio, she also listens to the news (402). But she is not affected by the news reported on the radio or in the newspapers that she reads; the novel does not even mention the content of this news. Given that Petry was a print journalist, one might expect newspapers to play a significant role in the novel; however, they are more likely to be blowing in the wind with the other trash of the street, as in the opening scene of the novel. Newspapers are also associated with deception and danger in *The Street*, whether they misrepresent events in accordance with racist preconceptions or offer false hope for opportunities that do not exist, as Lutie finds out when she answers the advertisement for the Crosse School for Singers. But newspapers and magazines seem to have little effect on the communal life of Harlem; they are more likely to be read in isolation, and on the subway they even function as physical walls for passengers to create "small private worlds" (27). In suggesting that the Junto is a better source of "news" than the mass media, the novel associates news with the social space of conversation, with the dialogic sound of voices and the sound of jazz, rather than with the disembodied "voice" of print journalism.

21. Ellison's essay is also a reflection on the discipline and practice necessary to become an artist; he compares his own memory of learning to play the trumpet with his response to a singer who practices above his apartment each day. While Ellison desires quiet in order to practice his craft as a writer, he also appreciates the singer's need to practice. The essay resolves this conflict through a musical dialogue between the music Ellison plays on his stereo with the music performed by the singer upstairs.

22. For a brief but cogent explanation of the principle of repetition in African diasporic cultures, see Snead.

23. Grandt discusses this specific reference as well as the trope of the circle in African American literature and culture more generally in *Kinds of Blue*, page 119, note 6.

24. The novel's conclusion reiterates the opening image of the street with its storm of blowing trash. Yet the concluding snowfall is calming, unlike the dangerously icy snow of *Native Son*: "The snow fell softly on the street. It muffled sound. It sent people scurrying homeward, so that the street was soon deserted, empty, quiet. And it could have been any street in the city, for the snow laid a delicate film over the sidewalk, over the brick of the tired, old buildings; gently obscuring the grime and the garbage and the ugliness" (435). This conclusion actually suggests the streets of another city, James Joyce's Dublin. With its melancholy tone, which corresponds with Lutie's regretful departure from her son, this conclusion resembles the conclusion of "The Dead," the final story of *Dubliners*. As that story's protagonist, Gabriel Conroy, recognizes that "the time had come for him to set out on his journey westward," the snow is "falling faintly" all over Ireland, which is described in similarly descriptive detail (194).

Chapter 4. "Cultural Exchange"

1. Hughes, *Montage of a Dream Deferred*, *Collected Poems* 387. Further references to Hughes's poetry are to this edition and will be cited parenthetically in the text as *CP*.

2. For a more extensive inquiry into the socio-aesthetics of bebop in *Montage of a Dream Deferred*, see my chapter on Hughes in *History, Memory, and the Literary Left* (99–127).

3. For exemplary criticism that relates *Ask Your Mama* to jazz performance, see M. Jones, "Listening"; Kun 162–83; and Saul 129–43. Kun makes an especially compelling case for the cross-cultural blend of African American and Cuban jazz forms that distinguishes *Ask Your Mama* from other jazz poetry. For recent essays that perceptively relate the jazz poetics of *Ask Your Mama* to *Montage of a Dream Deferred*, see Higgins; Lenz; and Marcoux, "'Blues Connotation.'" M. Jones and Marcoux relate Hughes's jazz poetics to subsequent poetry in *The Muse Is Music* and *Jazz Griots*, respectively. See also Piedra's essay on the "neo-African logic of performance" (113) evoked by *Ask Your Mama* and the poetry of Nicolás Guillén.

4. Amiri Baraka (LeRoi Jones) made his influential case for bebop's social and political significance in *Blues People* (188–202). For more recent considerations of the social historical implications of bebop, see Lott and Ramsey 96–130. See, also, DeVeaux's measured and insightful consideration of bebop in his introduction to *The Birth of Bebop*, titled "Stylistic Evolution or Social Revolution?" (1–31).

5. Rampersad discusses the circumstances of Hughes's composition of *Ask Your Mama* in *The Life of Langston Hughes*, vol. 2, 316–19. For an incisive historical analysis of the 1960 Newport Jazz Festival, see Saul 99–129. Saul examines *Ask Your Mama* as a response to the Newport riots on pages 129–43. For a comprehensive documentary history of the festival, see Goldblatt, especially 71–91, where he discusses the 1960 festival. Hentoff's account of the Rebels festival is also valuable for its insights on the politics and economics of jazz that prompted the counter-festival. See *The Jazz Life* 98–113.

6. For a detailed account of Lumumba's symbolic importance for African Americans, especially after his assassination, with the complicity of the CIA, see Meriwether 208–240. In addition to Meriwether's book, the most thorough accounts of the evolving importance of Africa for African Americans during this time period are Plummer, *Rising Wind*, and Von Eschen, *Race against Empire*. The historical studies of the civil rights movement by Borstelmann, Dudziak, and Singh are also especially useful for their considerations of U.S. Cold War foreign policy and African American anticolonialism. My understanding of Hughes's literary, musical, and political conceptualization of the African diaspora is influenced as well by Brent Hayes Edwards's astute analyses of earlier moments of his career, especially in *The Practice of Diaspora* and "Langston Hughes and the Futures of Diaspora."

7. Rampersad, *Life of Langston Hughes*, vol. 2, 305–306.

8. Ibid., 344. The initial reviews of *Ask Your Mama* concentrated on its two most notable features: (1) its challenging blend of poetry and jazz, and (2) its densely allusive texture. The most dismissive reviews questioned whether it could be considered

literature, given the explicit directions for performance on each page. Most notoriously, Dudley Fitts wrote in the *New York Times Book Review* that "Langston Hughes' twelve jazz pieces cannot be evaluated by any canon dealing with literary right or wrong. They are non-literary—oral, vocal compositions to be spoken, or shouted, to the accompaniment of drum and flute and bass." Fitts considered *Ask Your Mama* to be "stunt poetry; a nightclub turn," comparable to Vachel Lindsay's "Congo" (636). Paul Engle agreed that *Ask Your Mama* was written primarily for performance and added, as many reviewers noted, that the book's allusions to current events were also problematic: the poems were "full of topical references, some of them already out-of-date in a rapid world" (636–37). Reviewers who were more familiar with jazz and with African American vernacular traditions more generally were more appreciative of Hughes's formal innovations. See, for example, the reviews by Rudi Blesh, Carl Bloice, Ulysses Lee, Alma Parks, and J. Saunders Redding that are reprinted in *Langston Hughes: The Contemporary Reviews*. Underlying these disagreements about *Ask Your Mama* are, of course, contrasting expectations of "literature," and poetry more specifically. Reviews that dismissed *Ask Your Mama* as a script for performance rather than a poem that was meant to be read were defending, whether explicitly or implicitly, a canon of poetry that privileged the autonomous written work. *Ask Your Mama* doubly fails such formalist criteria; it "cannot be evaluated by any literary canon dealing with literary right or wrong," as Fitts wrote, because it was written explicitly for performance, and it is furthermore "non-literary" in its extraordinary range of topical references. In contrast, John Henrik Clarke, like other African American critics who initially reviewed *Ask Your Mama*, made a different case for the book's universality and for the significance of its temporality: "Langston Hughes has used the pattern of jazz, poetry and the dozens to bring another dimension to the Afro-Americans' long and agonizing struggle to have his art and the dignity of his personality accepted in a nation that proclaimed, so long ago, that all men were created equal" ("Book Reviews" 640–41). *Ask Your Mama* was thus both timeless, in its appeal to the supposedly universal ideals of individual dignity and equality that were inscribed in the nation's founding documents, and timely, in its reminder of how these ideals continued to be unfulfilled.

9. The earliest scholarly essays that explain the structure of *Ask Your Mama* and its implications are (listed chronologically) Wagner 461–74; Jemie 79–91; Johnson and Farrell; and Miller, "Framing and Framed Languages." While subsequent criticism has variously addressed its jazz form, and while critics have likewise historicized many of its allusions or references, readings of the poem tend to be selective rather than comprehensive in their scope. The most ambitious recent attempts to explain the formal and dramatic entirety of *Ask Your Mama* are Marcoux, *Jazz Griots* (25–67), and Scanlon.

10. Hughes acknowledges this difficulty through "liner notes" that implicitly mock Eliot's scholarly notes for *The Waste Land*. These liner notes are more often supplementary rather than explanatory and complicate rather than explain the poem's allusions. See Scanlon 50–51 for a persuasive interpretation of *Ask Your Mama*'s intertextual relation to *The Waste Land*.

11. Alexander G. Weheliye's incisive analysis of *The Souls of Black Folk* as the "first literary sound recording (phono-graph) of sonic Afro modernity" (83) is also pertinent for the structure of *Ask Your Mama*. As Weheliye argues, *Souls* is comparable to the DJ's creative act of combining different records through its blend of so many literary genres, initiated by the juxtaposition of musical bars from the African American "sorrow songs" with excerpts from European poetry at the beginning of each chapter. Like the DJ's mix, *Souls* "highlights the amalgamation of its components, or rather the process of this (re)combination, as much as it accentuates the individual parts from which it springs" (Weheliye 73). Du Bois also accentuates the "fissures" in the mix through the bars of music that initiate each chapter. Through this process, he redefines the significance of the spirituals, combining them with quotations from Western canonical texts and adapting them to black modernity (Weheliye 82–83). The structural similarity of *Souls* to *Ask Your Mama* is especially evident in the juxtaposition of musical notes and words in Hughes's introduction but also in the subsequent interplay of poetry and musical directions, both of which expand the scope of Du Bois's African American geography to a multinational African diaspora geography. Like *Souls*, *Ask Your Mama* channels an array of African diaspora voices through the mix of sonic materials, from the blues and jazz to a range of African and Caribbean musical forms, and forms of written notation. And like Du Bois, Hughes does so to accentuate the creative power of black vernacular forms of expression to translate and transform the social conditions to which they testify.

12. Ingrid Monson, *Freedom Sounds* 118. The jazz tours produced unexpected results, partly because they were often haphazardly organized and partly because musicians resisted their official roles. The "open-ended and unpredictable nature of cultural exchange" that characterized the tours resulted from the musicians' own ideas about their music and from the interactions between artists and audiences (Von Eschen, *Satchmo* 24). According to Von Eschen, the musicians resembled the narrator of *Invisible Man* in that they were visible as cultural ambassadors but invisible "as actors with social concerns and political viewpoints that were ignored by State Department bureaucracy" (24).

13. One result of the State Department jazz tours to Africa was the growth of interest in and opportunities for collaboration between African American and African musicians. The first two Pan-Africanist symphonic jazz compositions emerged as Hughes was writing *Ask Your Mama*: Max Roach's *Freedom Now Suite* (1960) and Randy Weston's *Uhuru Afrika* (1961), which featured lyrics by Hughes. Musicians such as Art Blakey, Horace Silver, and Roach had already become known for their blending of African, Caribbean, and African American musical traditions by the late 1950s. As more African nations achieved their independence, however, the association of African liberation with black freedom in the United States inflected Pan-Africanist jazz experiments with a more pronounced political purpose.

14. See Plummer, *Rising Wind* 269–77, on the notorious experience of racial discrimination and hostility experienced by African national leaders visiting the United States in the 1950s.

15. Charles Bernstein defines the concept of the hinge, as a line break that functions differently from either enjambment or disjunction, in an essay on George Oppen's *Of Being Numerous* titled "Hinge, Picture."

16. Von Eschen discusses the politics of Price's tour in *Satchmo* 4–5.

17. According to the Rampersad and Roessel endnote in *The Collected Poems of Langston Hughes*, "Ça Ira" "was a popular song during the French Revolution. It originally celebrated national unity and France's resistance to her enemies, but a refrain added later spoke of hanging aristocrats from lamp posts" (674).

18. James Smethurst documents Hughes's ongoing association with leftist organizations throughout the 1950s, contrary to widespread perceptions of his acquiescence to Cold War anticommunism, in "'Don't Say Goodbye to the Porkpie Hat.'"

19. For detailed studies of housing discrimination in the metropolitan New York area after World War II, see Biondi and Wiese.

Chapter 5. *"A Silent Beat in Between the Drums"*

1. The above quotation from *Golden Sardine* is from the reprinted edition of the book in *Cranial Guitar*.

2. The program for *Black, Brown, and Beige* is reprinted *The Duke Ellington Reader*, edited by Mark Tucker, 161–64, along with introductory promotional material about the Carnegie Hall performance.

3. Hammond's review is included in *The Duke Ellington Reader* (171–73) among several reviews of *Black, Brown, and Beige* from the jazz press, including Leonard Feather's angry retort to Hammond's article.

4. A good example is Paul Bowles's review in the *New York Herald-Tribune*, where he praises individual pieces of *Black, Brown, and Beige* but concludes that "as one number it was formless and meaningless. . . . The whole attempt to fuse jazz as a form with art music should be discouraged. The two exist at such different distance from the listener's faculties of comprehension that he cannot get them both clearly into focus at the same time" (166). See the reprint of this review in *The Duke Ellington Reader*, 165–66.

5. Gaines's essay on *Black, Brown, and Beige* and the cultural politics of race discusses Ellington's response to criticism of the composition. Emphasizing Ellington's "self-conscious construction of historically situated narratives of African-American group consciousness as part of a progressive, antiracist agenda during World War II," Gaines makes a compelling case against purely formalist understandings of jazz history. The most comprehensive and incisive analysis of the reception of *Black, Brown, and Beige* is DeVeaux, "*Black, Brown, and Beige* and the Critics." This essay is included in an informative special issue of *Black Music Research Journal* on *Black, Brown, and Beige*, edited by Mark Tucker. See, also, Cohen's chapter on *Black, Brown, and Beige* in *Duke Ellington's America*, 203–243.

6. Ellington discusses *My People* in *Music Is My Mistress*, 197–99. See Cohen 392–97 for a detailed overview of *My People*.

7. As Gaines notes, Ellington actually recorded an album with Mingus and Roach, *Money Jungle*, which was released by United Jazz Artists in February 1963. See Gaines

598–99 for a lucid discussion of how this album exemplifies the misleading consequences of formalist periodizations of jazz history.

8. The most comprehensive biographical information about Kaufman's early years can be found in Damon, *Dark End,* and in David Henderson's introduction to *Cranial Guitar,* which includes testimony by Kaufman's family and closest associates. Much of the evidence of Kaufman's early activism is anecdotal, however. As Smethurst writes, specific documentary evidence of Kaufman's wartime union activism and postwar labor organizing has not been found, although it is clear that the National Maritime Union leadership was avowedly communist prior to the Cold War. See Smethurst, "'Remembering,'" for the most detailed consideration of Kaufman's radical activism. Smethurst also expands on the significance of Kaufman's Popular Front social consciousness for the Black Arts movement in *The Black Arts Movement,* especially 265–74.

9. See Rampersad, *The Life of Langston Hughes,* vol. 1, 116–17, on Lindsay's "discovery" of Hughes. It is ironic that the New Directions narrative locates this transformative moment of Kaufman's life as a Beat poet in Los Angeles, given Kaufman's often comically exaggerated Bay Area disdain for L.A. In the "Abomunist Manifesto," Los Angeles represents the anti-Abomunist: "Abomunists who feel their faith weakening will have to spend two weeks in Los Angeles" ("Notes Dis- and Re- Garding Abomunism," *Solitudes* 79). Los Angeles figures similarly in "Unholy Missions": "I want to prove that Los Angeles is a practical joke played on us by superior beings on a humorous planet" (*Solitudes* 10). The most thorough indictment of Los Angeles, however, is directed specifically at Hollywood, the *"artistic cancer of the universe"* ("Hollywood," *Solitudes,* 26).

10. Since Thomas's insightful essay on the jazz poetics of Kaufman's and the Black Arts poets, there has been considerable work on jazz and the "black Beats." See especially T. J. Anderson III, Kohli, Lee, and Saloy. Anderson's *Notes to Make the Sound Come Right* is especially important for his comparative study of jazz poetry by African American writers, including Kaufman, Stephen Jonas, Jayne Cortez, and Nathaniel Mackey.

11. See Lindberg; Nielsen, "'A Hard Rain'"; and Smethurst, "'Remembering.'" Although he does not discuss Kaufman specifically, Kelley's articulation of the radical implications of black surrealism is especially valuable for considering Kaufman in a black internationalist, anticolonialist context. See Kelley, *Freedom Dreams* 157–94.

12. For additional information, and informed speculation, on Kaufman's life, see Damon, *Dark End* 32–76; Introduction to "Bob Kaufman"; and "Unmeaning Jargon."

13. See, for example, the collection of musicians' memoirs on Parker assembled by Reisner. Giddins also incisively discusses the influence of Parker as well as his development as a musician in *Celebrating Bird.*

14. See Panish 71–75 for his perceptive comparison of "Sonny's Blues" and *Dutchman.*

15. See Feinstein, *Jazz Poetry* 104–105 for a brief but incisive discussion of Kaufman's approximation of jazz improvisation.

16. Kaufman was more interested in performing his poems than publishing them in books, although City Lights Press published several Kaufman broadsides before

the publication of *Solitudes: Abomunist Manifesto* (1959), *Second April* (1959), and *Does the Secret Mind Whisper?* (1967). Kaufman's wife, Eileen, compiled and edited the manuscript of *Solitudes* for submission to New Directions. Eileen Kaufman's significant role as an editor and writer, like that of other Beat women, is underappreciated. Excerpts from her memoir, *Who Wouldn't Walk with Tigers?*, can be found in Charters 273–80 and Peabody 108–114. See also Knight's chapter on Eileen Kaufman in *Women of the Beat Generation* 103–114. In addition to these collections on Beat women, see the excellent collection of essays edited by Johnson and Grace.

17. See Damon, "Triangulated Desire."

18. John Hoffman was a promising San Francisco Beat poet who became legendary after he traveled to Mexico and died mysteriously at the age of twenty-one in 1950 or 1951. A collection of his poems titled *Journey to the End* was published in the City Lights Press Pocket Poets series in 2008 in an edition with Phillip Lamantia's *Tau*.

19. The poem is alluding to Bessie Smith's notorious death following a 1937 car accident in Mississippi. While the exact circumstances of the accident and its aftermath are not certain, it was widely believed that she bled to death because the closest hospitals did not admit black patients. Her death became a legendary example of the destructive costs of Jim Crow segregation.

20. Kohli's elucidation of the "martyrdom of black America, and the inability or unwillingness of white America to recognize its own sins" (178) is especially pertinent here. See his "Saxophones and Smothered Rage," which also discusses Kaufman's fictionalized biographical portrait of Charlie Parker in "Hank Lawler: Chorus."

21. T. J. Anderson III makes a compelling case for the fragmentation of the African diaspora suggested by "O-JAZZ-O" in *Notes* 94.

22. See "War Memoir: Jazz, Don't Listen to It at Your Own Risk," *Ancient Rain* 32–33. This version of the poem consistently replaces "they" with "we," beginning with the line that begins "Suddenly." The final lines of the revised poem add the first-person-plural subject as well: "And we Listen / And we feel / and live" (33).

23. "Bird Lives and Bob Still GIVES" was published in Andrae et al.

24. See Andrae et al. and Damon, "Bob Kaufman."

25. Kevin Young relates his own intense interest in Kaufman to the Dark Room Collective poets in *The Grey Album* 227–49. Given the current prominence of Dark Room Collective poets, Young's argument for Kaufman's exemplary dedication to poetry suggests how influential he has been for contemporary African American poetry: "For us, Bob Kaufman was an avatar of sorts—and incarnation of poetry in what may be called its purest form, or perhaps, more accurately, its most useful, impure form, complete with a sense of music and line that can be hard to find. Rare, but not rarefied" (227). The Dark Room Collective was initially formed by Thomas Sayers Ellis and Sharan Strange in Cambridge, Massachusetts, in 1998. Originally conceived as a local reading series, it eventually supported a community of younger black writers who have since achieved substantial recognition, including Young, Major Jackson, Carl Phillips, and Pulitzer Prize–winning poets Tracy K. Smith and Natasha Trethewey.

Conclusion

1. Pettis and Denniston each underscore this narrative trajectory of Marshall's novels in their important early books about her writing. Pettis emphasizes how this process of identification with Africa is fundamental to her protagonists' movement toward "psychic transformation" and "spiritual reintegration" (1). Denniston explores how Marshall's fiction reconciles her triple consciousness (as black, Caribbean, and American) through the "imaginative return to traditional African culture" (xiv).

2. Jackson briefly discusses Marshall's affiliation with the "indignant generation" in the final chapter of *The Indignant Generation* (494–96). Underscoring her importance as a writer who "outstripped the capacity of her audience," he asserts that *Brown Girl, Brownstones* was "the most significant narrative of the decade written after 1953" (496).

3. Although *Brown Girl, Brownstones* was published in 1959 and attracted favorable reviews, it was not widely recognized as an important feminist novel until Feminist Press republished it in 1981.

4. Prior to the publication of *The Fisher King*, few critics discussed the significance of music in Marshall's fiction. For thoughtful readings of how African diasporic music functions in *Praisesong for the Widow*, see Cartwright and Hoefel.

5. If jazz fiction is as notoriously difficult to define as jazz itself, Jürgen Grandt makes an important distinction between "how African American authors write *about* jazz" and "how African American narratives *are* jazz . . . how they . . . improvise a meaningful narrative of freedom over the dissonant sound clusters of the American experience" (xii). *The Fisher King* echoes previous African American narratives about jazz in its life story of a jazz musician, but it also *is* jazz in its adaptation of jazz performance practices, stylistically as well as structurally.

6. As Fischlin and Heble argue in their outstanding introduction to *The Other Side of Nowhere*, jazz improvisation is "less about original acts of individual self-creation . . . than about an ongoing process of community building, about reinvigorating public life with the spirit of dialogue and difference" (17). Their emphasis on the social implications of improvisation, in the introduction and in this collection as a whole, contests the popular association of improvisation with spontaneity. This important interdisciplinary anthology expands on previous studies of jazz improvisation by Berliner and Monson (*Saying Something*), both of which are based on extensive interviews with jazz musicians.

7. Toni Morrison's concept of "rememory" relates to the counter-hegemonic process of rethinking—and revising—the past exemplified in *Beloved*. My use of this term to describe Hattie's interpretation of jazz history alludes most specifically to Tucker's deployment of "rememory" in "'Where the Blues and Truth Lay Hiding': Rememory of Jazz in Black Women's Fiction."

8. Tucker emphasizes Bambara's "Medley" (1974), Maya Angelou's "Reunion" (1983), and Cartier's *Muse-Echo Blues* (1991) as examples of jazz narratives in which "Black women are remembered as producers and receivers of culture and knowledge" ("'Where the Blues and the Truth Lay Hiding'" 27). Her essay is important in jazz

studies for her emphasis on black women's fiction as a distinctive mode of testimony that supplements the work of "women-in-music historians" (26). She concludes that black women's fiction represents an alternative ethos to the masculinist emphasis on individual competition that dominates jazz historiography. Rather than emphasizing "technical superiority over somebody else," black women's jazz fiction celebrates "the power of jazz as a vehicle to arrive at personal and social conclusions, connections, and articulations otherwise missed" (42).

9. Roach also recalls the impact of Garvey on the Bedford-Stuyvesant black community. He attributes his own early interest in African music to Garvey: "Well, that all came about from Marcus Garvey, you know. Marcus Garvey was in the black community—and still is—one of the major heroes, even though he went to jail and all that kind of stuff. He really was very revolutionary" (Interview with Ingrid Monson, qtd. in Monson, *Freedom* 142).

10. Weston's father, Frank Edward Weston, owned a small business himself, a restaurant named Trios that was also an important gathering place for jazz musicians. In the late 1940s, after serving in the army during World War II, Randy Weston managed this restaurant.

11. Abdurahman's memoir of Bedford-Stuyvesant, *In the Key of Me: The Bedford-Stuyvesant Renaissance, 1940s-60s Revisited,* is discussed in Kelley's "Brooklyn's Jazz Renaissance." See also Monson, *Freedom* 140–47.

12. This correlation of Sonny's art with jazz improvisation is accentuated through the juxtaposition of scenes of his drawing with scenes that feature his grandfather's music. The first chapter that features the memory of the Putnam Royal, the club where Sonny-Rett had made his name, begins with a scene of Sonny drawing. As Edgar, Hattie, and the musicians who had played with Sonny-Rett are planning the memorial concert, Sonny recalls his development from tracing medieval castles and fortresses in a book to "making up his own" (74). And when the musicians later reconvene at the Putnam Royal before the concert, reminiscing about Sonny-Rett's breakthrough performance, Sonny draws a sketch of the building, "complete with its turrets and battlemented roof" (141), a picture that his uncle Edgar promises to have framed and put on his office wall, "right next to the picture I have of the place before we restored it. This will be the 'After' picture of the Before-and-After of Putnam Royal" (141).

13. The Brooklyn neighborhood that Sonny first encounters closely resembles the wartime street of brownstones perceived by Selina in the opening pages of *Brown Girl, Brownstones.* The resemblance of the two novels extends beyond this setting, however, as Selina's father, Deighton, is also a jazz musician, albeit an unsuccessful one. Marshall herself reminds us of the correspondence of Sonny-Rett with Deighton in her interview with James C. Hall and Heather Hathaway: "They are both artists. True, Deighton couldn't play the trumpet, but he had an artistic temperament. He was the one who made Selina aware of nature and of values apart from the material. These two are liabilities in the eyes of their community. Society can't afford them! . . . They can't afford the threat he [Deighton] represents to their notion of the American

dream. He is the sacrificial lamb to that dream. That's really one of the major themes of that first novel and of most of my work" (188).

14. As Griffin asserts, portrayals of Holiday that emphasize "her tragedy, sexuality and appetites sustain and reproduce ideologies of black womanhood and of jazz music. She is not only a woman who paid the price for living on the edge, not only a tragic victim who had to die, but also a black woman who suffered the fate of the jazz genius in a racist American society—substance abuse and underappreciation" (*In Search* 33). Griffin explains how this image of the tragic victim demeans talented black women more generally, as it assumes that such victimhood is inherent. The distinction Griffin makes between the "victimization" Holiday endured and more stereotypical perceptions of her as an inherently tragic victim apply to Hattie's characterization as well. See also O'Meally, *Lady Day*, who likewise contests the tragic image of Holiday that is most notoriously evident in her autobiography, written with William Dufty.

15. Many writers, of course, such as Richard Wright and Chester Himes, also sought refuge from anticommunist persecution in the United States. And others, most notably James Baldwin, chose to live in Paris because it was more accepting of homosexuals than New York.

16. Bebop became popular especially after a Paris concert by Dizzy Gillespie in 1948 and the International Jazz Festival the following year, which featured Charlie Parker as well as more traditional musicians such as Sidney Bechet. See Stovall 163–81 on the French reception of bebop at this time.

17. In her interview with Hall and Hathaway, Marshall notes that JoJo's discovery of sexual intimacy between Hattie and Cherisse is perhaps traumatic but is also left unresolved (164–65). The reasons for JoJo's departure from home are certainly complicated, given the preceding death of her father and mother and her pregnancy at the age of fourteen. This scene, like the scene of Sonny-Rett's death, also accentuates the limitations of Hattie's narrative consciousness. Even her intimate knowledge of the life of Sonny-Rett—and of Cherisse—as invaluable as her testimony to this jazz life is, is not presented as *the* truth. The counterpoint of public and private narratives enacts the narrative method of the novel more generally, which presents contrasting perceptions of Sonny-Rett's legacy, especially as they appear through the consciousness of Sonny.

18. "The Roots of Jazz" was probably written in 1958. It is inscribed "For the Stratford Souvenir Program," which suggests that Hughes wrote the essay for the July 22 and 23, 1958, Stratford, Ontario, Shakespeare Festival, in which he performed his poetry with Henry "Red" Allen and his All Stars. See the endnote by Christopher C. De Santis to "The Roots of Jazz" in Hughes, *Collected Works*, vol. 9, 583.

Works Cited

Abdurahman, Bilal. *In the Key of Me: The Bedford-Stuyvesant Renaissance, 1940s-60s Revisited*. Contemporary Visions Press, 1993.

Albert, Richard N. *An Annotated Bibliography of Jazz Fiction and Jazz Fiction Criticism*. Greenwood Press, 1996.

"America's India." Editorial. *The Messenger* 4 (June 1922): 418–19.

Anderson, Paul Allen. *Deep River: Music and Memory in Harlem Renaissance Thought*. Duke UP, 2001.

Anderson, T. J., III. *Notes to Make the Sound Come Right: Four Innovators of Jazz Poetry*. U of Arkansas P, 2004.

Andrae, Tomas, Bernard Augst, Jalal Toufic, and Trinh T. Minh-Ha, editors. *The Silent Beat*. Spec. issue of *Discourse* 20.1/2 (1998).

Armstrong, Louis. *Swing That Music*. 1936. Da Capo, 1993.

Baker, Houston A., Jr. *Modernism and the Harlem Renaissance*. U of Chicago P, 1987.

Baldwin, Davarian L. *Chicago's New Negroes: Modernity, The Great Migration, and Black Urban Life*. U of North Carolina P, 2007.

———. "Introduction: New Negroes Forging a New World." Baldwin and Makalani, pp. 1–27.

Baldwin, Davarian L., and Minkah Makalani, editors. *Escape from New York: The New Negro Renaissance beyond Harlem*. U of Minnesota P, 2013.

Baldwin, Kate A. *Beyond the Color Line and the Iron Curtain: Reading Encounters between Black and Red, 1922–1963*. Duke UP, 2002.

Baraka, Amiri (LeRoi Jones). *Blues People: Negro Music in White America*. William Morrow, 1963.

Barnhart, Bruce. *Jazz in the Time of the Novel: The Temporal Politics of American Race and Culture*. U of Alabama P, 2013.

Bassett, John E. *Harlem in Review: Critical Reactions to Black American Writers, 1937–1939*. Susquehanna UP, 1992.

Bauman, Zygmunt. "The Left as the Counter-Culture of Modernity." *Telos* 70 (1986–87): 81–93.

Beatitude 7.4 (1959). Beatitude Poetry. www.beatitudepoetry.com/beatitudemagazine.html. 14 Oct. 2016.

Bell, Bernard. "Ann Petry's Demythologizing of American Culture and Afro-American Character." 1985. Rpt. Ervin, pp. 68–76.

Bellegarde, Dantès. "Haiti under the Rule of the United States." Translated by Rayford Logan. *Opportunity* 5 (Dec. 1927): 354–57.

Bennett, Gwendolyn. "Blue-Black Symphony." Review of *Home to Harlem*. *New York Herald Tribune*, 11 March 1928, pp. 5–6.

Berliner, Paul. *Thinking in Jazz: The Infinite Art of Improvisation.* U of Chicago P, 1994.

Bernstein, Charles. "Hinge, Picture." *Ironwood* 26 (1985): 240–44.

Biondi, Martha. *To Stand and Fight: The Struggle for Civil Rights in Postwar New York City.* Harvard UP, 2003.

Bone, Robert, and Richard A. Courage. *The Muse in Bronzeville: African American Creative Expression in Chicago, 1932–1950.* Rutgers UP, 2011.

Borstelmann, Thomas. *The Cold War and the Color Line: American Race Relations in the Global Arena.* Harvard UP, 2001.

Bostic, Joe. "Radiograph." *People's Voice*, 14 Feb. 1942, pp. 36.

Bourne, Randolph. "Trans-National America." *War and the Intellectuals: Collected Essays, 1915–1919*, edited by Carl Resek. Harper, 1964, pp. 107–23.

Bowles, Paul. "Duke Ellington in Recital for Russian War Relief." *New York Herald-Tribune*, 25 Jan. 1943, 25. Rpt. in M. Tucker, *Duke Ellington Reader*, pp. 165–66.

Brennan, Timothy. *Secular Devotion: Afro-Latin Music and Imperial Jazz.* Verso, 2008.

Brickell, Herschel. Review of *Home to Harlem*. *Opportunity* 6 (May 1928): 151–52.

Brown, Sterling A. *The Collected Poems of Sterling A. Brown.* Edited by Michael S. Harper. TriQuarterly, 1989.

———. "The Literary Scene: Two Negro Poets." Review of *Black Thunder*, by Arna Bontemps, and *Black Man's Verse*, by Frank Marshall Davis. *Opportunity* 14 (March 1936): 217, 220.

———. "Portrait of a Jazz Giant: 'Jelly Roll' Morton." *Black World* 23.4 (1974): 28–48.

Capeci, Dominic J., Jr. *The Harlem Riot of 1943.* Temple UP, 1977.

Carby, Hazel V. "Policing the Black Woman's Body in an Urban Context." *Critical Inquiry* 18.4 (1992): 738–55.

"A Caribbean Issue." Editorial. *Opportunity* 4 (Nov. 1926): 334.

Cartwright, Keith. "Notes toward a Voodoo Hermeneutics: Soul Rhythms, Marvelous Transitions, and Passages to the Creole Saints in *Praisesong for the Widow*." *Southern Quarterly* 41.4 (2003): 127–43.

Cataliotti, Robert H. "African American Music in Chicago during the Chicago Renaissance." Tracy, pp. 424–47.

———. *The Music in African American Fiction.* Garland, 1995.

Charters, Ann, editor. *What Was the Beat Generation?* Penguin, 2001.

Chauncey, George. *Gay New York: Gender, Urban Culture, and the Making of the Gay Male World, 1890–1940*. Basic/HarperCollins, 1994.

Christian, Barbara. "A Checkered Career—*The Street* by Ann Petry." 1992. Rpt. Ervin, pp. 14–19.

———. "Whatever Happened to Bob Kaufman?" 1972. Rpt. in *The Beats: Essays in Criticism*, edited by Lee Bartlett. McFarland, 1981, pp. 107–14.

Churchill, Suzanne W. *The Little Magazine Others and the Renovation of Modern American Poetry*. Ashgate, 2006.

Clark, Keith. "A Distaff Dream Deferred? Ann Petry and the Art of Subversion." 1992. Rpt. Ervin, pp. 166–78.

Clarke, John Henrik. "The Afro-American Image of Africa." *Black World* 23.4 (1974): 4–21.

———. "Book Reviews." *Freedomways* 2 (1962). Rpt. Dace, pp. 640–41.

Cohen, Harvey G. *Duke Ellington's America*. U of Chicago P, 2010.

Cooper, Wayne F. *Claude McKay: Rebel Sojourner in the Harlem Renaissance*. Louisiana State UP, 1987.

Corsi, Jerome. *Obama Nation: Leftist Politics and the Cult of Personality*. Threshold/Simon & Schuster, 2008.

Cullen, Countee. *My Soul's High Song: The Collected Writings of Countee Cullen, Voice of the Harlem Renaissance*. Edited by Gerald Early. Anchor/Doubleday, 1991.

Dace, Tish, editor. *Langston Hughes: The Contemporary Reviews*. Cambridge UP, 1997.

Damon, Maria, editor. "Bob Kaufman: Poet: A Special Section." *Callaloo* 25.1 (2002): 105–231.

———. *The Dark End of the Street*. U of Minnesota P, 1993.

———. Introduction. Damon, "Bob Kaufman: Poet," pp. 105–11.

———. "Triangulated Desire and Tactical Silences in the Beat Hipscape: Bob Kaufman and Others." *College Literature* 27.1. (2000): 139–57.

———. "'Unmeaning Jargon'/Uncanonized Beatitude: Bob Kaufman, Poet." *Artifice and Indeterminacy: An Anthology of New Poetics*, edited by Christopher Beach. U of Alabama P, 1998.

Dash, J. Michael. *Haiti and the United States: National Stereotypes and the Literary Imagination*. 2nd ed. St. Martin's, 1997.

Davis, Frank Marshall. *Black Moods: Collected Poems*. Edited by John Edgar Tidwell. U of Illinois P, 2002.

———. "Jazz in New Orleans." 1955. Davis, *Writings*, pp. 19–21.

———. *Jazz Interludes: Seven Musical Poems*. Black Cat, 1977.

———. *Livin' the Blues: Memoirs of a Black Journalist and Poet*. Edited by John Edgar Tidwell. U of Wisconsin P, 1992.

———. "Mirror of Jazz." Davis, *Writings*, pp. 28–29.

———. "Poems by Frank Marshall Davis." *Black World* 23.4 (1974): 22–26.

———. *Writings of Frank Marshall Davis: A Voice of the Black Press*. Edited by John Edgar Tidwell. U of Mississippi P, 2007.

de Barros, Paul. "'The Loud Music of Life': Representations of Jazz in the Novels of Claude McKay." *Antioch Review* 57.3 (1999): 306–17.

De Jongh, James. *Vicious Modernism: Black Harlem and the Literary Imagination.* Cambridge UP, 1990.

DeLamotte, Eugenia C. *Places of Silence, Journeys of Freedom: The Fiction of Paule Marshall.* U of Pennsylvania P, 1998.

Denning, Michael. *The Cultural Front: The Laboring of American Culture in the Twentieth Century.* Verso, 1996.

Denniston, Dorothy Hamer. *The Fiction of Paule Marshall: Reconstructions of History, Culture, and Gender.* U of Tennessee P, 1995.

DeVeaux, Scott. *The Birth of Bebop: A Social and Musical History.* U of California P, 1997.

———. "*Black, Brown and Beige* and the Critics." M. Tucker, *Duke Ellington's Black, Brown, and Beige*, pp. 125–46.

———. "Constructing the Jazz Tradition." *Black American Literature Forum* 25.3 (1991): 525–60.

Dodson, Nell. "Negro Orks Must Battle for Jobs." *People's Voice*, 14 Feb. 1942, p. 28.

Domingo, W.A. "Gift of the Black Tropics." Locke, pp. 341–49.

Domingo, W.A., and Chandler Owen. "The Policy of *The Messenger* on West Indian and American Negroes: W. A. Domingo vs. Chandler Owen." *The Messenger* 5 (March 1923): 639–45.

Douglas, Ann. *Terrible Honesty: Mongrel Manhattan in the 1920s.* Farrar, Straus, and Giroux, 1995.

Doyle, R. E. "All Over Creation." Review of *The Fisher King*, by Paule Marshall. *Black Issues Book Review* 2.5 (2000): 72.

Drake, Kimberly. "Women on the Go: Blues, Conjure, and Other Alternatives to Domesticity in Ann Petry's *The Street* and *The Narrows*." 1998. Rpt. Ervin, pp. 240–63.

D'Souza, Dinesh. *The Roots of Obama's Rage.* Regnery, 2010.

Du Bois, W. E. B. Editorial. *The Crisis* 19 (April 1920): 297–98.

———. *The Souls of Black Folk.* 1903. Rpt. Norton Critical Edition. Norton, 1999.

———. "Two Novels: Nella Larsen, *Quicksand* and Claude McKay, *Home to Harlem.*" *The Crisis* 35 (June 1928): 202.

Dudziak, Mary L. *Cold War Civil Rights: Race and the Image of American Democracy.* Princeton UP, 2000.

Editorial. *People's Voice*, 8 May 1943, pp. 16.

"Editorial Policy." *People's Voice*, 14 Feb. 1942, pp. 21.

Edwards, Brent Hayes. "Langston Hughes and the Futures of Diaspora." *American Literary History* 19 (Fall 2007): 689–711.

———. *The Practice of Diaspora: Literature, Translation, and the Rise of Black Internationalism.* Harvard UP, 2003.

Ellington, Edward Kennedy. *Music Is My Mistress.* Da Capo, 1973.

Ellison, Ralph. *The Collected Essays of Ralph Ellison.* Edited by John F. Callahan. Modern Library, 2003.

―――. *Invisible Man.* 1947. Vintage, 1990.

―――. "Living with Music." 1955. Rpt. Ellison, *Collected Essays*, pp. 227–36.

―――. "On Bird, Bird-Watching, and Jazz." 1962. Rpt. Ellison, *Collected Essays*, pp. 256–65.

Engle, Paul. "Critic Approvingly Views Seferis, Ciardi, and Hughes." *Chicago Tribune Magazine of Books,* 29 Oct. 1961. Rpt. Dace, pp. 636–37.

Erenberg, Lewis A. *Swingin' the Dream: Big Band Jazz and the Rebirth of American Culture.* U of Chicago P, 1998.

Ervin, Hazel Arnett, editor. *The Critical Response to Ann Petry.* Praeger, 2005.

Evans, Nicholas M. *Writing Jazz: Race, Nationalism, and Modern Culture in the 1920s.* Garland, 2000.

Fabre, Michel. *From Harlem to Paris: Black American Writers in France, 1840–1980.* U of Illinois P, 1991.

Faulkner, Anne Shaw. "Does Jazz Put the Sin in Syncopation?" 1921. Rpt. Walser, pp. 32–36.

Feinstein, Sascha. *Jazz Poetry: From the 1920s to the Present.* Praeger, 1997.

Feinstein, Sascha, and Yusef Komunyakaa, editors. *The Jazz Poetry Anthology.* Indiana UP, 1991.

―――. *The Second Set: The Jazz Poetry Anthology,* Vol. 2. Indiana UP, 1996.

Fischlin, Daniel, and Ajay Heble, editors. Introduction. Fischlin and Heble, pp. 1–42.

―――, editors. *The Other Side of Nowhere: Jazz, Improvisation, and Communities in Dialogue.* Wesleyan UP, 2004.

Fitts, Dudley. "A Trio of Singers in Various Keys." *New York Times Book Review* 29 Oct. 1961. Rpt. Dace, pp. 636.

Floyd, Samuel A., Jr. *The Power of Black Music: Interpreting Its History from Africa to the United States.* Oxford UP, 1995.

―――, editor. *Black Music in the Harlem Renaissance.* Greenwood, 1990.

Foley, Barbara. *Spectres of 1919: Class and Nation in the Making of the New Negro.* U of Illinois P, 2003.

Gabbard, Krin, editor. *Jazz among the Discourses.* Duke UP, 1995.

―――. *Representing Jazz.* Duke UP, 1995.

Gaines, Kevin. "Duke Ellington, *Black, Brown, and Beige,* and the Cultural Politics of Race." *Music and the Racial Imagination*, edited by Ronald Radano and Philip V. Bohlman. U of Chicago P, 2000, pp. 585–602.

Garvey, Johanna X. K. "That Old Black Magic? Gender and Music in Ann Petry's Fiction." *Black Orpheus: Music in African American Fiction from the Harlem Renaissance to Toni Morrison*, edited by Saadi A. Simawe. Garland, 2000, pp. 119–51.

Gates, Henry Louis. "The Trope of a New Negro and the Reconstruction of the Image of the Black." *Representations* 24 (1988): 129–55.

Gendron, Bernard. "'Moldy Figs' and Modernists: Jazz at War (1942–1946)." Gabbard, *Jazz*, pp. 31–56.

Gennari, John. *Blowin' Hot and Cool: Jazz and Its Critics.* U of Chicago P, 2006.

———. "'A Weapon of Integration': Frank Marshall Davis and the Politics of Jazz." *Langston Hughes Review* 14.1/2 (1996): 16–33.

Giddins, Gary. *Celebrating Bird: The Triumph of Charlie Parker*. Beech Tree/Morrow, 1987.

Giles, James R. *Claude McKay*. Twayne, 1976.

Gilmore, Glenda Elizabeth. *Defying Dixie: The Radical Roots of Civil Rights, 1919–1950*. Norton, 2008.

Gilroy, Paul. *The Black Atlantic: Modernity and Double Consciousness*. Harvard UP, 1993.

Gold, Russell. "Guilty of Syncopation, Joy, and Animation: The Closing of Harlem's Savoy Ballroom." *Of, By, and For the People: Dancing on the Left in the 1930s*, edited by Lynn Garafola. Spec. issue of *Studies in Dance History* 5.1 (1994): 50–64.

Goldblatt, Burt. *Newport Jazz Festival: The Illustrated History*. Dial, 1977.

Gosciak, Josh. "Most Wanted: Claude McKay and the 'Black Specter' of African American Poetry in the 1920s." *Modernism on File: The FBI and American Writers*, edited by Claire Culleton and Karen Leick. Palgrave Macmillan, 2008, pp. 80–120.

———. *The Shadowed Country: Claude McKay and the Romance of the Victorians*. Rutgers UP, 2006.

Grandt, Jürgen E. *Kinds of Blue: The Jazz Aesthetic in African American Narrative*. Ohio State UP, 2004.

Green, Adam. *Selling the Race: Culture, Community, and Black Chicago, 1940–1955*. U of Chicago P, 2007.

Greene, Bob (Frank Marshall Davis). *Sex Rebel, Black: Memoirs of a Gourmet Gash*. San Diego: Greenleaf, 1968.

Griffin, Farah Jasmine. *Harlem Nocturne: Women Artists and Progressive Politics during World War II*. Basic Civitas/Perseus, 2013.

———. *If You Can't Be Free, Be a Mystery: In Search of Billie Holiday*. Free Press, 2001.

———. "'It Takes Two People to Confirm the Truth': The Jazz Fiction of Shirley Ann Williams and Toni Cade Bambara." *Big Ears: Listening for Gender in Jazz Studies*, edited by Nichole T. Rustin and Sherrie Tucker. Duke UP, 2008, pp. 348–60.

———. *"Who Set You Flowin'?" The African-American Migration Narrative*. Oxford UP, 1995.

"Haiti: What Are We Really Doing There." *The Crisis* 32 (July 1926): 125–27.

Hall, Jacquelyn Dowd. "The Long Civil Rights Movement and the Political Uses of the Past." *Journal of American History* 91.4 (March 2005): 1233–63.

Hammond, John. "Is the Duke Deserting Jazz?" *Jazz* 1/8 (May 1943): 15. Rpt. in M. Tucker, *The Duke Ellington Reader*, pp. 171–73.

Hanchard, Michael. "Afro-Modernity: Temporality, Politics, and the African Diaspora." *Public Culture* 11 (1999): 245–68.

Hathaway, Heather. *Caribbean Waves: Relocating Claude McKay and Paule Marshall*. Indiana UP, 1999.

Henderson, David. Introduction. Kaufman, *Cranial Guitar*, pp. 7–28.

Henderson, Stephen. *Understanding the New Black Poetry: Black Speech and Black Music as Poetic References*. William Morrow, 1973.

Hentoff, Nat. *The Jazz Life*. 1961. Da Capo, 1985.

Higashida, Cheryl. *Black Internationalist Feminism: Women Writers of the Black Left, 1945–1995*. U of Illinois P, 2011.

Higgins, Scarlett. "How Long Must We Wait?: Langston Hughes's Cryptic Collage." *Langston Hughes Review* 23 (2009): 5–18.

Hine, Darlene Clark. Introduction. *The Black Chicago Renaissance*, edited by Darlene Clark Hine and John McCluskey Jr. U of Illinois P, 2012, pp. xv–xxxiii.

Hoefel, Roseanne. "Praisesong for Paule Marshall: Music and Dance as Redemptive Metaphor in *Brown Girl, Brownstones* and *Praisesong for the Widow*." *MaComère: Journal of the Association of Caribbean Women Writers and Scholars* 1 (1998): 133–44.

Holcomb, Gary Edward. *Code Name Sasha: Queer Black Marxism and the Harlem Renaissance*. U of Florida P, 2007.

Holder, Brian. "Ragtime and Anti-Bolshevism." *IASPM Journal* 2.1/2 (2011): 75–86.

Holliday, Robert Cortes. "The Negro in King Christophe's Haiti, in Sir M. Garvey's Harlem, in Sunday School and at Large." *New York Evening Post*, 21 April 1928, sec. 3, p. 12.

Horne, Gerald. "Rethinking the History and Future of the Communist Party." Tamiment Library, New York University, New York. 10 June 2008. Speech. *Socialism: Theory and Practice*. http://www.politicalaffairs.net/rethinking-the-history-and-future -of-the-communist-party-41925, 29 March 2007.

Hughes, Langston. *The Best of Simple*. Illustrated by Bernhard Nast. Hill and Wang, 1961.

———. *The Collected Poems of Langston Hughes*. Edited by Arnold Rampersad and David Roessel. Knopf, 1994.

———. "Jazz as Communication." *Collected Works of Langston Hughes*. Vol. 9: *Essays on Art, Race, Politics, and World Affairs*, edited by Christopher C. DeSantis. U of Missouri P, 2002, pp. 368–70.

———. "The Negro Artist and the Racial Mountain." 1926. *Within the Circle: An Anthology of African American Literary Criticism from the Harlem Renaissance to the Present*, edited by Angelyn Mitchell. Duke UP. 1994, pp. 55–59.

———. *Not without Laughter*. 1930. Scribner, 1995.

———. "The Roots of Jazz." *The Collected Works of Langston Hughes*. Vol. 9: *Essays on Art, Race, Politics, and World Affairs*, edited by Christopher C. DeSantis. U of Missouri P, 2002, pp. 370–71.

Hutchinson, George. *The Harlem Renaissance in Black and White*. Belknap of Harvard UP, 1995.

Jackson, Lawrence P. *The Indignant Generation: A Narrative History of African American Writers and Critics: 1934–1960*. Princeton UP, 2011.

Jackson, Travis A. "Jazz Performance as Ritual: The Blues Aesthetic and the African Diaspora." Monson, *African Diaspora*, pp. 23–82.

James, C.L.R. *The Black Jacobins: Toussaint L'Ouverture and the San Domingo Revolu-tion.* 2nd ed., rev. Vintage/Random House, 1989.

James, Winston. *A Fierce Hatred of Injustice: Claude McKay's Jamaican Poetry of Rebellion.* Verso, 2001.

———. *Holding Aloft the Banner of Ethiopia: Caribbean Radicalism in Early Twentieth-Century America.* Verso, 1998.

"The Jazz Problem." *The Etude.* 1924. Rpt. Walser, pp. 41–54.

Jemie, Onwuchekma. *Langston Hughes: An Introduction to the Poetry.* Columbia UP, 1976.

Jimoh, A. Yemisi. *Spiritual, Blues, and Jazz People in African American Fiction: Living in Paradox.* U of Tennessee P, 2002.

Joans, Ted. *Teducation: Selected Poems, 1949–1999.* Coffee House, 1999.

Johnson, James Weldon. "Harlem: The Culture Capital." Locke, pp. 301–311.

———. Preface. *The Book of American Negro Poetry.* 1921. Rev. ed. Harcourt, 1969, pp. 9–48.

———. "Self-Determining Haiti." *The Nation* 111.2878–80 and 2882 (28 Aug.–25 Sept. 1920), 4 parts.

———. "The Truth about Haiti." *The Crisis* 20 (Sept. 1920): 217–24.

Johnson, Patricia A., and Walter C. Farrell Jr. "The Jazz Poetry of Langston Hughes: A Reflection." *Minority Voices* 4 (1980): 11–21.

Johnson, Ronna C., and Nancy M. Grace, editors. *Girls Who Wore Black: Women Writing the Beat Generation.* Rutgers UP, 2002.

Jones, Gayl. *Liberating Voices: Oral Tradition in African American Literature.* Harvard UP, 1991.

Jones, Meta DuEwa. "Listening to What the Ear Demands: Langston Hughes and His Critics." *Callaloo* 25.4 (2002): 1145–75.

———. *The Muse Is Music: Jazz Poetry from the Harlem Renaissance to Spoken Word.* U of Illinois P, 2011.

Joyce, James. *Dubliners.* 1914. Norton Critical Edition. Norton, 2006.

Karpman, Laura. Program Notes, *Ask Your Mama!* Co-created by Jessye Norman and Laura Karpman, Carnegie Hall, New York, 16 March 2009.

Kasinitz, Philip. *Caribbean New York: Black Immigrants and the Politics of Race.* Cornell UP, 1992.

Kaufman, Bob. *The Ancient Rain: Poems, 1956–1978.* New Directions, 1981.

———. *Cranial Guitar: Selected Poems of Bob Kaufman.* Edited by Gerald Nicosia. Coffee House, 1996.

———. *Solitudes Crowded with Loneliness.* New Directions, 1965.

Kaufman, Eileen. "From *Who Wouldn't Walk with Tigers?*" *Beat Down to Your Soul: What Was the Beat Generation?,* edited by Ann Charters. Penguin, 2001, pp. 273–80.

———. "From *Who Wouldn't Walk with Tigers?*" *A Different Beat: Writings by Women of the Beat Generation,* edited by Richard Peabody. Serpent's Tail, 1997, pp. 108–14.

Kelley, Robin D. G. *Africa Speaks, America Answers: Modern Jazz in Revolutionary Times.* Harvard UP, 2012.

———. "Brooklyn's Jazz Renaissance." *Institute for Studies in American Music Newsletter* 33.2 (2004): 4–5.

———. *Freedom Dreams: The Black Radical Imagination.* Beacon, 2002.

———. *Hammer and Hoe: Alabama Communists during the Great Depression.* U of North Carolina P, 1990.

———. *Race Rebels: Culture, Politics, and the Black Working Class.* Free Press, 1994.

Kengor, Paul. *Dupes: How America's Adversaries Have Manipulated Progressives for a Century.* Intercollegiate Studies Institute, 2010.

Kenney, William Howland. *Chicago Jazz: A Cultural History, 1904–1930.* Oxford UP, 1993.

Kent, George E. "Reflections on Stephen Henderson's *Understanding the New Black Poetry,* A Review Essay." *Black World* 23.4 (1974): 41–52, 73–77.

Kerouac, Jack. *Mexico City Blues.* Grove, 1959.

———. "The Philosophy of the Beat Generation." *Esquire.* March 1958, pp. 24–25.

Kesteloot, Lilyan. *Black Writers in French: A Literary History of Negritude.* Translated by Ellen Conroy Kennedy. Temple UP, 1974.

King, Rosamond S. "The Flesh and Blood Triangle in Paule Marshall's *The Fisher King.*" Review of *The Fisher King,* by Paule Marshall. *Callaloo* 26.2 (2003): 543–45.

Klein, Aaron, and Brenda J. Elliott. *The Manchurian President: Barack Obama's Ties to Communists, Socialists, and Other Anti-American Extremists.* WND Books, 2010.

Knight, Brenda. *Women of the Beat Generation: The Writers, Artists, and Muses at the Heart of a Revolution.* Conari, 1996.

Knupfer, Anne Meis. *The Chicago Black Renaissance and Women's Activism.* U of Illinois P, 2006.

Kohli, Amor. "Saxophones and Smothered Rage: Bob Kaufman, Jazz, and the Quest for Redemption." *Callaloo* 25.1 (2002): 165–82.

Kun, Josh. *Audiotopia: Music, Race, and America.* U of California P, 2005.

Kurtz, Stanley. *Radical-in-Chief: Barack Obama and the Untold Story of American Socialism.* Threshold/Simon & Schuster, 2010.

Larsen, Nella. *Quicksand.* 1928. Penguin, 2002.

Lattin, Vernon E. "Ann Petry and the American Dream." 1978. Rpt. Ervin, pp. 33–41.

Lee, A. Robert. "Black Beats: The Signifying Poetry of LeRoi Jones/Imamu Amiri Baraka, Ted Joans, and Bob Kaufman." *Beat Down to Your Soul: What Was the Beat Generation?,* edited by Ann Charters. Penguin, 2001, pp. 303–28.

Lenz, Günter H. "'The riffs, runs, breaks, and distortions of the music of a community in transition'—Redefining African American Modernism and the Jazz Aesthetic in Langston Hughes' *Montage of a Dream Deferred* and *Ask Your Mama.*" *Massachusetts Review* 44.1–2 (2003): 269–82.

Lewis, David Levering. *When Harlem Was in Vogue.* Oxford UP, 1979.

Lewis, George. "Afterword to 'Improvised Music after 1950': The Changing Same." Fischlin and Heble, pp. 163–72.

———. "Improvised Music after 1950: Afrological and Eurological Perspectives." Fischlin and Heble, pp. 131–62.

Lindberg, Kathryne V. "Bob Kaufman, Sir Real, and His Revisionary Surreal Self-Presentation." *Reading Race in American Poetry: "An Area of Act,"* edited by Aldon Lynn Nielsen. U of Illinois P, 2000, pp. 163–82.

Lindsay, Vachel. "The Congo." *Collected Poems.* MacMillan, 1925, pp. 178–84.

Lock, Graham. *Blutopia: Visions of the Future and Revisions of the Past in the Work of Sun Ra, Duke Ellington, and Anthony Braxton.* Duke UP, 1999.

Lock, Graham, and David Murray, editors. *Jazz and Blues Influences in African American Literature and Film.* Oxford UP, 2009.

———, editors. *Jazz and Blues Influences in African American Visual Art.* Oxford UP, 2009.

Locke, Alain. "Deep River, Deeper Sea: Retrospective Review of the Literature of 1935." *Opportunity* 14 (Jan. 1936): 6–10.

———. "Jingo, Counter-Jingo, and Us: Retrospective Review of the Literature of 1937." *Opportunity* 16 (Jan. 1938): 7–11, 27.

———. *The Negro and His Music.* Associates in Negro Folk Education, 1936.

———. "The New Negro." Locke, *The New Negro,* pp. 3–16.

———, editor. *The New Negro.* 1925. Atheneum, 1992.

Logan, Rayford W. "The New Haiti." *Opportunity* 5 (April 1927): 101–103.

López Ropero, Lourdes. "'Some of All of Us in You': Intra-racial Relations, Pan-Africanism, and Diaspora in Paule Marshall's *The Fisher King.*" *Miscelánea* 26 (2002): 39–57.

Lott, Eric. "Double V, Double-Time: Bebop's Politics of Style." Gabbard, *Jazz,* pp. 243–55.

Lowney, John. *History, Memory, and the Literary Left: Modern American Poetry, 1935–1968.* U of Iowa P, 2006.

Lubin, Alex, editor. *Revising the Blueprint: Ann Petry and the Literary Left.* UP of Mississippi, 2007

Lutz, Tom. "Music, Sexuality, and Literary Cosmopolitanism." *Black Orpheus: Music in African American Fiction from the Harlem Renaissance to Toni Morrison,* edited by Saadi A. Simawe. Garland, 2000, pp. 41–65.

Major, Clarence, editor. *Juba to Jive: A Dictionary of African-American Slang.* Penguin, 1994.

Marcoux, Jean-Phillipe. "'Blues Connotation': Bebop Jazz and Free Jazz as Idioms Expressive of African American Culture in *Montage of a Dream Deferred* and *Ask Your Mama.*" *Langston Hughes Review* 21 (2007): 13–29.

———. *Jazz Griots: Music as History in the 1960s African American Poem.* Lexington, 2012.

Marsh, John. *Hog Butchers, Beggars, and Busboys: Poverty, Labor, and the Making of Modern American Poetry.* U of Michigan P, 2011.

Marshall, Paule. *Brown Girl, Brownstones.* 1959. Feminist Press, 1981.

———. *Conversations with Paule Marshall.* Edited by James C. Hall and Heather Hathaway. UP of Mississippi, 2010.

———. *The Fisher King.* Scribner, 2000.

———. Interview with James Hall and Heather Hathaway. "The Art and Politics of Paule Marshall: An Interview." 2001. Marshall, *Conversations with Paule Marshall*, pp. 57–88.

———. *Praisesong for the Widow*. Dutton, 1983.

———. *Triangular Road: A Memoir*. BasicCivitas/Perseus, 2009.

Maxwell, William J. "Banjo Meets the Dark Princess: Claude McKay, W.E.B. Du Bois, and the Transnational Novel of the Harlem Renaissance." *The Cambridge Companion to the Harlem Renaissance*, edited by George Hutchinson. Cambridge UP, 2007, pp. 170–83.

———. "Claude McKay—Lyric Poetry in the Age of Cataclysm." Introduction. McKay, *Complete Poems*, pp. xi–xliv.

———. "F. B. Eyes: The Bureau Reads Claude McKay." *Left of the Color Line: Race, Radicalism, and Twentieth-Century Literature of the United States*, edited by Bill Mullen and James Smethurst. U of North Carolina P, 2003, pp. 39–65.

———. *F. B. Eyes: How J. Edgar Hoover's Ghostreaders Framed African American Literature*. Princeton UP, 2015.

———. *New Negro, Old Left: African American Writing and Communism between the Wars*. Columbia UP, 1999.

McBrien, William. *Cole Porter: A Biography*. Knopf, 1998.

McCann, Paul. *Race, Music, and National Identity: Images of Jazz in American Fiction, 1920–1960*. Fairleigh Dickinson UP, 2009.

McDuffie, Erik S. *Sojourning for Freedom: Black Women, American Communism, and the Making of Black Left Feminism*. Duke UP, 2011.

McKay, Claude. *Banjo*. 1929. Harvest-Harcourt, 1957.

———. *Complete Poems*. Edited by William J. Maxwell. U of Illinois P, 2004.

———. *Harlem: Negro Metropolis*. Dutton, 1940.

———. *Home to Harlem*. 1928. Northeastern UP, 1987.

———. *A Long Way from Home*. 1937. Harvest-Harcourt, 1970.

———. "A Negro Extravaganza." Review of *Shuffle Along*. *Liberator* 4.12 (1921): 24–26.

———. "A Negro Writer to His Critics." 1932. Rpt. *The Passion of Claude McKay: Selected Poetry and Prose, 1912–1948*, edited by Wayne F. Cooper. Schocken, 1973, pp. 132–39.

———. *The Negroes in America*. Translated by Robert J. Winter, edited by Alan L. McLeod. Kennikat, 1979.

McKay, Nellie Y. "Ann Petry's *The Street* and *The Narrows*: A Study of the Influence of Class, Race, and Gender on Afro-American Women's Lives." 1990. Rpt. Ervin, pp. 156–65.

Meriwether, James H. *Proudly We Can Be Africans: Black Americans and Africa, 1935–1961*. U of North Carolina P, 2002.

Miller, R. Baxter. "Framing and Framed Languages in Hughes's *Ask Your Mama: 12 Moods for Jazz*." *MELUS* 17.4 (1991–92): 3–13.

———. *On the Ruins of Modernity: New Chicago Renaissance from Wright to Fair*. Common Ground, 2012.

Monroe, Harriet. "A New Negro Poet." Review of *Black Man's Verse*, by Frank Marshall Davis. *Poetry* 48.5 (1936): 293–95.

Monson, Ingrid, editor. *The African Diaspora: A Musical Perspective*. Routledge, 2000.

———. *Freedom Sounds: Civil Rights Call Out to Jazz and Africa*. Oxford UP, 2007.

———. Introduction. Monson, *African Diaspora*, pp. 1–19.

———. *Saying Something: Jazz Improvisation and Interaction*. U of Chicago P, 1996.

Morgan, Stacy. *Rethinking Social Realism: African American Art and Literature, 1930–1953*. U of Georgia P, 2004.

Morrison, Toni. "Behind the Making of *The Black Book*." *Black World* 23.4 (1974): 86–90.

Mullen, Bill V. *Popular Fronts: Chicago and African-American Cultural Politics, 1935–46*. U of Illinois P, 1999.

Murray, Albert. *Stomping the Blues*. Da Capo, 1976.

Naison, Mark. *Communists in Harlem during the Depression*. Grove, 1983.

Nielsen, Aldon Lynn. *Black Chant: Languages of African American Postmodernism*. Cambridge UP, 1997.

———. "'A Hard Rain': Looking to Bob Kaufman." *Callaloo* 25.1 (2002): 135–45.

North, Michael. *The Dialect of Modernism: Race, Language, and Twentieth-Century Literature*. Oxford UP, 1994.

Obama, Barack. *Dreams from My Father: A Story of Race and Inheritance*. 1995. Three Rivers, 2004.

Ogren, Kathy J. *The Jazz Revolution: Twenties America and the Meaning of Jazz*. Oxford UP, 1989.

O'Meally, Robert, editor. *The Jazz Cadence of American Culture*. Columbia UP, 1998.

———. *Lady Day: The Many Faces of Billie Holiday*. Arcade/Little, Brown, 1991.

O'Meally, Robert, Brent Hayes Edwards, and Farah Jasmine Griffin, editors. *Uptown Conversation: The New Jazz Studies*. Columbia UP, 2004.

Omry, Keren. *Cross-Rhythms: Jazz Aesthetics in African-American Literature*. Continuum, 2008.

Osofsky, Gilbert. *Harlem: The Making of a Ghetto. Negro New York, 1890–1930*. 2nd ed. Harper, 1971.

Ottley, Roi. *"New World A-Coming": Inside Black America*. Houghton Mifflin, 1943.

Owen, Chandler. "The Cabaret—A Useful Social Institution." *The Messenger* 4 (1922): 461.

Panish, Jon. *The Color of Jazz: Race and Representation in Postwar American Culture*. UP of Mississippi, 1997.

Peabody, Richard, editor. *A Different Beat: Writings by Women of the Beat Generation*. Serpent's Tail, 1997.

People's Voice. Vol. 1, 14 Feb. 1942.

Petry, Ann. Interview with Hazel Arnett Ervin. 4 Feb. 1989. *Ann Petry: A Bio-Bibliography*, Hall, 1993, pp. 101–103.

———. "The Lighter Side." *People's Voice*, 21 Feb. 1942, p. 16.

———. "Marie of the Cabin Club." 1939. Rpt. *PMLA* 121.1 (2006): 245–54.

———. *Miss Muriel and Other Stories*. Beacon, 1989.

———. "The Novel as Social Criticism." *The Writer's Book*, edited by Helen Hull. Harper, 1950.

———. "Olaf and His Girlfriend." 1945. Rpt. Petry, *Miss Muriel*, pp. 181–97.

———. "An Open Letter to Mayor LaGuardia." *People's Voice*, 22 May 1943, 4.

———. "Solo on the Drums." 1947. Rpt. Petry, *Miss Muriel*, pp. 211–34.

———. *The Street*. Houghton Mifflin, 1946.

Pettis, Joyce. *Toward Wholeness in Paule Marshall's Fiction*. U of Virginia P, 1996.

Piedra, José. "Through Blues." *Do the Americas Have a Common Literature?*, edited by Gustavo Pèrez Firmat. Duke UP, 1990, pp. 107–29.

Plummer, Brenda Gayle. "The Afro-American Response to the Occupation of Haiti, 1915–1934." *Phylon* 43.3 (1982): 125–43.

———. *Rising Wind: Black Americans and U.S. Foreign Affairs, 1935–1960*. U of North Carolina P, 1996.

Porter, Cole. *The Complete Lyrics of Cole Porter*. Edited by Robert Kimball. Knopf, 1983.

Porter, Eric. *What Is This Thing Called Jazz? African American Musicians as Artists, Critics, and Activists*. U of California P, 2002.

"Program for the Ellington orchestra's 23 Jan. 1943 Carnegie Hall concert." Duke Ellington Collection, Smithsonian. Rpt. in M. Tucker, *Duke Ellington Reader*, pp. 160–64.

Pryse, Marjorie. "From 'Patterns against the Sky': Deism and Motherhood in Ann Petry's *The Street*." 1985. Rpt. Ervin, pp. 117–30.

Rampersad, Arnold. *The Life of Langston Hughes*. Vol. 1: *1902–1941: I, Too, Sing America*. Oxford UP, 1986.

———. *The Life of Langston Hughes*. Vol. 2: *I Dream a World*. Oxford UP, 1988.

Ramsey, Guthrie P., Jr. *Race Music: Black Cultures from Bebop to Hip-Hop*. U of California P, 2003.

Randall, Dudley, editor. *The Black Poets*. Bantam, 1972.

———. "'Mystery Poet': An Interview with Frank Marshall Davis." *Black World* 23.3 (1974): 37–48.

Razaf, Andy. "Guilty of Syncopation." *People's Voice*, 22 May 1943, p. 26.

———. "The Negro Speaks." *People's Voice*, 14 Feb. 1942, p. 3.

Redmond, Eugene B. *Drumvoices: The Mission of Afro-American Poetry*. Anchor/Doubleday, 1976.

Reed, Ishmael. *Mumbo Jumbo*. 1972. Scribner, 1996.

Reid, Ira. *The Negro Immigrant: His Background, Characteristics, and Social Adjustment, 1899–1937*. Columbia UP, 1939.

Reisner, Robert George. *Bird: The Legend of Charlie Parker*. Da Capo, 1975.

Renda, Mary A. *Taking Haiti: Military Occupation and the Culture of U.S. Imperialism, 1915–1940*. U of North Carolina P, 2001.

Rife, David. *Jazz Fiction: A History and Comprehensive Reader's Guide*. Scarecrow, 2008.

Roach, Max. *We Insist! Freedom Now Suite*. Candid, 1960. LP.

Robinson, Cedric J. *Black Marxism: The Making of the Black Radical Tradition*. U of North Carolina P, 1983.

Rogers, J.A. "Jazz at Home." Locke, *The New Negro*, pp. 216–24.

"Roosevelt's Deeds for the Negro: Things That Never Happened Before." *People's Voice*, 4 Nov. 1944, p. 2.

Rosenthal, Caroline. *New York and Toronto Novels after Postmodernism: Explorations of the Urban*. Camden House, 2011.

Rosenthal, David H. *Hard Bop: Jazz and Black Music, 1955–1965*. Oxford UP, 1992.

Rubin, Rachel, and James Smethurst. "Ann Petry's 'New Mirror.'" Lubin, pp. 15–34.

Rustin, Nichole T., and Sherrie Tucker, editors. *Big Ears: Listening for Gender in Jazz Studies*. Duke UP, 2008.

Saloy, Mona Lisa. "Black Beats and Black Issues." *Beat Culture and the New America, 1950–1965*, edited by Lisa Phillips. Whitney Museum of Art, 1995, pp. 153–67.

San Francisco Chronicle. 5 Oct. 1963.

Sandburg, Carl. "Chicago." *The Complete Poems of Carl Sandburg*. Rev. and expanded ed. Harcourt, 1969, pp. 3–4.

Sanders, Mark A. *Afro-Modernist Aesthetics and the Poetry of Sterling A. Brown*. U of Georgia P, 1999.

"Santo Domingo Protests." Editorial. *The Messenger* 3 (Aug. 1921): 226.

Saul, Scott. *Freedom Is, Freedom Ain't: Jazz and the Making of the Sixties*. Harvard UP, 2003.

Scanlon, Larry. "News from Heaven: Vernacular Time in Langston Hughes's *Ask Your Mama*." *Callaloo* 25.1 (2002): 45–65.

Schlabach, Elizabeth Schroeder. *Along the Streets of Bronzeville: Black Chicago's Literary Landscape*. U of Illinois P, 2013.

Schmidt, Hans. *The United States Occupation of Haiti, 1915–1934*. Rutgers UP, 1971.

Schuller, Gunther. *The Swing Era: The Development of Jazz, 1930–1945*. Oxford UP, 1989.

Schwarz, A. B. Christa. *Gay Voices of the Harlem Renaissance*. Indiana UP, 2003.

Singh, Nikhil Pak. *Black Is a Country: Race and the Unfinished Struggle for Democracy*. Harvard UP, 2004.

Small, Christopher. *Music of the Common Tongue: Survival and Celebration in African American Music*. Riverrun, 1987.

Smethurst, James. *The African American Roots of Modernism: From Reconstruction to the Harlem Renaissance*. U of North Carolina P, 2011.

———. *The Black Arts Movement: Literary Nationalism in the 1960s and 1970s*. U of North Carolina P, 2005.

———. "'Don't Say Goodbye to the Porkpie Hat': Langston Hughes, the Left, and the Black Arts Movement." *Callaloo* 25.4 (2002): 1225–36.

———. *The New Red Negro: The Literary Left and African American Poetry*. Oxford UP, 1999.

———. "The Red Is East: Claude McKay and the New Black Radicalism of the Twentieth Century." *American Literary History* 21.2 (2009): 355–67.

———. "'Remembering When Indians Were Red': Bob Kaufman, the Popular Front, and the Black Arts Movement." *Callaloo* 25.1 (2002): 146–64.

Snead, James A. "Repetition as a Figure of Black Culture." O'Meally, *Jazz Cadence*, pp. 62–81.

Solomon, Mark. *The Cry Was Unity: Communists and African Americans, 1917–1936.* UP of Mississippi, 1998.

Stander, Bella. Interview with Paule Marshall. *Albemarle* (Feb./March 2001). Bella Stander. http://www.bellastander.com/paule.htm. 8 Jan. 2013.

Stephens, Michelle Ann. *Black Empire: The Masculine Global Imaginary of Caribbean Intellectuals in the United States, 1914–1962.* Duke UP, 2005.

———. "Black Transnationalism and the Politics of National Identity: West Indian Intellectuals in Harlem in the Age of War and Revolution." *American Quarterly* 50.3 (1998): 592–608.

Stovall, Tyler. *Paris Noir: African Americans in the City of Light.* Houghton Mifflin, 1996.

Stowe, David W. *Swing Changes: Big-Band Jazz in New Deal America.* Harvard UP, 1994.

Street, Julian. "The Jazz Baby." 1922. Rpt. in Sascha Feinstein and David Rife, *The Jazz Fiction Anthology*, Indiana UP, 2009, pp. 415–46.

Takara, Kathryn Waddell. "Frank Marshall Davis." Tracy, pp. 161–84.

———. *Frank Marshall Davis: The Fire and the Phoenix.* Pacific Raven, 2012.

———. "Frank Marshall Davis: A Forgotten Voice in the Chicago Black Renaissance." *Western Journal of Black Studies* 26.4 (2002): 215–27.

Thomas, Lorenzo. "'Communicating by Horns': Jazz and Redemption in the Poetry of the Beats and the Black Arts Movement." *African American Review* 26.2 (1992): 291–98.

———. *Extraordinary Measures: Afrocentric Modernism and Twentieth-Century African American Poetry.* U of Alabama P, 2000.

Thompson, Emily. *The Soundscape of Modernity: Architectural Acoustics and the Culture of Listening in America, 1900–1930.* MIT Press, 2002.

Tidwell, John Edgar. "Alternative Constructions to Black Arts Autobiography: Frank Marshall Davis and 1960s Counterculture." *CLA Journal* 41.2 (1997): 47–60.

———. "'I Was a Weaver of Jagged Words': Social Function in the Poetry of Frank Marshall Davis." *Langston Hughes Review* 14.1/2 (1996): 65–78.

———. "An Interview with Frank Marshall Davis." *Black American Literature Forum* 19.3 (1985): 105–108.

———. Introduction. Davis, *Black Moods*, pp. xxi–lxv.

———. Introduction. Davis, *Livin' the Blues*, pp. xiii–xxxii.

Tillery, Tyrone. *Claude McKay: A Black Poet's Struggle for Identity.* U of Massachusetts P, 1992.

Tracy, Steven J., editor. *Writers of the Black Chicago Renaissance.* U of Illinois P, 2011.

Tucker, Mark. *Duke Ellington's Black, Brown, and Beige.* Spec. issue of *Music Research Journal* 13.2 (1993).

———. editor. *The Duke Ellington Reader.* Oxford UP, 1993.

Tucker, Sherrie. *Swing Shift: "All-Girl" Bands of the 1940s.* Duke UP, 1940.

———. "'Where the Blues and the Truth Lay Hiding': Rememory of Jazz in Black Women's Fiction." *Frontiers: A Journal of Women's Studies* 13.2 (1992): 26–44.

Vandercook, John. "Whitewash." *Opportunity* 5 (Oct. 1927): 289–93, 296.

Vernon, Grenville. "A Negro Explains Jazz." 1919. Rpt. Walser, pp. 12–14.

Vogel, Shane. *The Scene of Harlem Cabaret: Race, Sexuality, Performance.* U of Chicago P, 2009.

Von Eschen, Penny M. *Race against Empire: Black Americans and Anticolonialism, 1937–1957.* Cornell UP, 1997.

———. *Satchmo Blows Up the World: Jazz Ambassadors Play the Cold War.* Harvard UP, 2004.

Wagner, Jean. *Black Poets of the United States: From Paul Laurence Dunbar to Langston Hughes.* Translated by Kenneth Douglas. U of Illinois P, 1973.

Wald, Alan M. *Trinity of Passion: The Literary Left and the Antifascist Crusade.* U of North Carolina P, 2007.

Wall, Cheryl A. *Worrying the Line: Black Women Writers, Lineage, and Literary Tradition.* U of North Carolina P, 2005.

Wallhead, Celia M. "Myth, Ritual, and Racial Identity in Paule Marshall's *The Fisher King.*" *Revista Canaria de Studios Ingleses* 45 (2002): 205–214.

Walser, Robert, editor. *Keeping Time: Readings in Jazz History.* Oxford UP, 1999.

Weheliye, Alexander G. *Phonographies: Grooves in Sonic Afro-Modernity.* Duke UP, 2005.

Welburn, Ron. "James Reese Europe and the Infancy of Jazz Criticism." *Black Music Research* 7 (1987): 35–44.

Werner, Craig Hansen. *Playing the Changes: From Afro-Modernism to the Jazz Impulse.* U of Illinois P, 1994.

Weston, Randy, with Willard Jenkins. *African Rhythms: The Autobiography of Randy Weston.* Duke UP, 2010.

Weston, Randy. *Uhuru Afrika.* Roulette, 1960. LP.

Wiese, Andrew. *Places of Their Own: African American Suburbanization in the Twentieth Century.* U of Chicago P, 2004.

Wood, Clement. "The American Uplift in Haiti." *The Crisis* 35 (May 1928): 152–53, 173; *The Crisis* 35 (June 1928): 189–91.

Wright, Richard. *Native Son.* 1940. Harper Perennial, 2005.

Young, James O. *Black Writers of the Thirties.* Louisiana State UP, 1973.

Young, Kevin. *The Grey Album: On the Blackness of Blackness.* Graywolf, 2012.

Index

Abdurahman, Bilal, 165
Abraham Lincoln School (Chicago), 65
Adderley, Cannonball, 150
Addisleigh Park. *See* St. Albans
Africa: anti-colonial movements in, 19; liberation movements in, 23
African American literary modernism, 5
African Blood Brotherhood, 15
African diaspora: contexts in *Ask Your Mama*, 112; mix of people in Bedford-Stuyvesant, 164; musical traditions in Brooklyn, 164–65; music in *Banjo*, 54–57; scenes and sounds in *Ask Your Mama*, 117; songs, 40
African history, impact on U.S. black activists, 114
Afro-modernism, 7–9, 11–12, 18; Afro-modernity and correlation with, 6–7
American modernism, 7, 33
American Society of African Culture festival, 115
"American Southern Orchestra," 36
Amsterdam News: 92; coverage of the Savoy Ballroom, 95
Armstrong, Louis, 2, 14–16, 18, 59, 64, 66, 81–82, 84–85
Associated Negro Press, 60
Astaire, Fred, 99
Azikiwe, Benjamin Nnamdi, 24

Baldwin, James, 5, 141, 161–62
Baldwin, Kate, 10–11, 31

Bambara, Toni Cade, 162
Baraka, Amiri, 12, 17, 113, 138, 140, 158, 179
Basie, Count, 16, 126, 164
Beat movement, 140
Bellegarde, Dantes, 49
bebop: as an African American movement, 146; Beats obsession with, 132; Bob Kaufman's affiliation with, 24, 139; drug use among musicians of, 153; impact on jazz, 149; militancy associated with the sound of, 17; as a modern jazz movement, 17; movement after WWII 93; musicians, 18; poetry, 17; primary practitioners of, 153; as protest of commercialism, 113; as protest of swing music, 113; as rebellious expression of a black-subculture, 113; as revolutionary, 112–13; as a subculture, 17; ways of transforming jazz, 22
Bedford-Stuyvesant, 163; African diasporic mix of people, 164; as a site for jazz, 163; in *The Fisher King*, 160; jazz musicians in, 163–65; "Bedford-Stuyvesant Renaissance," 165
Beethoven, Ludwig van, 2
Bellegarde, Dantes, 49
Bernstein, Charles, 119
Bethune, Mary McLeod, 93
Black Aesthetic movement, 80
Black Arts movement, 6
black Atlantic theory (Paul Gilroy), 9–11; geography in Paule Marshall's writings, 159–60, 162

Black Chicago Renaissance, 21; as local African American and black internationalist movements 60

black internationalism, 11–12, 15, 51, 54, 137; identified with Paule Marshall's fiction, 260; internationalist consciousness, black, 158

Black Power movement, 9

Black World, 79

Blakey, Art, 17, 19, 66, 150

Bodenheim, Maxwell, 145

Bolshevik Revolution, 4, 7

Bolshevism, 3

Bontemps, Arna, 85

Bostic, Joseph, 94

Brennan, Timothy, 28

"Bronzeville Brevities," 65–66

Brooklyn: African diasporic mix of people in, 164; African diasporic music traditions in, 164–65; jazz clubs in, 165; jazz musicians in, 163–65

Brooks, Gwendolyn, 60, 80

Brown, Sterling, 39, 62–63, 67–68, 74, 77, 81

Buchanan, Charles P., 93–94

Burroughs, Margaret, 80

Carnegie Hall: Africa Freedom Day (1959), 114; performance of *Ask Your Mama*, 130; premier of *Black, Brown, Beige*, 133–34

Castro, Fidel, 122–23

Century of Negro Progress Exposition, 134

Cesaire, Amie, 32, 138–39

Charles, Ray, 149–152

Chicago: Abraham Lincoln School in, 65; as an alternative "black metropolis," 109; black-and-tan cabarets in, 64; black cultural institutions in, 60; Century of Negro Progress Exposition in, 134; jazz, 65; as a jazz mecca, 60, 188n1; as a migrant refuge, 109; Post–World War I, 109; as a site of black modernity, 21; South Side, 60, 64, 68–69, 127

Chicago Defender, 60, 92

Chopin, Frederic, 1

Christian, Barbara, 156

civil rights movement, African American, 5, 19, 115, 152; hard bop's commitment to, 152; jazz activist role in, 153; "long civil rights movement," 5–6; spiritual terms of freedom, 152–53

Cold War: 11, 18; jazz's role in 116; political implications in *Ask Your Mama*, 112; propaganda against Soviet communism, 152

Coleman, Ornette, 114, 129

Coltrane, John, 66, 83, 150, 165

Communism (American), 10–11; Communist Party, 17; in support of jazz, 15

Communist Party USA (archives), 87

Congo: assassination of Patrice Lumumba, 114, 195n6; Civil War (1960), 114

Constitution, Haitian: U.S. policy makers revising, 47

Corso, Gregory, 137

Cortez, Jayne, 158, 179

Cotton Club, Duke Ellington's association with, 16

Crisis, The, 27–28; on U.S. foreign policy in the Caribbean, 48

Cullen, Countee, 9, 71, 145

cultural memory, 148

cultural nationalism, 33

cultural studies, 5

Daily Worker, 92

Damon, Maria, 138, 147

Danner, Margaret, 80

Dark Room Collective, 158

Dash, Michael, 49

Davis, Frank Marshall, 5–6, 16, 21–22, 59–72, 74–88, 92, 177, 180

Davis, Helen Canfield, 79

Davis, Miles, 165

DeLamotte, Eugenia C., 171

Denning, Michael, 33

Dent, Tom, 158

DeVeaux, Scott, 113, 139, 140, 178

diaspora, African, 12

Dodson, Nell, 94

Domingo, W.A., 34

Double V Campaign, 113; in discussion of *The Street*, 96

Douglas, Ann, 33

Douglass, Frederick, 108

Down Beat, 92

"dozens, the," 23, 116

Du Bois, W.E.B., 11, 13, 27–29, 34, 46, 48, 58, 128

Dumas, Henry, 138

Edwards, Brent Hayes, 11–12, 31, 54

Eisenhower, Dwight, 121

Ellington, Duke, 15–16, 18, 24, 66, 68–70, 81–82, 85, 87, 132–34, 164

Ellington, Mercer, 126
Ellison, Ralph, 5, 12, 103–4, 131, 140
environmental determinism, 102
Eschen, Penny Von, 18–19, 116
Europe: modernism, 7, 158; musical traditions of, 64; reference to black jazz influence, 2; war against fascism in, 17; white supremacy in, 92
Europe, James Reese, 1, 8, 40, 15
European modernism, 7, 158

Fabre, Michel, 173
Fearing, Kenneth, 62
Federal Bureau of Investigation (FBI), 79
Feinstein, Sascha, 61, 84, 139
Festac '77, 160
Field, Marshall, 65
Field Museum of Natural History, 65
Fischlin, Daniel, 161
Fisher King, The, 160–63, 167–69
Fitzgerald, Ella, 87, 126, 164
Five Spot Café, 114
Floyd, Samuel, 12
Foley, Barbara, 11
folk, African American: expressions, 16; materials, culture, and music, 13; traditions, 13
folk life, Negro: Frank Marshall Davis dramatizing, 67–84
Ford, Kenneth, 84
Fourth Congress of the Communist International (1922), 37
Franklin, Benjamin, 100
Fuller, Hoyt, 80

Gaines, Kevin, 134
Garvey, Marcus, 34, 36, 57, 164; United Negro Improvement Association founded by, 15
Garvey movement, 33; Garveyism, 9, 32
Gay Divorce (1932 musical), 99
Gay Divorcee, The (1934 film), 99
Gennari, John, 65–66
Gershwin, George, 121
Gillespie, Dizzy, 17–18, 66, 112, 174
Gilmore, Glenda Elizabeth, 5
Gilroy, Paul, 5, 9, 10–12, 32
Ginsberg, Allen, 136–37
Grandt, Jurgen, 91
Great Migration, the, 8
Greenwich Village, 142
Grieg, Edvard, 2
Griffin, Farrah Jasmine, 162, 171

Hall, Jacquelyn Dowd, 5
Haiti: independence, 48; nationalism, 47–48; Revolution, 32; U.S. occupation of, 8, 46–47; U.S. policy in, 27, 28, 46–47; U.S. policy makers revising constitution, 47; uprising in 1919, 47
Haitian Revolution, 32
Hammond, John, 133
Hanchard, Michael, 6–7
Handy, W.C., 40, 63
Hansberry, Lorraine, 126
Hard bop: commitment to the Civil Rights Movement, 152; emergence of, 150; musicians of, 150
Harlem: as a cosmopolitan cultural capital, 33; Harlem Riot, 96, 113; as a multinational center of black culture, 34; nightclubs in, 113; as a site for jazz, 53
Harlem Renaissance, 6, 8, 11, 16, 46; fiction, 29, 101; as an international movement, 58; novels 108–9. *See also* New Negro Renaissance
Harlem Riot (1943), 96; due to lack of racial progress, 113
Hawaii, racial prejudice and discrimination in, 79
Heble, Ajay, 161
Hellfighters Band. *See* 369th Infantry Jazz Band
Henderson, David, 158
Henderson, Stephen, 80, 85
Henry, Ernie, 163
Hernton, Calvin, 158
Herskovits, Melville, 64–65
Hine, Darlene Clark, 60
history, African: impact on U.S. black activists, 114
history, jazz, 63; Charlie Parker as transformative figure in, 139; Bedford-Stuyvesant in, 165; Brooklyn in, 164–65; in *The Fisher King*, 160, 167–69
history, New World: of blacks in war, 133
Hoffman, John, 148
Holcomb, Gary, 31
Holiday, Billie, 25, 66, 81–82, 85–87, 99, 145–46, 162, 171
Holocaust: violence of, 148
Honolulu: African American culture in, 80; *Honolulu Record* (newspaper), 79
Hoppers, Lindy, 94
Horne, Gerald, 87
Hot Club of Chicago, 65

Hughes, Langston, 5–6, 12–18, 38, 40, 67–73, 77, 83, 98, 108, 120–30, 134–39, 158, 160, 165, 174, 177, 179; aware of political implications of bebop, 23–24; engagement with mass culture, 62–63; inventive adaptations of African American vernacular forms, 111–17
Hugo, Victor, 50
Hutchinson, George, 33

improvisation, 177. *See also* jazz
independence, Haitian, 48
internationalism: of jazz, 2; social, 4; Soviet, 11
internationalist organizations, black, 177. *See also* Garvey, Marcus; United Negro Improvement Association
international modernism, 7, 15; according to Claude Mckay, 37–38

Jackson, Lawrence P., 5
Jackson, Travis, 12
Jacquet, Illinois, 126
James, C.L.R., 47
James, Winston, 11
Japan, atomic bombing of, 148
Jay McShann Orchestra, 84
jazz: activist role in the Civil Rights Movement 153–54; African American, 73; as an Afro-modernist literary medium, 16; bebop's impact on, 149; Bedford-Stuyvesant as an important site for, 163; blend different forms of expression, 75; challenge to European musical concepts, 65; Cold War, 18; as a form of African American folk life, 68; as a form of protest music, 138, 155, 158; history of, 177; improvisation in *The Fisher King*, 161; as an intercultural mode of expression, 20; journals, 92; leftist jazz historians, 92; as life-affirming, 155; as a major weapon against white supremacy, 65; as a medium of African American folk culture, 68; post–World War II, 18; role in Cold War, 116; roots in Africa, 16; as 'un-American,' 153; associated with U.S. nationalism, 92. *See also* swing era
Jazz Age, 15; international appeal of, 60
jazz history, 63; Charlie Parker as transformative figure in, 139; Bedford-Stuyvesant in, 165; Brooklyn in, 164–65; in *The Fisher King*, 160, 167–69

jazz internationalism, 4–5, 9
Jim Crow era, 9; Double V campaign, 113; *People's Voice* headline on military policy, 93; practices, 18, 22; racial policies during, 113; racism, 113; South, 117, 123
Joans, Ted, 17, 140–42, 158
Johnson, Charles S., 49
Johnson, James Weldon, 13–15, 34, 38, 46–49, 161
Johnson, Lutie, 22
Jones, LeRoi, 140
Jones, Meta DuEwa, 115
journals, African American. See *Black World*; *Crisis, The*; *Liberator, The*; *Opportunity*
journals, jazz. See *Down Beat*; *Metronome*
journals associated with Popular Front. See *Daily Worker*; *Nation, The*; *New Masses*; *New Republic, The*

Karpman, Laura, 130
Kaufman, Bob, 5–6, 17, 23–24, 131–56, 177, 180; letter to editor of *San Francisco Chronicle*, 131, 132, 134; involvement in Society of Umbra, 138, 158; vow of silence in protest of Vietnam War, 132, 157–58
Kelley, Robin, 11, 19, 164–65
Kelley, William Melvin, 161
Kengor, Paul, 88
Kennedy, Jacqueline, 132
Kent, George, 80
Kerouac, Jack, 24, 84, 135–37, 141–42
King, Martin Luther, Jr., 23, 128, 134
Kohli, Amor, 154

Larsen, Nella, 27, 108
League of Nations, 8
Leopold, King, 123
Lewis, George, 177
liberation movements, black, 115, 177. *See also* Black Power movement; Garvey movement
liberation movements, Third World: in *Ask Your Mama*, 121–22; trans-national American culture immigrant claims for, 33; triangular relationship in *The Fisher King*, 161–62
Liberator, The, 35–36
Lincoln, Abby, 134
Lincoln, Abraham, 65
Lindberg, Katheryne V., 138

Lindsay, Vachel, 61, 67–69, 137
Liston, Melba, 165
literary studies, African American, 5
literature, African American: Alaine Locke's
    Opportunity review on, 67; impact of
    jazz on, 5–7; jazz narratives, 161; novels,
    85, 161
Lock, Graham, 177
Locke, Alain, 8, 14, 16–17, 33–34, 38, 67–68
Logan, Rayford W., 49
London, England: post-war race riots in,
    36, 43
"long" civil rights movement, 5–6
Lorca, Frederico Garcia, 138
Los Angeles Hilton 137
Lubin, Alex, 90
Lumumba, Patrice, 114, 123

Mackey, Nathaniel, 179
Madhubuti, Haki, 80
Major, Clarence, 158
Marshall, Paule, 5–6, 19–20, 24–25, 159–64,
    167, 172, 176, 180
Masters, Edgar Lee, 61–62
Maxwell, William, 10, 31
McKay, Claude, 5–6, 11, 20, 27–40, 42–44,
    47, 49, 52–59, 77, 108, 159–60, 180
McShann, Jay, 84
Messenger, The, 27; on U.S. foreign policy in
    the Caribbean, 48
Metronome, 92
Mingus, Charles, 24, 66, 114, 123, 134, 149–51,
    179
Minton's, 113
modernism. *See* African American Liter-
    ary modernism; American modernism;
    European modernism; international
    modernism
Monk, Thelonious, 17, 24, 149–50, 165
Monroe, Harriet, 67–68
Monson, Ingrid, 12, 18–19, 116, 164
Morocco bands, black, 2
Morrison, Toni, 80, 161–62
Morton, Jelly Roll, 59, 81
movements. *See* Beat movement; Black Aes-
    thetic movement; Black Arts movement;
    Black Power movement; liberation move-
    ments; Third World; Negritude move-
    ment; New Negro movement
Murray, Albert, 12
music, African American: Charlie Parker in
    the history of, 142

music, improvisation, 177

Nation, The, 27, 92
nationalism, Haitian, 47–48
nationalist organizations. *See* African Blood
    Brotherhood; National Urban League
National Maritime Union, 136–37
National Urban League, 49
Neal, Larry, 138
Negritude movement, 32
Negro Digest, 60; Frank Marshall Davis's
    poems in, 80; publishing African Ameri-
    can poets, 80
Negroes in America, The, 37
New Masses, 92
New Negro, 33; transnational implications
    of 34
New Negro movement. *See* Harlem Renais-
    sance; New Negro Renaissance
New Negro Renaissance, 6, 8, 11, 16, 46; as
    an international movement, 58; fiction,
    29, 101; novels, 108–9. *See also* Harlem
    Renaissance
New Orleans jazz, 65, 80; African and Afri-
    can American roots of, 15
Newport Jazz Festival, 114, 125
New Republic, The, 92
newspapers, African American. See *Amster-
    dam News*; *Chicago Defender*; *Pittsburgh
    Courier*. See also Associated Negro Press
New World history of blacks in war, 133
New York City Board of Education, 93
Nielson, Aldon Lynn, 138
Norman, Jessye, 130
North, Michael, 33

Obama, Barack, 21, 61, 86–88, 130
Occidental College, 86
Oliver, Joe "King," 59, 64
Opportunity, 27; Alaine Locke's literature
    review in, 67; attention to Haitian cul-
    tural politics, 49
oral tradition, 23, 116
Owen, Chandler, 38–39

Pan-African Conference (1919), 8
Pan-Africanism, 9, 32; Pan-African Confer-
    ence in Paris, 8; W.E.B. Dubois advocacy
    of, 28
Panish, Jon, 140
Paris, France: as a cosmopolitan site, 11;
    Pan-African Conference in, 8

Parker, Charlie, 17, 24, 66, 81–85, 112, 127–29, 132–33, 139–49, 153, 158, 161, 174; as transformative figure in jazz history, 139; recordings with Jay McShann Orchestra, 84; in the history of African American music, 142

Payne Cecil, 163

People's Voice, 22; coverage of closing the Savoy Ballroom, 94–95; coverage of popular entertainment, 94; headline on military policy, 93; against Jim Crow racism, 93

Petry, Ann, 5–6, 16, 22, 89–96, 111, 160, 162, 180

Pittsburgh Courier, 92

Poe, Edgar Allan, 145

poetry, jazz: as democratic, 7

Popular Front, 16: commitment to black and interracial cultural radicalism, 60; images of interracial solidarity, 72; international and interracial alliances of, 21; journals associated with, 92; overthrow Jim Crow practices, 22; value for jazz, 92

Porter, Cole, 99

Porter, Eric, 17, 30

Powell, Adam Clayton, Jr., 93, 95

Pozo, Chano, 17

Price, Leontyne, 120–21

Putnam Central, 165

Rampersad, Arnold, 115

Randall, Dudley, 80, 85

Razaf, Andy, 10, 94, 96

recording ban, 113

Redmond, Eugene, 61, 85

Reed, Ishmael, 158

rhythm and blues, popularity of, 150

Roach, Max, 19, 114, 134, 163, 165

Robeson, Paul, 11, 19

Robinson, Cedric, 11

Robinson, Jackie, 126

Rodgers, Carolyn, 80

Rodgers, Joel, 34

Rogers, Ginger, 99

Rogers, J.A., 14

Rollins, Sunny, 66, 150

Roosevelt, Theodore, 96

Rosenthal, David, 150

Russell, Ross, 141

Sandburg, Carl, 61–62, 67–70

San Francisco Chronicle, 131, 132, 134

Saul, Scott, 152

Savoy Ballroom: as a democratic symbol for the left, 96; closing of, 94–96

Schomburg, Arthur, 34

Second World Black and African Festival of Arts and Culture, 160

Semple, Jessie B., 135

Senghor, Leopold Sedar, 32

Shange, Ntozake, 162

Sharpeville Massacre, 114

Shepp, Archie, 66

Silver, Horace, 150

Singh, Nikhil Pak, 5

Small, Christopher, 12

Smethurst, James, 8, 11, 62, 138

Smith, Jimmy, 150

Smith, Mabel Louise, 124

Smythe, Billy, 40

Society of Umbra, 138, 158

South Africa: Sharpeville Massacre, 114

South Side Writers Group, 60

Soviet State Publishing House, 37

Soviet Union, 11; as a communist state, 8; formation of, 7; Fourth Congress of the Communist International, 37; postcolonial alliances with, 18; Soviet State Publishing House, 37

Stearns, Marshall, 92

Stephens, Michelle, 11, 31

Stovall, Tyler, 173

Stowe, Harriet Beecher, 50

Strauss, Richard, 1

Street, Julian, 1–2

swing era, 16, 82, 90; bebop as protest against swing music, 113; identified with American democracy, 92

Tamiment Library, 87

Thomas, Dylan, 145

Thomas, Lorenzo, 138, 158

369th Infantry Jazz Band, 1

Tidwell, John Edgar, 62, 68, 79

Toure, Sekou, 118

Trumbauer, Frankie, 64

Tubman, William, 117

Tucker, Sherrie, 90, 162

United Hot Clubs of America, 65

United Negro Improvement Association, 15

Uptown House, 113

U.S. State Department: briefing Paule Marshall, 160; sponsors international jazz tours, 18, 19, 116–17; sponsors 1965 cultural tour of Europe, 160

U.S. military, protest against racism in, 134

Vandercook, John, 49
Vechten, Carl Van, 28
Vietnam War, 132, 157–58
Vogel, Shane, 39

Waikiki, "the Jungle" (neighborhood), 86
Walker, Margaret, 60
Wall, Cheryl, 162
Wallace, Henry, 137
Walrond, Eric, 34
Weheliye, Alexander, 103
Whitman, Walt, 70
WJJD, 65; "Bronzeville Brevities" program, 65–66
Williams, John, 161
Williams, Mary Lou, 99

Williams, Shirley Anne, 162
Wilson, Woodrow, 53
Wood, Clement, 27
World War I, 1, 4, 7; League of Nations, 8; President Woodrow Wilson's administration's policy on, 47–48
World War II: New Negro Renaissance novels' conversation on, 109; racial prejudice and discrimination, 79; traumatic violence of, 148; U.S. nationalism during, 92
"worrying the line" (Cheryl Wall), 162
Wright, Richard, 22, 60, 67,108

X, Malcom, 23, 123

Young, Kevin, 158

Zola, Emile, 50

JOHN LOWNEY is a professor of English at St. John's University. He is the author of *The American Avant-Garde Tradition: William Carlos Williams, Postmodern Poetry, and the Politics of Cultural Memory* and *History, Memory, and the Literary Left: Modern American Poetry, 1935–1968.*

The New Black Studies Series

Beyond Bondage: Free Women of Color in the Americas   *Edited by David Barry Gaspar and Darlene Clark Hine*

The Early Black History Movement, Carter G. Woodson, and Lorenzo Johnston Greene   *Pero Gaglo Dagbovie*

"Baad Bitches" and Sassy Supermamas: Black Power Action Films   *Stephane Dunn*

Black Maverick: T. R. M. Howard's Fight for Civil Rights and Economic Power   *David T. Beito and Linda Royster Beito*

Beyond the Black Lady: Sexuality and the New African American Middle Class   *Lisa B. Thompson*

Extending the Diaspora: New Histories of Black People   *Dawne Y. Curry, Eric D. Duke, and Marshanda A. Smith*

Activist Sentiments: Reading Black Women in the Nineteenth Century   *P. Gabrielle Foreman*

Black Europe and the African Diaspora   *Edited by Darlene Clark Hine, Trica Danielle Keaton, and Stephen Small*

Freeing Charles: The Struggle to Free a Slave on the Eve of the Civil War   *Scott Christianson*

African American History Reconsidered   *Pero Gaglo Dagbovie*

Freud Upside Down: African American Literature and Psychoanalytic Culture   *Badia Sahar Ahad*

A. Philip Randolph and the Struggle for Civil Rights   *Cornelius L. Bynum*

Queer Pollen: White Seduction, Black Male Homosexuality, and the Cinematic   *David A. Gerstner*

The Rise of Chicago's Black Metropolis, 1920—1929   *Christopher Robert Reed*

Living with Lynching: African American Lynching Plays, Performance, and Citizenship, 1890—1930   *Koritha Mitchell*

Africans to Spanish America: Expanding the Diaspora   *Edited by Sherwin K. Bryant, Rachel Sarah O'Toole, & Ben Vinson III*

Rebels and Runaways: Slave Resistance in Nineteenth-Century Florida   *Larry Eugene Rivers*

The Black Chicago Renaissance   *Edited by Darlene Clark Hine and John McCluskey Jr.*

The Negro in Illinois: The WPA Papers   *Edited by Brian Dolinar*

Along the Streets of Bronzeville: Black Chicago's Literary Landscape   *Elizabeth Schlabach*

Gendered Resistance: Women, Slavery, and the Legacy of Margaret Garner   *Edited by Mary E. Fredrickson and Delores M. Walters*

Racial Blackness and the Discontinuity of Western Modernity   *Lindon Barrett, edited by Justin A. Joyce, Dwight A. McBride, and John Carlos Rowe*

Fannie Barrier Williams: Crossing the Borders of Region and Race
    Wanda A. Hendricks
The Pekin: The Rise and Fall of Chicago's First Black-Owned Theater
    Thomas Bauman
Grounds of Engagement: Apartheid-Era African American and
    South African Writing   *Stéphane Robolin*
Humane Insight: Looking at Images of African American Suffering
    and Death   *Courtney R. Baker*
Word Warrior: Richard Durham, Radio, and Freedom   *Sonja D. Williams*
Funk the Erotic: Transaesthetics and Black Sexual Cultures   *L. H. Stallings*
Spatializing Blackness: Architectures of Confinement and Black Masculinity
    in Chicago   *Rashad Shabazz*
Painting the Gospel: Black Public Art and Religion in Chicago
    Kymberly N. Pinder
Radical Aesthetics and Modern Black Nationalism   *GerShun Avilez*
Sex Workers, Psychics, and Numbers Runners: Black Women in New York City's
    Underground Economy   *LaShawn Harris*
Slavery at Sea: Terror, Sex, and Sickness in the Middle Passage
    Sowande' M. Mustakeem
Booker T. Washington in American Memory   *Kenneth M. Hamilton*
Black Post-Blackness: The Black Arts Movement and Twenty-First-Century
    Aesthetics   *Margo Natalie Crawford*
Archibald Motley Jr. and Racial Reinvention: The Old Negro in
    New Negro Art   *Phoebe Wolfskill*
Building the Black Metropolis: African American Entrepreneurship
    in Chicago   *Edited by Robert E. Weems Jr. and Jason P. Chambers*
Jazz Internationalism: Literary Afro-Modernism and the Cultural Politics
    of Black Music   *John Lowney*

The University of Illinois Press
is a founding member of the
Association of American University Presses.

University of Illinois Press
1325 South Oak Street
Champaign, IL 61820-6903
www.press.uillinois.edu